Time-Bound Words

Also by Peggy A. Knapp

ASSAYS: Critical Approaches to Medieval and Renaissance Texts (volumes I-IX) (*editor*)

CHAUCER AND THE SOCIAL CONTEST

THE STYLE OF JOHN WYCLIF'S ENGLISH SERMONS

Time-Bound Words

Semantic and Social Economies from Chaucer's England to Shakespeare's

Peggy A. Knapp
Professor of English
Carnegie Mellon University
Pittsburgh

First published in Great Britain 2000 by
MACMILLAN PRESS LTD
Houndmills, Basingstoke, Hampshire RG21 6XS and London
Companies and representatives throughout the world

A catalogue record for this book is available from the British Library.

ISBN 0-333-75379-8

 First published in the United States of America 2000 by
ST. MARTIN'S PRESS, INC.,
Scholarly and Reference Division,
175 Fifth Avenue, New York, N.Y. 10010

ISBN 0-312-22404-4

Library of Congress Cataloging-in-Publication Data
Knapp, Peggy A., 1937–
Time-bound words : semantic and social economies from Chaucer's England to
Shakespeare's / Peggy A. Knapp.
p. cm.
Includes bibliographical references and index.
ISBN 0-312-22404-4 (cloth)
1. Economics—Terminology—History. 2. English language—History. I. Title.

HB62 .K57 1999
330'.01'4 21—dc21
99-042134

This book is printed on paper suitable for recycling and made from fully managed and sustained
forest sources.

10 9 8 7 6 5 4 3 2
09 08 07 06 05 04 03 02

Printed and bound in Great Britain by
Antony Rowe Ltd, Chippenham, Wiltshire

Contents

Preface		vi
1	Introduction: Philology in a New Key	1
2	Corage/Courage	13
3	Estat/Estate	28
4	Fre/Free	48
5	Gloss	66
6	Kynde/Kind	80
7	Lewid/Lewd	98
8	Providence	113
9	Queynte/Quaint	130
10	Sely/Silly	143
11	Thrift	158
12	Virtù/Virtue	172
	After Words	189
	Notes	194
	References	207
	Index	221

Preface

This book is concerned with the ways semantic change comes about as the world people imagine (by which I mean both "observe" and "impose") changes. Cases differ. Sometimes large-scale economic, social, or religious movements inflect language change, sometimes influential texts do, and sometimes a long, silent logic slowly works itself out.

I expect the book to be read in different ways by different readers. For some, its interest may lie in its argument about language generally. In the Introduction (Chapter 1), I pose the general question which has permeated so much discussion in the humanities over the last two or three decades: what is the best way to represent the relationship between words and texts on the one hand, and what "really" went on in social and cultural life on the other. My contribution to that ongoing discussion focuses on a series of specific cases—words errant—rather than an overarching philosophical inquiry.

For other readers, the usefulness of the book will rest on the array of verbal instances it presents, their patterned variousness and their remarkable saturation with meanings. I hope the work will provide new vantage points from which to develop readings of both familiar and marginalized texts. Contrary to the shibboleth of a few years ago, we do not need more readings of texts, since we are always finding ourselves in new relations to their conditions of production.

For still other readers, this book will be primarily a resource for teaching. I identified these wandering words while I was acquainting students with the broad contexts for medieval and early modern texts and reading passages closely with them. Since a language is the product of slow, communal, cultural work, certain words have often provided a pedagogically useful focal point where social possibilities and constraints meet textual designs. The semantic register is complicated at any given moment, and the changes words undergo are less predictable and more volatile than those of syntactic structures, which can often be studied in terms of general linguistic and historical principles.

I have depended, of course, on the indispensable *Oxford English Dictionary* and *Middle English Dictionary*, but as starting points only; I do not always find myself in agreement with their readings of passages, and the majority of instances I cite or refer to were found through my own reading. I have also depended on the record of commentary which accompanies these primary materials to the present. I wish to acknowledge, but have not been able to footnote, all those literary analysts who influenced my readings of early texts; collectively, they have constructed the language of my vantage point.

I wish to thank the people at the *Middle English Dictionary* library in Ann Arbor, Michigan, for allowing me to use the (then) unpublished citation slips with which they are preparing the T U and V fascicles of the *Dictionary*. (I have printed the Middle English thorn as "th" throughout; otherwise spelling follows the manuscripts and editions listed in the bibliography.) The chapter entitled "Thrift" appeared in a somewhat different form in *Art and Context in Late Medieval English Narrative*, edited by Robert R. Edwards; I am grateful to Boydell & Brewer for permission to use it here. Robert Hinman, Jean Carr, and Mary Ann Ferguson offered insightful readings of the whole manuscript at some stage of its development, and Paul Hopper advised me on Chapter 6. Gatherings at the Claremont Graduate School and the University of Rochester proved helpful audiences to part of my argument. My huge, unrepayable debt is to James Franklin Knapp for reading every draft, discussing everything, and helping me in every way. I use my husband's full name to distinguish him from our son, James Andrew Knapp, with whom I have had a number of useful discussions of this material.

P.K.

1
Introduction: Philology in a New Key

For last year's words belong to last year's language
And next year's words await another voice

T.S. Eliot, *Four Quartets*

The boy did not know he was hearing Ovid, and it would not have mattered if he had known. Grandfather's stories proposed to him that the forms of life were volatile and that everything in the world could as easily be something else. The old man's narrative would often drift from English to Latin without his being aware of it...so that it appeared nothing was immune to the principle of volatility, not even language.

E.L. Doctorow, *Ragtime*

This book is about the volatility of some late medieval and early modern words and the "forms of life" to which they testify. It is also about the conditions under which the interpretation of verbal texts and social experience can take place. For "the boy," as he is called in Doctorow's novel, the world seems to "compose and recompose itself constantly in an endless process of dissatisfaction," and he responds to the recomposition with wonder and wide-eyed pleasure, but what response is available to scholars and teachers concerned with historically distant texts? What does the prevailing mix of theories and methods offer to cope with the simultaneous imperatives to see texts as part of a complex social formation, to recognize the fluidity of that formation, and to hear "last year's words" and "next year's" as spoken in different social voices?

One branch of traditional philology has approached linguistic

1

change by isolating language events from larger social and cultural histories, by, for example, charting the first occurrences of words and syntactic structures, their geographical range, and their transmission from one language group to another.[1] Deconstructive analysis, which I think has important connections with philology, attempts to show the slippage between signifier and signified, the unexpected lurking of traces of "hostile" within the friendly invitation of the "host," to cite the example of J. Hillis Miller's influential "The Critic as Host." I intend here a direct contribution to neither of these projects, although I depend from time to time on the insights and methods of both. My "new key" for philology frames the general problem of our access to the cultural formations of past eras in terms of a celebrated debate between Hans-Georg Gadamer and Jürgen Habermas, and, attentive to the common maxim that the deity or the devil—at any rate something of great importance—is in the details, attempts to "put you a case," in Thomas More's lawyerly phrasing, by citing instances of eleven words through a couple of centuries of wear and tear and using these semantic histories to both track ideological forces and reread complex texts.

The Gadamer–Habermas problem space

The study of texts from the past may situate itself as a Gadamerian emphasis on hermeneutics and interpretation or a Habermasian emphasis on "critical theory." Each position enables certain kinds of insight, and each brings with it certain untenable assumptions. Gadamer's insistence on language as "being which is understood" allows him to posit the possibility of a "fusion of horizons" between past culture, which "bears the imprint of its historical tradition," and present interpretation made possible by the sharing of a common language. He argues that the past can be understood, although each succeeding generation will understand it differently, and elevates hermeneutics to a privileged place among the human sciences (*Philosophical Hermeneutics* 31, 39). The price for this optimism is its suggestion of an overarching continuity between a natural and closed "tradition" and an unspecified contemporary interpreter—a suggestion we are less comfortable with now than thirty years ago. Hermeneutics makes little space for the struggle among groups divided by class, gender, religious affiliation or the like in either the past or the present. The array of the possible for both traditional and contemporary positions seems too easily unified across Gadamer's horizons.

Habermas centers his attack on Gadamer's claim that hermeneutics is a universal science, which can report on social problems as well as canonized art. He allows that common language does provide "a kind of metainstitution on which all social institutions are dependent" (a proposition with which I heartily agree). But he objects that it is "*also* a medium of domination and social power" in which normal communicative functions are distorted into legitimations of domination ("Review of Gadamer's *Truth and Method*" 360). As a result, he argues, we are deeply estranged from the life of previous eras and prevented from a rapprochement through hermeneutics by the unreliability of language. As John Brenkman puts it, Habermas is claiming that the machinations of ideology already lurk within the process of "cultural symbolizations and representations" (*Culture and Domination* 46). Gadamer's response has been that his model can also account for the social relations of labor and domination, since they also are recorded in language. Brenkman doubts this, says it "rings hollow" because Gadamer himself never includes this step in his own hermeneutic practice. No logical necessity, however, precludes interrogations of power relations within Gadamer's model.

Habermas himself seems willing to leave the field of art and literature to Gadamer's sense of the hermeneutic project, but to approach the rest of culture with a deep distrust of its systematically deformed language. Habermas's suggestion of a "two-tiered" approach in which hermeneutics is adequate to the languages of art, but fails for those which bear more directly on the public sphere (since then language will be deformed by power relations) can be re-formulated in this light. For if language itself is distorted by relations of power and labor, these relations will always distort it; there can be no valid reason for granting some special status to "high art." (I have, therefore, chosen instances of linguistic change from various kinds of practical and polemical discourse as well as from texts thought of as art.) The result of Habermas's method is that he must posit a place *above* or outside of language in order to describe its systematic deforming powers over the "normal" or "ideal" speech situation, into which the distortions which signal power relations do not intrude. The predication of normalcy as egalitarian not only suggests that language might attain an unmediated access to human intention (a proposition contemporary semioticians might take exception to), but also supposes that past generations must have shared such a hope. For example, the post-enlightenment idealness of a level speech situation must assume the bad faith of medieval estates theory, with its assumptions of differing "natural" responsibilities, talents, and discourses.

I do not expect this account of semantic and social change to settle the Gadamer–Habermas debate, for I do not think the issue can be directly resolved theoretically in favor of either hermeneutics or critical theory. Hermeneutics takes too passive a stance toward the discourses of the past, assuming too unproblematically their potential for capturing something true in social relations and communicating that something to the future, albeit differently to each new era. But critical theory takes too aggressive a stance, assuming that some standard we adopt now is the norm against which the deformations of medieval or early modern discourse must be measured. What I want to propose is that cultural study of the older periods necessarily takes place in the problem space of the Gadamer–Habermas debate, which is to say that Gadamerian hermeneutics and Habermasian critical theory form the opposed correctives to one another in terms of which cultural inquiries may be conducted. At stake is whether the supposition that analysis of early texts can produce valid (though not unchanging) knowledge of past life-worlds can be entertained at the same time as the acknowledgment that linguistic forms are shaped under pressure from prevailing ideology.

In order to avoid working out these word-histories under the shadow of a direct contradiction, I want to appeal to some propositions which can be seen as commensurate, in different ways, with both hermeneutics and critical theory. The first is the familiar observation that linguistic art depends on distortion, paronomasia, and play in general to accomplish its ends, an idea that Dominick LaCapra has introduced into the Gadamer–Habermas controversy. The second, associated with the work of Stuart Hall, is that the ideologically colored terms of a particular discourse can be detached and made use of in others. And the third is Raymond Williams's notion of social change at the level of "structures of feeling."

It is my contention that linguistic "distortion" (for a moment setting aside the objection that Habermas's term assumes the possibility of perfectly transparent representation) can either simply encode prevailing ideology or enable critique of it. LaCapra's discussion in "Habermas and the Grounding of Critical Theory" insists that the conventional expectation of distortion in verbal art prevents the "automatic" and therefore mystifying distortion Habermas posits. As LaCapra puts it, "The critical question is the nature of the distortion, for one can distinguish between playfully creative ambiguity (including humor, irony, and parody) and destructive equivocation—although in any real context the two will interfere with one another" (262). I would argue that this "creative ambiguity" is not limited to "art"; although it is often found in imaginative texts, voices in the public sphere also exhibit it. The verbal playfulness of many medieval and early modern texts seems quite deliberately concerned with the linguistic distortions present in the discourses of their societies, distortions they unmask by punning with key terms. For example, feudal ideology supporting the three medieval estates makes *gentle* a moral honorific as well as an indication of status conferred by birth and fortune, but John Ball's famous little verse "When Adam delved and Eva span, where then was the gentleman" provides both an enactment and a critique of common usage. Before the fall, Adam and Eve were in perfect harmony with God's design for human welfare and innocence; they were, therefore, perfectly *gentle*—as "worthy." Yet they were active workers in their Edenic garden, and not *gentle*—as "idle"—making visible the usually unseen link between aristocratic exemption from labor and genteel behavior. This trope is revisited often (although rarely so concisely) in various social documents; Thomas Dekker evokes it somewhat irreverently in *The Wonderful Yeare* by asking why he should flatter his reader, who has "no more gentilitie in him than Adam had (that was but a gardener)" (in Wilson's edition 4). LaCapra's "critical question"—"the nature of the distortion"—is exactly what is at stake in the interpretation of both the aesthetic and social effects of such "art." Merely recognizing the linguistic intricacy of passages like these is only a starting point; the full analysis must attempt to distinguish playful usages which enable social insight from equivocations which merely naturalize subjugation. Habermasian deformation is evident in terms like *gentle,* but it is sometimes traceable through Gadamerian assumptions about linguistic readability across generations.

The second mediating proposition is Hall's notion of "articulation." A term belongs to a discourse in the sense that it is "articulated" with the domain of that discourse, as Hall explains, the way the cab and trailer of an articulated lorry are joined, but can also be detached ("Postmodernism and Articulation"). Verbal histories may be construed, therefore, as witnesses in the struggle among social groups to "detach one meaning of a concept...from public consciousness and supplant it within the logic of another political discourse" (53). What joins and what detaches particular terms from the larger social discourses available is a logic which produces or seems to produce a coherent reading of the world for a particular group of people. Three points of interest arise from this way of looking at ideology and language which define the new key of the philology I propose: 1) that

ch.

e Y

ideologies are not intrinsically coherent, but are articulated by a logic specific to their time and place, 2) that the elements of which they are constructed can come apart and be re-articulated in different configurations to meet new circumstances and social projects; and 3) that people, subjects, create the logic which joins ideas to create new coherences and animate social struggles—they are not unconscious or entirely "falsely conscious" of their situation, although their understanding may be partial ("Marxism without Guarantees" 37). Hall's sense of articulation acknowledges the power of ideology to deform language, but its stress on the impermanence of any particular deformation renders that power visible during periods of change and thus available to hermeneutic analysis.

"Art," particularly fiction-making art, however a particular milieu defines it, is an especially empowered participant in the struggle to reconfigure key terms. It does not stand outside ideology, as Habermas's "two-tiered" approach seems to suggest, but it often renders semantic change and struggle visible because of its heightened attention to language and history. I therefore make no apology for lingering over the explication of specific passages in well-known texts. As Colin MacCabe has argued, linguistic historians working at the level of meaning must attend to influential texts, where "the examples produced do not just analyze specific uses of particular meanings but constitute those meanings in the analysis." In such cases, it is not a question of "specifying a meaning and then a use but rather of an account in which that meaning is in the process of changing as a word gets articulated in new, or in opposition to new, discourses" (*Tracking the Signifier* 123). Semantic and social changes must be seen in a dynamic and fluid relationship, in which new social formations modify the range or inflection of verbal signs and those signs in turn impel or retard social change. Sharply bifurcated terms provide the occasion for the playfulness and punning LaCapra describes. Hall's formulation posits a concerted intention by groups to seize a powerful term for their program, and some of the words in this study answer to that description quite well, for example, the shift from a primary meaning for *thrift* as feudal propriety to one which stressed economic frugality under Calvinist influence. But other kinds of semantic participation in social transformation are more gradual and diffuse. *Kynde,* for example, slowly loses its medieval connection with *kin,* and its early modern spelling *kind* begins to appear as the neutral "category" or "sort," in an intellectual climate inclining toward systematicity and away from birthright.

The work of Raymond Williams supplies another term for the way language and art may be seen to participate in social change. In *Marxism and Literature,* Williams defines "structures of feeling" as "characteristic elements of impulse, restraint, and tone...a social experience which is still in process, often indeed not yet recognized as social but taken to be private." Art and literature are "often among the very first indications that such a new structure is forming" (132, 121–27, 133),[2] and I would add, often conducive to its formation. Structures of feeling are both social and personal. Williams describes his own attempts to discover older structures and present them in the fictional characters of his "Welsh trilogy" as felt "in the way that important actual relationships are felt, but also...a structure...a particular kind of response to the real shape of a social order" (*Writing in Society* 264). As both author and literary theorist, he posits that such structures can be recovered from the evidence left us by earlier social formations. (Hall too argues for the recoverability of the lived conditions of the past—"common sense" logics that hold ideas together at a particular time, the "spontaneous, vivid but not coherent or philosophically elaborated, instinctive understanding of its basic conditions of life" ["Marxism without Guarantees" 20–21]). But of course no social formation elicits the same responses from all its subjects. In order to signal unevenness in the acceptance of change and contention over it between groups, I will call Williams's terms "dominant," "residual," and "emergent" into service. To trace the movement of these eleven words from one discursive domain to another, is to observe an important, and difficult-to-get-at, aspect of historical change. Some of this semantic change and resistance to change is the result of authorial craft, and I will posit that Chaucer or Shakespeare is "using" a word in creating a particular effect. But "authors," as authorities, are by no means the whole story. Nobody owns ideas (Hall, "Marxism without Guarantees" 39), and nobody owns words. I want to see historical change as both created by those who participate in it and limited and occluded by the social formation, including the linguistic formation, in which they live.

Time-bound words

> I once was lost, but now am found,
> Was bound, but now I'm free.
> "Amazing Grace," traditional American hymn

This train is bound for glory, this train.
                Traditional African-American spiritual

The words in this study are time bound in two senses. Like all language, they are bound to and bounded by the social formation in which they occur, the horizon of what is imaginable in a particular time and place (like the Christian soul in "Amazing Grace" before being set free by God). They are also headed somewhere—not necessarily for glory, like the train—but headed for new territory none the less. Each of these eleven words points to both the horizon it helps define in the Middle Ages, and to a new understanding of society and culture as new conditions arise in what we have come to call the early modern period. But these words also influence societal and cultural change, sometimes impeding it, as James I's insistence on the old reading of the estates did, and sometimes impelling it, as Providence did in Calvinist hands.

"Thou hast frighted the word out of his right sense, so forcible is thy wit," says Benedick to Beatrice in *Much Ado about Nothing*. The words in this study were frighted out of their medieval senses between the late fourteenth and the early seventeenth centuries, roughly between 1380 and 1611. The words are: *corage, estat, fre, gloss, kynde, lewed, providence, queynte, sely, thrift,* and *virtù*. Each of these words is either captured fully for the logic of a new social discourse, gradually sloughing off its old meaning, or, if it contained dual significances in the Middle Ages, greatly altered in the balance between coexisting meanings. *Thrift*, for example, is of the first type, early signaling "propriety" in whatever venue, but losing that implication by 1600 for most everyday purposes in favor of "frugality," its surviving sense. *Virtù* is of the second type, "goodness" and "power" coexisting in the term but "power" showing up less and less often in later decades. It is not my claim that these particular semantic changes are the *inevitable* results of proto-capitalist pressures on the economy, Protestant theology, or shifts in conceptions of gender—here as elsewhere in history contingency and systematicity both operate. What I do want to claim is that close attention to the range and tone of words is important evidence of how social change is being naturalized into the life-worlds of men and women, and therefore how tightly linguistic and social histories are woven together.

This description of linguistic change does not lie in the domain of a history of ideas, like that of C.S. Lewis in *Studies in Words*, partly because Lewis's reliance is exclusively on major works and partly because he tends to see "his" words functioning in one of their two or three significations at a time; that is, he pays too little attention to paronomasia and linguistic play. Nor would I align this project with William Empson's very full description of verbal implication in *The Structure of Complex Words*, since he makes so little reference to the social world in which his texts are implicated. Raymond Williams's *Keywords* is consistently worldly and historical, but it deals so briefly with each term that it cannot attend to linguistic play within specific texts. Play is, of course, meat and drink to Jacques Derrida and deconstructionists in his line. Derrida's "Plato's Pharmacy" and J. Hillis Miller's "The Critic as Host" remark on some flip-flops in signification very like those I want to discuss. My argument diverges from theirs in that I want to rely not on a theory presenting linguistic "slippage" or "duplicity" as general and inevitable, but rather on one stressing social hegemony, resistance, and change. My nearest neighbor in the attempt to account for responses to the decline of feudalism in the linguistic register may be Michael Nerlich, in his working out of the trope *adventure*, and for certain linguistic effects of the Reformation in England, Janel Mueller's *Native Tongue and Word*.

In *Ideology of Adventure*, Nerlich traces a history of those changes by means of the metamorphosis of *aventure* ("that which happens to a person," Old French) through its appropriation as the key term in an ideological construction which privileged the quest for (rather than the mere suffering of) events, extraordinary events which required bold forays into the unknown. He follows the trajectory of this construction from twelfth-century social formations in much of Europe, which demanded of its ruling class the courage and endurance epitomized in and encouraged by "courtly-knightly" tales of adventure (5). As knight-errantry declined into "freebooting" (14), the aristocracy was no longer the only or most obvious candidate for adventuring. The mounted *chevalier* yielded to the sea-faring merchant adventurer, who provided the needed risk-taking ventures of opening and using the new trade routes around the Cape of Good Hope and to the Americas, winning the right to a coat of arms in 1490 and garnering a kind of business monopoly on sea traffic for hundreds of years. The still later turn on the adventure trope is that by the late sixteenth century the merchant adventurer, "royal merchant," as Shakespeare calls his character Antonio in *Merchant of Venice*, does not personally go anywhere. He has become a capitalist pure and simple. Nerlich thus traces the steps by which *adventure* becomes detached from its twelfth-century chivalric context and "supplanted within the logic" (Hall) of an early capitalist style which is deeply antithetical to its "original" sense.

Ideology of Adventure introduces the mix of social, discursive, and textual issues I want to observe, but I differ from Nerlich in attempting to represent, in so far as possible, everyday, practical usage as well as that of influential texts. In some cases, with the help of the Middle English Dictionary Library, I will have been able to see every found occurrence of a word (*thrift* and *virtue*, for example) before 1550. Even then, of course, only usage which has found its way into texts which happen to have been preserved will stand as evidence, and that record falls far short of what the living language must have offered.[3] I also regard social change itself as more uneven than Nerlich does. The international economic changes on which he predicates his readings turned up early in some sectors of English life—notably in the wool trade—but old practices and old loyalties hung on stubbornly in others. Then too, I will not be looking at textual art as merely reflecting changes in the economic base, but as potentially (often simultaneously) registering, inciting, critiquing, opposing, and generally playing with the discourses of experienced life.

The other major upheaval in English "structures of feeling" during these centuries is, of course, the Protestant Reformation. Janel Mueller finds traces of new "structures," in the "urgently affective" prose of William Tyndale and his heirs: "a soul justified by faith begins to think and express itself entirely differently than it did before" (199). The traces of the change she describes are by and large syntactic. She contrasts, for example, Tyndale's personal, oral style (which makes use of "binary conjunctions, correlatives, and comparatives" to link human faith with God's plan for salvation) with the complex subordinate clause construction of Thomas More's Latinate style (201–04). The importance we now place on Chaucer's English makes it easy for us to forget how thoroughly the authorized word was Latin during the whole period of this study—the universities could be addressed formally only in Latin as late as Elizabeth's reign, and in 1605 only 60 of the 6,000 volumes in the Oxford University Library were in English. The challenge to Latin was voiced as early as the defense by Wycliffites like Purvey of their English Bible translations as more accurate than Latin versions, but Latin was still being valorized in 1527, when Robert Ridley wrote to the archbishop of Canterbury's chaplain to protest vernacular scripture: "It becummyth the people of truste to obey and folowe their rewellers which hath geven study & is lerned in such matters as thys. People showd heer & beleve, thai showd not judge the doctrine of paule ne of paules vicares & successors" (quoted by Mueller 208). Well into the sixteenth century, writers were still learning (prodded by the English Bibles and Books of Common Prayer in local churches) to use their mother tongue for serious religious, legal, and courtly discourse, and their readers and hearers had to learn to regard it in those domains.

The debate Mueller charts is of course also over specific items of vocabulary and was understood by the contestants themselves. Tyndale "recognized that centuries of accrued usage would operate to give clerical authority and the Catholic sacrament of ordination a claim to Scriptural warrant if he translated *ekklesia* as 'church' and *presbuteros* as 'priest,'" and More "saw so clearly and said so roundly that the Scripturalism (and Lutheranism) of Tyndale would undermine the established rule and prerogatives of the papacy and the Roman Church" (207). Ridley, More and Tyndale are all thoroughly self-conscious about linguistic effects, and their self-consciousness reinforces Hall's sense of the at least partly willed nature of articulation. A dramatically increased awareness of such linguistic power, experienced in public controversy, is one legacy of the Reform.

Another is a sense of religious loyalties entwined with national identities and interests. Benedict Anderson's *Imagined Communities* argues that one condition necessary for the nation to become an imagined community is that the sacral language of the larger empire (in this case Latin) lose ground to national languages, which then provide a single instrument for conveying religious and historical truth (11–50). This condition was met most dramatically in the allowed translation and dissemination of the English Bible, which broke the link between Latin and religious truth, the supposition that the Latin words were themselves part of that truth. A third legacy is the thoroughgoing re-inflection of practices and values in which Protestantism became, in Alan Sinfield's words, "the most fully articulated [here in the sense "sharply, distinctly spoken"] system of belief" in England, having the "authority of state, church and educational system" (*Literature in Protestant England* 3). These effects of the English Reformation in turn influenced the politics and semantics of gender, as women's relations to the language, the nation and the family were gradually redefined by it, as well as by an increasingly urbanized, proto-capitalist national economy.

I have stopped chronicling instances of these eleven words after 1611, the date of the Authorized Version, but the embedded medieval implications of many English words extend their cultural resonance far beyond that date. For example, consider the social logic of one of the most memorable lines in nineteenth-century American popular culture, "I can read his righteous sentence in the dim and flaring lamps" from the "Battle Hymn of the Republic." Behind its force stands a history of the Civil War, of slavery and abolition in the United States, and of a very specific brand of Protestant scripturalism. Not the least interesting features of this line inhere in the polyvalence of the word *sentence*. *Sentence* immediately conjures up the raw literal image of men (perhaps boys) reading the sentences of the printed Bible in a military camp. But the apocalyptic makes its appearance through the resonance of the medieval sense of *sentence* as "kernel meaning, visionary truth behind or above appearances." This medieval sense is preserved by the language of the Authorized Version to which the literal campfire reading refers, and leads to an image of the Civil War as Armageddon itself, whose watchfires both illuminate and become instances of God's *sentence*, as "final judgment." Such entwined historical, linguistic, and social issues sound the new key of the philology I hope to explore.

2
Corage/Courage

"Temperament" is used [for women] where, with men, we would probably have found the word "courage".
　　　　　　　　　　Klaus Theweleit, *Male Fantasies*, p. 145

Couragio!
　　　Dan Rather on the CBS *Nightly News* during a strike by employees of the network

Viewers around the country must have speculated over Dan Rather's intensely uttered—almost whispered—sign of encouragement of or solidarity with his coworkers. As a battle cry, it had a distinguished precedent: "Couragio, my hearts! S. George for the Honour of England!" dates from 1605, when *courage* had largely become a term for manly valor and resolution. Klaus Theweleit is commenting on Heinrich Teuber's denial of the term *courage* to women in his 1927 article "Miners' Wives," which attributes commitment to a cause, "enormous energy," and realistic assessment of risks to working-class women, but withholds the word most appropriate to those qualities: *courage*. Instances of *corage/courage* serve as particularly apt test cases for Habermas's contention that language is inherently a "medium of domination and social power," deformed in its ability to convey truth because it protects the dominant group, in this case male, and difficult for later hermeneutic efforts to unmask. This chapter follows *corage*, initially associated with inwardness (*corage* appears early in Middle English directly from Old French and ultimately Latin: *cor* "heart") to its identification with specifically male, and often military, exploits.
　　In medieval usage *corage* has three quite distinct senses: "heart,"

"valor," and "lust." As "heart" in the sense of "seat of the emotions," John Gower writes in the Prologue to *Confessio Amantis* of a semblance which "scheweth outward a visage / Of that is noght in the corage" (448) and Lydgate in *Siege of Troy*: "Tresour non so nygh his herte stood, / Nor was so depe graue in his corage" (3245). This sense includes the idea of will as in Gower's "Hanybal...hadde set al his corage / Upon knithod" (*Confessio Amantis*, 5.2057), or Malory's "To drynke of that water I have grete currage" (*Works*, 563.5). Lydgate's *Troy Book* implies valor: "ʒif...gret hardines, / Corage of wil, Meven thin herte...to darreyne here betwene vs two thilke quarel" (3.3955), but not many Middle English instances are unequivocal in that use.[1] (The adjective *corageous*, as "brave" is somewhat better represented; in *Firumbras*, for example, we find: "Hym dredeth nothyng of Olyuer, nomore than of flye; / For he was strong & coraious" [438].) Battle fields are the most predominant venue for this sense, and males are far more often said to possess it—I have only found two women described with the word *corage* as "valor," and one of them is Judith as she kills Holofernes. The Yonge *Secretum Secretorum* is quite explicit about the male inflection: "He that is wyse and hardy...Sum men hym callyth a corageous man or a manful man" (170.38). Yet overall *corage* as "valor," which of course becomes the main surviving meaning, is less frequent in Chaucer's time than the third sense: "lust," usually sexual.

Corage as "lust" is decidedly somatic, sometimes drug induced, and attributed to both men and women. Trevisa's *Bartholomeus* describes a potion thus: "Seed therof ydronke with wyn moeueth venus and exciteth courage [Latin source: *vrina*]" (258a). In *Handlyng Sin*, Mannyng warns that "In drunkenes men wyl rage, / And Ragyng wyl reyse Korage" (9714). Old men worry about its loss, as in *Lessons of the Dirige*,"My spyryt shal be feble and feynt...When I am fallen in any age; My dayes, make I neuer so queynt, / Shullen abrege and a somwhat swage, / And I ful sone shal be atteynt / Whan I haue lost myn hote corage" (447). They may try to get it back, as Lydgate's narrator in *Fall of Princes* charges: "Thou vsist many riche restoratiff / In swiche vnthrifft tencrece thi corage" (vii.477–78), much like Chaucer's Merchant's January, of whom more later. The Wycliffite *Lanterne of Liȝt* explains how these bodily urges can be tamed: "Fastars in Cristis chirche abstynen hem from lustis for to tempir the coragenes of the reble fleishe & kepe her bodi clene chast" (48.15), and in the "Sermon of Dead Men" this thought experiment is urged on every man:

and specialy men in her myddil age when lust and likyng of corage stirith hem most awey fro the seruise of God, make a jornay in her thou3t to the 3atis of helle, to se hou hydously synne is vengid in that plase.

(962–65)

The Brut or the Chronicles of England tells of certain over-sexed women who "For hete they woxen wondir coraious of kynde...so that they desirid more mannys cumpanye than eny other solas or merthe" (4.21), and it is not the only chronicle to do so.

By 1600 *corage* as sexual appetite is a residual trace. The sense "bravery" is clearly predominant and has become a straightforward honorific. It is this privileged term that Theweleit objects to denying to the bold, committed women in Teuber's article. The cultural work performed by *corage* in the Middle Ages was to facilitate an exploration of interior intellectual and emotional states, will and desire. Its post-medieval instances focus on outward conduct, especially in combat. The deflection of the word to its least prevalent medieval usage—"bravery"—in the sixteenth century suppressed its entanglement with lust and promoted its appropriateness in defining male norms. But in Sidney's *New Arcadia* and a number of Shakespeare's plays, especially *Troilus and Cressida* and *Cymbeline*, the term reinstates the older link with sex with which its history is marked.

Interiority, will, and Chaucer

From the early translations to the complex late tales, Chaucer's texts probe the gaps between action and motive, often making use of the word *corage* to do so. The translations *Boece* and *Romaunt of the Rose* tend to use *corage* primarily to distinguish internal from public action, and they account for more than half of the 98 instances of *corage* in Chaucer's corpus.[2] Chaucer's translation of the *Romaunt* also uses the word this way, but in its discussion of the nature of Youth, the internal is strongly sexualized, as in the sudden awakening of Narcissus to his own beauty (1614) and the "unthrifty" follies of young people's changeable *corages* (4928). In *The Canterbury Tales*, though, several tales rest on nuanced play with the most prominent medieval senses: "interiority" and "lust." The range of effects available for *corage* throughout the *Tales* is prefigured in its condensed force in the *General Prologue*. When Nature "so priketh hem...in hir corages" that they desire pilgrimage, and when the pilgrims take up the road to

Canterbury "with ful devout corage," a polyvocal play of piety and
irony toward both flesh and spirit is set in motion. Reading these two
lines with both implications in mind enables the most inclusive comic
and philosophical reading of *The Canterbury Tales*. Chaucer's pilgrims,
men and women alike, are governed by both the nature whose spring-
time libidinous restlessness keeps the birds awake all night and the
spirituality that acknowledges the timely help of Saint Thomas.

The *Clerk's Tale* produces strong tensions between these two senses
of *corage*. The tale is about Walter's stubborn disbelief that the outward
demeanor of his wife could possibly match her inmost heart. The
Clerk/narrator assures us early that Griselda's *corage* is "sad and rype"
(220), and later that she came to prepare the house for the second wife
"with no swollen thoght in hire corage" (950). Readers are privy to her
inmost heart, but Walter, until the very end, is not; he wants "the
utterest preeve of hir corage" (787). The contribution of the term
corage to the shape of the plot is to establish it as the stable center for
personality (the sense it often bears in *Boece*), when it is used of
Griselda, but to slant it toward "lust" when Janicula accuses his son-
in-law of abandoning his daughter once he "fulfild hadde his corage"
(907). Although Janicula's charge of a wandering eye is not exactly
what the reader knows about Walter from the rest of the tale, this
suggestion tinges his overbearing masculine willfulness with the
erotic.

The inner/outer perspective is just as probing in *The Merchant's Tale*,
although its mode is comic, sometimes broadly so. The first of its five
occurrences of *corage*—"swich a greet corage / Hadde this knyght to
ben a wedded man" (1254)—could be construed as "will" or even
"valor" (it is the phrase used to define fortitude in *The Parson's Tale*).
But when Placebo asserts that it is "heigh sentence" January has
uttered and "heigh corage" in general for an old man to take a young
wife, the implication veers sharply toward *corage* as "lust" (1513);
anyone who, like Placebo, thinks January has been making sense
would also be likely to mistake lust for fortitude. Venus's speculation
as to whether her knight's *corage* will hold up as well in marriage as in
"libertee" (1725–26) clearly refers to sexual powers. In the darkly
comic wedding-night scene it is January himself who uses *corage* to
mean sexual prowess; first he warns May of its ferocity, then drinks a
concoction to increase it (1759, 1808). From an ethical standpoint,
January's conduct is blameworthy in two quite different ways: his
corage is willful without being steadfast (as his willingness to buy into
May's lies at the end suggests), but as boasted sexual capability, it is

undercut by his need for an aphrodisiac. His is "sex-in-the-head" in D.H. Lawrence's phrase, "not worth an olde shoe" in Alisoun of Bath's. Both as a Christian and as a lover, his *corage* is wanting.

In *Troilus and Criseyde,* the narrator's attribution to Criseyde of a "slydyng corage" in Book V (825) requires a retrospective reconsideration of both sex and will in the poem. Pandarus's use of *corage* to awaken Troilus's passive will, once when he first falls in love and later when he is in despair over the exchange of "prisoners" (I.564, IV.619), seems at first like right-minded encouragement (the surviving sense, *encourage,* has that cast). His assurance that Troilus's beloved is worthy and therefore ought to produce the peace of mind that comes with "noble corage and wel ordeyne" (I.892) is similarly positive. The "noble and heigh corage" Pandarus urges on his friend just before the consummation scene (III.897) is advice to overcome a love-sick paralysis in favor of sexual momentum, and, again, potentially positive. If sexual love is posited as a natural good (and the narrator is at pains to locate the story in a pre-Christian dispensation, "the tyme of the lawe of kynde"), the linchpin of the plot is that Criseyde's sexual imagination was not steadfast enough—it slid from one object to another, and the poem reports how the "slydyng" occurred. But the pattern of uses for *corage* in *Troilus* can be used to underwrite a quite different reading. Sex itself, when it becomes the dominant feature of will, may be the motive force of the tragedy, as the same narrator insists in the "epilogue," when he abandons his identification of Troilus as pre-Christian. In this view, it is his capitulation to *corage* as sexual desire that spells his doom, and would have marked his affair as tragic even if Criseyde had remained faithful to him. Troilus sought certainty, and sexual affections are by nature unanchored, blown about by warm winds.

Making courage male: Malory to Marlowe

Thomas Malory's retrospective celebration of English chivalry, *Morte D'Arthur,* involves none of these Chaucerian ambiguities. Malory inflects *courage* in ways that continue through most of the sixteenth century; retaining the sense of *courage* as strongly physical as well as mental, he suppresses its medieval sense "lust" in favor of bravery on the battlefield and uses it as the verb "encourage." The verb *corage* was just coming into favor late in fifteenth-century usage. In one of the *Paston Letters* we read: "It shall be ... the gretter ... shame to all your frendis, and the grettest coragyng and plesere ... to your elmyse [enemies]" (5.130) and John Bale's character Sedicyon instructs Dissymulation to drink with the king "to corage hym to drink" (*King Johan*, 1982). Malory's use of the verb throws emphasis on the way one knight's actions enspirit the group's. In the *Tale of Gareth*, Lynet tries to rally her allies from their dismay at the sight of the corpses of their predecessors: "abate nat youre chere for all this syght, for ye muste corrage youreself, other ellys ye bene all shente" (VII.15; 196.18–19).[3] In *The Healing of Sir Urry*, King Arthur offers to search Urry's wounds, "for to corrayge all other knyghtes I woll pray the sofftely to suffir me to handyll thy woundis" (XIX.40; 665.1–2). Such instances stress the importance of martial solidarity and by implication indict Malory's own fractious milieu. The spirit-kindling verb *courage* seems stronger than the merely suasive *encourage*, which supplanted it by the end of the sixteenth century.

Malory's usage includes no instances of what we now call "moral courage" which does not result in some sort of public action and no attributions of *courage* to female characters. *Courage* is the inner will to perform outward actions in Malory's description of Sir Severause; according to the Freynshe book, he "had never corayge nor grete luste to do batayle ayenste no man but if hit were ayenste gyauntis and ayenste dragons and wylde bestis" (XIX.11; 665.42–44). Trystram's qualities are similarly public; the Kynge with the Hundred Knyghtes offers to withdraw, having seen his opponent's "corayge and curtesye" (IX.31; 323.29). A vivid passage that reveals Malory's sense of what *courage* is describes the battle between Gawain and Lancelot at the siege of Benwick:

> But whan sir Launcelot felte sir Gawaynes myght so mervaylously encres, he than wythhylde hys corayge and hys wynde, and so he kepte hym undir coverte of hys myght and of hys shylde: he traced and traverced here and there to breake sir Gawaynys strokys and hys currayge.
>
> (XX.22; 706.16–20)

Such *courage* is both a constitutional factor among the knight's powers, like strength, and a willed stance which can be offered or withheld and even weakened in one's enemy. Knowing that Gawain's strength increases until noon like that of the sun, Lancelot makes a conscious decision to husband his own valuable *courage* until his chances of defeating Gawain are better. The *courage* of both men is treated as a supply which will be spent in battle.

Malory's usage would be interesting even if it were simply idiosyncratic, but the lexicon of the rather unlikely Thomas Elyot, seldom concerned with military matters, replicates the idea of a supply of *corage* to be managed. Together the two writers suggest a bridge between inwardness and valor. In his *Castle of Health,* Elyot gives the physiological explanation of the fleumatic complexion, in which cold and moisture predominate, as "dulness in learning, smallness of courage" (119). There *courage* seems a quality rooted in the disposition of the somatic person. It is not altogether denied to women, as *The Defence of Good Women* shows (50.5–6), but men's constitutions are "more strong and couragiouse," women's "more circumspecte," suggesting compensating virtues (36.5–8).[4] Much of the advice in *The Book Named the Governor* is aimed at strategically managing a youngster's store of *courage.* Elyot implies that it uses up *courage* to read and study (32.35) and schoolmasters should be sparing with grammar lessons lest those "too long or exquisite" for the young child "mortifieth his courage." He also argues at some length for the value of reading Latin and Greek authors, for thereby *"courage* is inflamed in virtue" (24.36) and desire to experience noble action (33.19); proper poetry can "inflame" a young man's "martial courage," while grammar and law lessons can kill a child's "courage to study" (29.5–6, 52.6). The *courage* of the young must be both aroused by reading histories and "bridled with reason" by reading philosophy. There are several sorts of *courage*: "gentle" (14.30, 17.22), but also "martial" (33.28), "valiant" (37.30), and even "furious" (64.27). But whether discerning or daring, *courage* carries a positive valence, not to be confused with avaricious, loose-tongued "fury or rage, which they [gamblers] call courage" (89.24). (Note here Elyot's awareness of the appropriation of language to enhance an activity.) Malory's sense of a commodity to be deployed in battle is moved indoors to the classroom in *Book of the Governor,* where vital energy is none the less shaped and rationed out.

But an interesting set of Elyot's instances hark back to the medieval sense "lust" as Malory's do not. Certain scents, for example, might move a man toward "wanton courage" (*Governor* 49.23), and as the child approaches 14 or 15, *courage* increases (51.17 and 59.30) and must be channeled (39.5) or "assuaged" (50.3). Considering these uses as signaling at least general gusto, and probably sexual energy, Elyot's defense of dancing as a ritual of right order provides an interesting crux:

And the moving of the man would be more vehement, of the

woman more delicate, and with less advancing of the body, signifying the courage and strength that ought to be in a man, and the
pleasant soberness that should be in a woman.

(78.7–11)

Certainly bravery and vigor are cited as the man's part, but *courage* as
"desire" may also be implicated in the general meaning this social
ritual enacts: "*shamefastness* joined to *appetite of generation* maketh
continence, which is a mean between *chastity* and *inordinate lust*"
(78.17–18, italics in the edition). Even when Elyot's instances allow
themselves to be read with their medieval suggestion of "lust," his
usage fixes *corage* as a male-inflected term, as strongly as Malory's,
although exceptional women like Zenobia in *The Defence of Good
Women* (1.7; 51.14–15) are said to demonstrate valor and resolution.

Courage in Christopher Marlowe's plays is once more a call to battle.
Like Malory's, Marlowe's sense of *courage* is both the constitutional
equipment of worthy men and a managed resource of fighters and their
leaders. His range for the term is suggested by its heavy concentration
in the two parts of *Tamburlaine,* where 16 of the 19 dramatic uses are
found. In all 19 cases, "valor" is the predominant meaning, often in
phrases like "fight [or "martch"] couragiously."[5] Tamburlaine's ethos is
based on *courage,* which he thinks of as both inborn (in his case, given
by Providence) and able to be inspired. He curses his eldest son thus:

> Bastardly boy, sprong from some cowards loins,
> And not the issue of great *Tamburlaine*:
> Of all the provinces I have subdued
> Thou shalt not have a foot, unlesse thou beare
> A mind corragious and invincible
>
> (Part II, I.iii.69–73)

Courage here is the direct opposite of cowardice. The son fails to
exhibit such a mind, and is killed and denied a proper burial;
Tamburlaine himself unfailingly returns to the field and requires that
behavior of his soldier-companions. *Courage* fills the hearts of warlike
men; the implication "lust" is not only not attached to it, but becomes
in effect its counter-term. Tamburlaine chides his sons with looking
"amorous, / Not martiall," which "Argues their want of courage and of
wit," they might "play the lute, dance, or hang the arms about a Ladies
neck" (Part II, I.iv.21–30). Tamburlaine deals out women to his soldiers
as spoils of battle after an enemy's defeat, linked no more than the

gold with which they are paid to the *courage* that has "earned" them. These plays present a stance toward women not far from that which Klaus Theweleit observed in the Freikorps writing which prepared Germany for fascism after World War I. "Love of women and love of country are at opposite poles" seems to be a non-ironic motif of this writing, and Theweleit concludes that "evil," sexually tempting women are vilified and killed while the mother/sister figure of the "white nurse" is "rendered lifeless", being turned into a distanced idea, with inspirational power but no agency (like Zenocrate, both living and dead). The soldier must exclude both kinds of women from his serious work in defense of his own purity and autonomy.

The practice of other sixteenth-century writers falls close to the patterns set by Malory, Elyot, and Marlowe. Thomas More's *Dialogue of Comfort* frequently uses *corage* as the verb "encourage," as in Malory, and therefore links it with comfort, which itself means strengthen, and William Tyndale does too, both in *The Obedience of a Christian Man*, when the members of the early church are said to have "couraged them [Paul and Barnabas]...bidding them to be strong in God" (275.25) and in the chapter summary for Joshua I in his translation of the Old Testament when "The Lord courageth Josua to invade the land of promise." The word in this sense becomes a leitmotif for both men, since both attempted, as Tyndale puts it in *Obedience,* to "apply our myndes to the gatheryng of comfort & corage agaynst such persecutions" (296.10).[6] In the political sphere *courage* is inflected as "valor" and marked as masculine even more single-mindedly. Robert Thorne's "Declaration" urging Henry VIII to colonize the New World argues that other nations will regard England as wanting "the noble courage and spirit" to compete for colonies, while Henry's subjects are "without activity or courage in leaving to do this glorious and noble enterprise" (quoted in Jeffrey Knapp's *Empire Nowhere* 27, 31).

It would seem that in establishing the positive, masculine, public sense of valor, Early Modern English all but lost the most prominent Middle English aura of *corage* as inward inclination, especially sexual desire. But in their project to establish English as a literary language capable of sophisticated effects for original works and the translation of the ancients, some writers raided the word-hoards of other European languages, of street language and specialized dialects, and, in the case of *courage* particularly, of medieval English. The effect of this raid is to evoke a structure of feeling in which the positive, public, masculine virtue of courage does not entirely lose touch with the older sign *corage* as "sexual desire." Sometimes this appears as readable *double entendre*, and sometimes as a telling, but less definite, feature of the emotional tone of a passage.

Return of the repressed: Spenser, Sidney, and Shakespeare

In *A Midsummer Night's Dream* Peter Quince worries that if the company practices its play in the city, its clever dramatic "devices" will not be able to be kept secret. Bottom agrees that they should meet in the forest to "rehearse most obscenely and courageously" (I.ii.110). By "obscenely" he "means" obscurely (or so the notes say), but also, as the event will prove, "obscenely." His "courageously" reinforces the double entendre in his malapropism and suggests that a residue of *courage* as "lust" was discernible to London theater-goers. So do a few other examples of London writing. Thomas Dekker's *The Gul's Horn-booke* uses the word in his praise of midday naps, "they set a russet colour on the cheekes of young women, and make lusty courage to rise in men" (22.18–20), just what medieval sermons often warned against.[7] In Thomas Middleton's *Michaelmas Term*, the Country Wench who has been persuaded to come to London to be Lethe's mistress explains to her father (whom she does not recognize in disguise), "there's no courageous sinner amongst us, but was a gentle-woman by the mother's side, I warrant you" (4.3.22), suggesting both "bold" or open sinners, like herself and "lustful" though perhaps less public sinners who are still accounted "gentlewomen."[8] But it is in Spenser's *Faerie Queene*, Sidney's *New Arcadia*, and several of Shakespeare's plays that the residual sense is most strongly marked.

In Edmund Spenser's work the three medieval strands of implication for *courage* are all present. *The Faerie Queene* sometimes uses *corage* as valor: "with steadfast eye and courage stout" (III.xii.37.5) and "Nor yet has any knight his courage crackt" (II.i.12.5), and sometimes as sexual desire: "When courage first does creepe in manly chest" (I.ix.9.2). But usually the strands of implication are tightly woven together. An idea like "resolve" is basic to such passages, but it is often linked syntac-tically with "eager," "greedy," "flaming," "enflamed," or, most frequently, "kindled," blurring the distinction between *courage* as constitutional valor (in either a male or female) and as the result of erotic stimulation (usually in a male). Early in Canto XI of Book I, Una attempts to embolden Redcrosse for his encounter with the dragon. Her encouraging speech mixes gratitude for his faithful sufferings with the lure of renown for his exploit and a subtle promise of herself as prize in urging him to "awake" "the sparke of noble courage" (2.6). In a comic tone the mixed strands are evoked in would-be abductor Trompart's shrinking before Belphebe's "great words," which "did apall his feeble courage" (II.iii.44.5–6). In such passages, and there are many in *The Faerie Queene*, Spenser signals a sense of the connectedness of these strains in male psychology and discourse.

Midway through Book I, a cluster of instances of *corage* explores that connection with particular focus. In Canto VIII, the giant Orgoglio fights for Duessa "with courage fild, / And eger greedinesse through every member thrild" (6.8–9), and the stress falls heavily on the erotic sense of *courage*. A few stanzas later Duessa aids her giant-lover by sprinkling poyson from her golden cup on Arthur's "courageous" squire who impedes her from attacking his master. The poyson "his sturdie courage soone...quayd / And all his senses were with suddeine dread dismayd" (viii.13–14). The "poyson" from her golden cup is the Eucharist polluted by the Catholic doctrine of transubstantiation in the historical allegory this section establishes, but in the literal fiction, it dulls the valor and conviction of a simple, righteous man. The literal tale presents a vivid scene of the Squire's loyal boldness mysteriously incapacitated; allegorically, the practicing Christian is incapacitated by the magical priestly mediation (somehow associated with female seductiveness) which is claimed to transform wine into sacred blood.

Philip Sidney's *New Arcadia* generally treats courage as "bravery" and gives it a distinct masculine, even martial, inflection. The neat put-down Zelmane/Pyrocles offers the peasants is a good example of this usage: how can it be that "so many valiant men's courages can be inflamed to the mischief of one silly woman" (285.31–32). At first glance, its rhetorical strategy seems appropriate to Malory or Marlowe's terrain, where masculine *courage,* valor, is contrasted with the weakness (and perhaps innocence—see chapter 10, "Sely/Silly") of the feminine. But although such notions are taken for granted by Zelmane's appeal, the effects of the speech turn out to be quite subtle and contradictory, in part because the "silly woman" involved has just exhibited extraordinary valor, in part because *courage* is situated textually between "valiant men" and "inflamed" (suggesting aroused lust), and in part because "Zelmane" is Prince Pyrocles in drag.[9]

Musidorus explains how "full of tormenting desire...my courage stirred up my wit to seek for some relief" (108.18–19), and wit provided the ruse of the rustic disguise in which he could see Pamela. Plangus's stepmother praises the "valiantness of his courage," a seemingly straightforward enough commendation, but then she puts a sexual spin on the word by wondering "whether his wit were greater in winning [his subjects'] favours, or his courage in employing their favours" (218.17, 25 27).[10] The passage in which the lust-besotted Amphialus looks around him on the battlefield and sees horror without its flattering mask refects on the duplicity of the term *courage*. Danger was not dreadful to his "undismayable courage" and he found himself "rather inflamed than troubled with the increase of dangers, and glad to find a worthy subject to exercise his courage" (345.6, 8–10). It would seem that, if we allow the old meaning of *courage* to operate subtly, the text invites a reflection about sexual prowess culturally connected to military valor through a well approved dynastic pride. The passage goes on to comment on the odd connection between Eros and combat through an epic simile: "as in two beautiful folks love naturally stirs a desire of joining, so in their two corages hate stirred a desire of trial" (345.18–20). Nature is alleged as the source of both sex and aggression, but culture has provided the similitude which frames their connection.

Shakespeare's cross-dressed heroines in the comedies acknowledge the male inflection of the word *courage* and subvert its straightforward effects through their brave conduct, rendering that inflection both visible and constructed rather than "natural." Although the trope of female cowardice in these plays is consistently belied by the principled fortitude of the heroines—Portia, Viola, Rosalind, Imogen—it is presented through the Middle English courage-as-arousal and sword-as-phallus, as in Rosalind's "make them think I am furnished with that which I lack." Male impersonation is invoked in a darker way in Lady Macbeth's "screw your courage to the sticking place" (I.vii.60). Lady Macbeth is tauntingly presenting herself as more manly than her husband in this scene; whether she has actually borne the children she refers to is less important than her assertion that her female constitution would be equipped for the murderous task from which his shrinks. Her diction stresses the link between violence and sex (as well as gender) through the innuendoes in "screw" and "sticking," both of which were already sexual puns in 1600. In a different style, Cleopatra's "Husband I come / Now to that name my courage prove my title! / I am fire and air" (V.ii.290–92) enacts maleness by assuming the role of Antony (now dead) and his distinctive Roman virtue. She follows him in suicide and repeats as she does so the word associated with his "noble" and "Roman" death as it is reported earlier in Act V by Decretas: "that self hand / Which writ his honor in the acts it did / Hath with the courage which the heart did lend it, / Spitted the heart" (V.i.21–24). She proclaims herself entitled to call Antony "husband" by her "courage," now made of fire and air, the two elements conventionally associated with maleness and mind, ridding herself of the female-inflected water and earth (V.ii.290–93).

In different ways the words written for Rosalind, Lady Macbeth, and Cleopatra directly acknowledge that *courage* has a male province in these social formations. *Troilus and Cressida* and *Cymbeline* provide extended studies in the macho temperament. They complicate the significances of *courage* by posing embarrassing questions about the constellation independence, warlikeness, and chivalric courage-as-bravery and its connections with sexual desire, possessive jealousy and courage-as-lust.

In *Troilus and Cressida*, Nestor is the spokesman for the idealized military sense of *courage* as the brave and steady defiance of the odds. He encourages the continuation of the siege by urging that a storm which lays oak trees low inspires "the thing of courage / As roused with rage with rage, doth sympathize...Retires to chiding Fortune" (I.iii.50–54). This sounds just like Malory—one man's daring responding to another's and seasoned warriors conserving their store, as Aeneas does when he postpones his "black defiance" and "courage" to welcome Diomede on a diplomatic mission (IV.i.14). (The passage reads, "Health to you, valiant sir, / During all question of the gentle truce. / But when I meet you armed, as black defiance / As heart can think or courage execute" [IV.i.10–13]). Troilus's argument that nothing should be allowed to "deject the courage of our minds" (121) because Helen is "the theme of honor and renown, / A spur to valiant and magnanimous deeds / Whose present courage may beat down our foes" (199–201), relies on male solidarity the occasion of which is sexual desire. Troilus's warmth toward Paris's keeping Helen is in large measure based on his own desire for Cressida, as Hector points out (without knowing the specifics) in calling their argument that of "young men...unfit to hear moral philosophy" (166–67). Thus the deployment of the word *courage* plays an important part in the more general subversion, by Thersites and by the plot itself, of patriotic battle rhetoric. As a result, Agamemnon's cheerful greeting to the Greek warriors that they anticipate the battle with "starting courage" and Ulysses' "Oh courage, courage, princes" on the approach of the final day of the war, cannot be taken quite at their speakers' valuations.

If *courage* is steadily de-valorized, in part by its connection with sex in *Troilus*, it begins at the bottom in *Cymbeline*. Explaining why he seems cool while enduring gambling losses and "hot" in winning, the churlish Cloten says that "winning will put any man into courage. If I could get this foolish Imogen, I should have gold enough" (II.iii.7). Cloten is a fool, a village explainer; yet discredited as the play holds him, his little speech here renders explicit one thrust of the fable of the whole: winning (getting the tribute back, asserting military superiority over Caesar) produces valor and is routed through sex ("If I could *get* Imogen"). Jachimo also gets money and ascendancy in the male peer group by seeming to *get* Imogen, and in the end Posthumus and Cymbeline do the same thing. The *courage* of the Britons, as Posthumus (II.iv.22–24) and the Queen (III.i.33) both tell the story, was legendary. Briton or not, women don't have courage—that is the point of the by-play in III.iv concerning Imogen's disguise as a youth. Imogene is urged to adopt "a waggish courage, / Ready in gibes, quick-answered, saucy, and / As querulous as the weasel" (160–62), a description that fits the men in this play pretty well.

   In spite of this familiar comic irony, when Imogene faces the danger she is courting she calls herself a "soldier" to it, who "will abide it with / A prince's courage" (183–84), defining her constitution by referring to her lineage. In this she spoke as Queen Elizabeth had throughout her reign: "I care not for death, for all men are mortal and though I be a woman I have as good a courage answerable to my place as ever my father had" and "I am armed with a better courage than is common in my sex, so as whatsoever befalls me, death shall never find me unprepared."[11] The chivalric pretensions of the military aristocracy are as roughly handled by the events of this play as by *Troilus and Cressida*. The kidnapped princes aristocratic *blood* (as "genetic inheritance" and as "thirst for battle") is proved by their untaught yearning for violence: "What thing is't that I never / Did see man die.... I am ashamed to look upon the holy sun" (IV.iv.35–41). The play seems to let the macho, boasting, violence-loving, women-distrusting ethos run its course. And finally, with no convincing conversion experiences to account for the change, all the men still alive at the end of the play make peace: they have all *got* Imogen, each in a different way.

   There is no question that Shakespeare expects *courage* to be inflected as male, even as *Troilus and Cressida* and *Cymbeline* undermine the term as the straightforward honorific "valor" to which it had been elevated during the preceding century. The deep distrust of military rhetoric these plays carry reactivates residual traces for the word, especially its earlier sense "lust." This residual sense does not return, of course, with its original, straightforward significance intact. It returns as something usually occluded, something important for an emerging nation-state to occlude, especially a state still contemplating the after-image of an imposing female monarch. It appears in puns and fables, but these indirections point out directions readable in semantic history. For Theweleit, the denial of the privileged term *courage* to women signaled an important feature of the fantasy life of the clearly misogynous German "patriots" he studied, but he argues that less extreme forms of these notions characterize all patriarchal mentalities. Although language itself is inflected by such notions, as Habermas claims, sometimes the subtleties of language can be probed, as Gadamer argues, to reveal them.

3
Estat/Estate

Time, that rearranger of estates
Anne Sexton, "The Division of Parts"

You would have Mr. Casaubon because he had such a great
soul, and was so old and dismal and learned; and now you
think of marrying Mr. Ladislaw, who has got no estate or
anything.
George Eliot, *Middlemarch*

Anne Sexton's choice of "estate" relies on a general sense of "standing"
or "condition," which is derived straightforwardly from its Latin
precursors *status*, "standing," and *stare*, "to stand," but it also involves
a deliberate pun on "holdings." That first sense—"condition"—runs
through the whole period of this study; for example, a will in 1392
reads "I...in hool estat of my body and in good mynde beynge, make
my testament" (*Earliest English Wills* 4). But dying and wills were not
the primary site for the word; "man's estate," "the estate of virginity
[or widowhood]" (Queen Elizabeth refers to her virgin "kind of life" as
"this estate" [in Rice's edition 115]) and "estate of grace" were more
common. *The Castle of Perseverance* contains the memorable couplet,
urged against Man's salvation by Justicia: "But whanne he was com to
man's a-state / All his behestis he thanne for-gate" (3402–03). Even the
departed saints are thought of in status hierarchies; as the *Mirror of
Salvation* says, "Marie superexcellis of all seints, the state / Of patriarkes
and Prophetes and Postles Dignitee, / Of Martirs and confessoures and
virgines in Degree" (39). A touching fictional example is found in *The
Pearl*. The bereaved father cannot believe his daughter is a queen in

28

heaven, a countess or lesser lady "wer fayr in heuen to halde asstate" (490), but the girl asserts that God has made her a queen by the same logic that pays the last-hired worker in the parable in Matthew the wage of the first-hired. In another register, "My belly farys not weyll, it is out of astate" (123.228) from the *Towneley* suggests the colloquial reach of the word. Middle English usage, however, is dominated by a more specific sense, that of the three estates into which dominant social theory imagined England's population divided.

For the late Middle Ages, the division of the social world into three estates was one of those ideas so self-evident that they "do not need evidence, yet they create it," as Michael Mendle puts it in *Dangerous Positions*. Estates theory granted each person membership in a productive group with a particular function—the clergy to pray and study, the knighthood to fight and rule, and the peasantry to work—however awkward it may have been at accounting for some late medieval careers. The tripartite division was acknowledged as early as a gloss by King Alfred in his translation of Boethius's *Consolation of Philosophy*, insisting that the king needs "gebedmen" who pray, "fyrdmen" who fight, and weorcmen" who labor (Book II, prosa 7).[1] Such *estate* was generally conferred by birth, not choice, exertion, or talent, except in the case of the clergy, where priestly celibacy complicated the inheritance system. There were, of course, within each of the three, gradations of status, in which some opportunities for mobility and impersonation were available. In 1362, the commons presented Edward III a petition urging him to correct the outrage that "divers people" were appropriating the garb of their betters; the resulting statute sought to discipline dress and prevent upstarts from assuming a demeanor "against their estate and degree" (Baldwin 46–47). Time was not, for most people, expected to rearrange estates. Among the hundreds of examples of *estate* in the *Middle English Dictionary*, only one suggests the possibility of working toward a particular *estate,* and even that in a style emphasizing hierarchy. "The Constitutions of Masonry" promises beginners, "Whose wol conne thys craft and com to astate, / He most love wel God, and Holy Churche algate / And his mayster also, that he ys wyth" (265–67). A woman could marry up, as Russell's *Book of Norture* explains.[2] Although estates theory came to reflect neither lived careers in an increasingly fluid economy nor rationales for the make-up of Parliament, it none the less grounded discussion of medieval social relations in secular and religious discourses, both orthodox and heterodox.

By 1600 the role of estates theory in everyday usage was merely residual.[3] In governmental circles, estates theory had gradually become tangled with issues of the role and make-up of Parliament. The Reformation cast doubt on the obviousness of the clergy as an estate, and some Presbyterian factions reinterpreted the estates as king, lords, and commons. The matter came to a head as James VI of Scotland brought the quarrel with him on ascending the English throne, insisting that the three old estates defined the constitution of Parliament, which, under the rule of the king, defined England's government. In Scotland he declared deviation from it treasonous, and as James I of England he called that deviation sedition (see Mendle, Chrimes, and Weston and Greenberg). Less visible, but perhaps more influential than these deliberate personal and factional maneuvers, economic changes, fed by new gold from the Americas, which rearranged the old inherited estates joined the strand of Protestant thought which de-emphasized birthright. Most instances of *estate* by James's time had come to involve ownership of property.[4] That sense was so general that Hermia's father Egeus in *A Midsummer Night's Dream* can use it to give away his possession Hermia: "She is mine, and all my right of her / I do estate unto Demetrius" (I.i.97–98), and Iris in Prospero's masque offers "some donation freely to estate / On the blest lovers" (*Tempest*, IV.i.85–86). This reference to holdings, of course, becomes the surviving meaning, and it is what George Eliot's status-obsessed Celia means by chiding Dorothea for making a marriage that will not advance her heritable wealth.

However we assess the balance of economic and social forces, the fact that *estate* lost its medieval reference "who one is" and took on its early modern reference "what one has" is surely a semantic example of what Marx refers to in *The Communist Manifesto* when he writes: "All fixed, fast-frozen relations, with their train of ancient and venerable prejudices and opinions, are swept away.... All that is solid melts into air, all that is holy is profaned" by the cash nexus (58).

The medieval consensus and its material signs

The pervasiveness in late medieval social theory of largely inherited membership in one of the three estates is nicely demonstrated by the similarity between orthodox and Lollard commentators on work and duty. As Raymond Williams argues, hegemonies are sustained in dynamic processes, "renewed, recreated, defended, and modified" to meet new conditions (*Marxism and Literature* 112), and this must certainly be true of a large-scale hegemony like estates theory. Today

Wyclif's ideas are generally held to be socially liberatory and in advance of their time—and in many ways they are—but in their insistence on the importance of the estates they are indistinguishable from the social thinking of the mainstream—Wyclifittes take part in the renewal of estates theory. On the orthodox side, Thomas Wimbledon's sermon at Paul's Cross in 1387, for example, explains I Corinthians 7.20, which Wimbledon translates: "euery man see what astaat God hath clepid hym and dwelle he ther inne" (98–99). As long as a horse or sheep has access to his proper food, says Wimbledon, he can survive quite well, but human beings cannot survive without social organization. Without clerics the people would "waxe wilde in vices, and deyen gostely," without knights "no man shold live in peace," and without laborers the other estates would lapse while everyone became "acre men and herdis" (48–66).[5] The Wycliffite tract *Lanterne of Liȝt* defends estates theory in an equally thoroughgoing way. "This is the lowest astaat that we clepen comunes.... [Knyȝthod] is clepid the seconde astate in hooli chirche.... The hiȝe ordir of presthood... this astate representith the seconde persoone in trinite.... Vpon thise three astatis standith the chirche" (33–34; cf., *de Officio Regis* 58–59 and many sermons). Wyclif argued his case for dominion (an important focus of the controversy surrounding his positions) on the basis of a very discrete separation of the powers of the estates, which led to the conclusion that the lords temporal must rule temporal affairs, including some management of ecclesiastically held property, especially that of the monastic orders.[6] Far from being a leveler in the matter of the estates, Wyclif out-Heroded Herod—or rather Wimbledon.

Both Lollard and anti-Lollard tracts of the early fifteenth century respect medieval estates theory. In *Jack Upland,* the Lollard position is that the religious orders "lyve idilli bi ipocrisie and disceive alle the statis ordeyned bi God" (Dean's edition 120.37–38). The orthodox rejoinder, *Friar Daw's Reply,* accuses Wycliffite factions of destabilizing the estates (Dean 150.4) and teaching the "hindring of states" by attacking friars' right to poverty, and presumably therefore to begging (150.17–18). The attack *The Plowman's Tale* launches against the clerical estate, while loyal to estates theory, perches its implications for the word precariously between the God-ordained social role and the emergent, secular "holdings." Consider, for example, the neat couplet: "Priours, abbottes of great estates. Of hevyn and hell they kepe the yates" (Dean 60.64–65). By invoking a clever mix of potential meanings the lines can suggest the great manorial lords that contemporary abbots often were, commanding the opening and closing physical gates, or the holders of a spiritual charge exercising their duties, depending on the reading of *gates* and *estates*. The prelates who "weld hye estates" (71.416) later in the argument are being admonished that their *estates* have dwindled from spiritual callings into secular, pride-fully-held real estate. And at the climactic finish, after the Gryffon representing the institutional church has threatened the Lollard Pellycan with death and hell, the Pellycan answers, "I drede nothynge your hye estate" (97.1259). *Estate* has thus structured the argument of the poem; early it is ambiguous, later accusatory. The force of the poem, none the less, rests on the natural rightness of the true estates; current claimants to the first estate are only landlords who can legislate for the body but not the soul. These broad, naturalized understandings are what melt into air when the cash nexus takes over, in Marx's vision of the end of the Middle Ages.

What Marx described as sacred obligation also required routine material demonstration. Stabilized as they were by birth, estates divisions were also openly and constantly marked with visible signs. The sumptuary laws of Edward III's time have already been mentioned, and documents concerning late medieval great households are equally precise about the ideological connection between the standing a person is granted and the property he or she can display. Sir John Fortescue puts it thus:

> it shall nede that the kyng haue such tresour, as he mey...bie hym riche clothes, riche furres,...and other juels and ornaments conueyent to his estate roiall....Ffor yff a king did not so, nor myght do, he lyved then not like his estate, but rather in miseire, and in more subgeccion than doth a priuate person.
>
> (Myers 10)

The *Liber Niger* or *Black Book* of Edward IV's household accounts (1471 or 1472) exemplifies the blessed rage for order and degree in a king's household, an order that was threatened by an increasingly fluid and competitive arrangement of duties and honors intended to produce the no-longer-functional appearance of a chivalric court. Late-medieval princes like Edward IV were expected to appear more and more grandly magnanimous, while becoming in fact more competently managerial by bringing their expenditures within predictable limits. The arrangement of the *Liber Niger* supports this claim by being divided into two distinct parts: the "Domus Regie Magnificencie," about how to look resplendent, and the "Domus Providencie," about how to buy, prepare, and lay out as little as possible to produce the aura of *richesse*. The key term in the first section is *estate*, often followed by *degree*, and the frequency with which it turns up witnesses the continual pressure on the account to define the "estate and degree" of every office and visitor discussed and to insure the granting of servants, food, fuel, and candles for each according to his or her *estate*. Each rank is distinguished from those above and below it—the thesaurere is "the second astate next the steward in this honorable court" (Myers 144.25–26)—in an orderly subcategorization of the three medieval orders. The term also refers to the proper displays and ceremonies of *estate*, as when "the king kepe astate in his chambyr" (115.21). Just how these categories must have intruded on people's self-definition can be seen in two stipulations:

ITEM, that none astate, hygh nor lowe degree, kepe within thys court mo personez than be to hym appoynted vppon the payne of houshold.

ITEM, that none officer nor knyȝt nor esquier charged depart from thys court any tym without hys dew lycence...

(161.37–41)

The king's household, it would seem, endeavored to prescribe everything worn, eaten, or used, everyone commanded, every place inhabited. No matter how unsuccessful this attempt may ultimately have been, it must have slowed the momentum toward the personal and social fluidity that characterizes modernity.

Assuming and resigning estate in Chaucer

There were few ways, outside of ordination and (largely for women) marriage, to advance one's estate, but it was possible to be downwardly mobile. Trevisa's *Higden* reports that "[Pope] Formosus...was degraded anon to the staat of a lewed man" (6.391). The casual statement is interesting in that it shows both how far one could be lowered by a disgrace or unfortunate political alliance and how firmly *lewed* referred, at this date, primarily to a social, rather than a moral, category.[7] Presumably, Formosus did not immediately forget all the Latin he knew when he was "lerned," but without institutional favor, his learning was withdrawn from his public identity. Chaucerian usage evokes a rich and subtle mix of social and introspective emphases with the word *estate*. *The Clerk's Tale*, *The Parson's Tale*, and *Troilus and Criseyde* all contain an unusually large number of instances of the term (*Clerk's Tale* 11, *Parson's Tale* 16, and *Troilus* 21), and each works out, I want to claim, an internally coherent attitude toward it. In each, it comes to question whether and how *estate* can be assumed and resigned, and that, in turn, suggests the range of *estat* in Chaucer's lexicon.

The interrogation of *estat* in *The Clerk's Tale* begins as Walter's people urge him to marry, since death smites in "ech estaat" (123), and they need an heir to rule them. They respect the claims of blood—their next ruler must be *his* heir—but they imagine his wife will be "Born of the gentilleste and of the meeste / Of al this land." Walter agrees to marry, but makes an argument for natural nobility (155–61), and acts on it by choosing Griselda from a "povre estaat ful lowe" (473). The unconditional obedience he demands of her rests on the fact that he took her out of her poor array "And putte [her] in estaat of heigh noblesse / Ye have nat that forgeten, as I gesse?" (467–69). A neutral use of *estaat* marks the passing of four years (610), and then Walter sends for his saved, but hidden children to rejoin them in "honorable estaat al openly" (767). Griselda's final trial—her repudiation—begins. Her father, hearing of her walking back home stripped to her smock, confirms his earlier doubts about the marriage: that once Walter had sated his "corage," he would think it a "disparage / To his estaat so lowe for t'alighte" (909). But Griselda herself returns to her life of poverty as if none of this had happened, because, the narrator tells us, "in hire grete estaat / Hire goost was evere in pleyn humylitee" (925). Walter then orders her back to the house to provide for "every wight in his degree / Have his estaat, in sittyng and servyse" (957–58). When Walter finally concludes his cruel test, he acknowledges her steadfastness both in "greet estaat and povreliche arrayed" (1055). *Estaat* has thus turned up in connection with all the major plot developments.

I am not concerned here to work out a psychology for Walter and Griselda so much as to discern in their story a kind of thesis about *estaat*. The instances of *estaat* in *The Clerk's Tale* refer to the distinction between those who work and those who rule, and the tale is told by one of those who pray. Everyone—Walter, Walter's "people," the sergeant who takes the children, Griselda, Griselda's father Janicula, and even the off-stage sister who keeps the children hidden from their mother for 12 years—takes for granted social distinctions and the right of the high-born to control the lived conditions of the low-born. If this is an egalitarian fable—and it is insofar as peasant Griselda proves a capable ruler—it backs into its egalitarianism after a false start in which Walter preached "natural nobility" early in the tale only to pull rank soon afterward. Walter quickly succumbed to the temptations of high estate, imagining that his temporal power gave him some rights over other people's *inner* lives, but Griselda entertained no such illusion. Griselda's "goost was ever in pleyn humylitee," untouched by temporal *estaat*, without staging an open rebellion against it. It is the tale as a whole that hints rebellion, told as it is by a poor philosopher hard-pressed to explain Walter's obsessive actions (617–23, 701–07), one who may be imagined as having run into some advanced social thinking at Oxenford.

The Parson's Tale concurs in the general consensus that temporal high and low are ordained by God and "everich sholde be served in his estaat and in his degree," but that entails mutual obligations, the man to the lord and the lord to the man (770–71). (The Parson even mentions that some converts to the faith set their chattel slaves free.) To the person placed in "heigh estaat," that gift is like God's other gifts, given to test human ability to resist sin (152). The very definition of "veyneglorie" is "to have pompe and delit in his temporeel hynesse, and glorifie hym in this worldly estaat" (405). The *Parson's Tale* acknowledges clothing as a sign of *estaat* (as do the sumptuary laws) and treats them as providing an occasion for sin, but not that of social overreaching—the tale rebukes the wastefulness and immodesty of current styles. They use scarce materials, are easily dirtied and cannot be given to the poor as it is "nat convenient to were for hire estaat" being so "pownsoned and dagged" (pierced and slit) that they will scarcely keep an outdoor worker warm.

Here is what I want to note about the Parson's view of the estates: 1) like the Clerk, he acknowledges their rightness for temporal governance; 2) he considers membership in the ruling estate to provide temptations to pride and indulgence; and 3) the particulars of his rebukes to those who misuse social power show a detailed sense of the lives of the poor. Looked at as a commentary on the story of Walter and Griselda—not as the moral solution to the opposed perspectives of *The Canterbury Tales* or Chaucer's personal "take" on social morality— *The Parson's Tale* may help locate the disputed point of *The Clerk's Tale*. It limits what Walter has done for Griselda (or could do for anyone) by raising her social estate, since ultimately the state of grace in which Griselda remains is higher than her title as marchesa, and she maintains it from beginning to end. It demonstrates that support for social hierarchies does not empower the high to do as they will to the low with impunity, nor does it inhibit empathy with the lives of the poor. The Parson's emphasis on clothing as a mark of estate is matched in *The Clerk's Tale* by the three scenes stripping Griselda, first for her marriage, later for her repudiation, and finally for her re-instatement. The Clerk's story, like the Parson's sermon, insists that clothes mean something and confer function, but they may be put on and taken off, assumed and resigned.

As might be expected in a courtly tale, *Troilus and Criseyde* is also deeply cognizant of the decorum of *estate*. The implications of Troilus's resignation of his "estat roial" into his lady's hands in a striking passage in Book I is central to a reading of the moral import of the whole story. After her father's treachery, Criseyde somehow "Kepte hir estate" among the Trojans (I.130), and Troilus noted his lady's "Honour, estat, and wommanly noblesse" when she first caught his eye (I.287). *Estat* in this poem is used (on the surface, at least) for aristocratic standing; it is an honorific, like several words discussed by C. S. Lewis, which mean the high end of a scale when unmodified. *Estat* in this sense is an issue for Criseyde throughout. Fearful of losing the *estat* she holds onto so precariously after her father's treason, she refers to it often, telling Pandarus in Book II to keep his love letter "To myn estat have more reward [regard], I preye / Than to his lust!" (1133–34). (This phrasing can be reconsidered in the light of the "epilogue" as "spiritual estate," but its immediate implication is literally "standing"—her glance in the temple where Troilus first sees her says "may I not stonden here?"). Moreover, she is fully aware of the attractions of Troilus's *estat*; Pandarus stresses it, and she ponders it privately (II.205, 661). In Book IV she reassures Troilus that she would never forsake him for considerations like "estat, delit, or for weddynge" (1536), but when the test of her loyalty comes, she does count Diomede's *estat* in his favor (V.1025). "Estat roial" figures in the story from Criseyde's point of view early and late. Only Book III, which describes the lovers' mutual enjoyment, contains no mention of *estat* at all.

The turning point of Book I is Troilus's capitulation to the god of love, and it is performed in terms of *estate*.

> Wherefore, lord, if my service or I
> May liken yow, so beth to me benigne;
> For myn estat roial I here resigne
> Into hire hond, and with ful humble chere
> Bicome hir man, as to my lady dere.
>
> (430–34)

This passage describes an important gesture of feudal fealty. Troilus derives his "estat roial" from his birth in a social hierarchy, but he resigns it in a prayer to a deity (or mock deity). Justice William Thirning's formal declaration to Richard II that he had been deposed and deprived of the "Astate of King" would provide a spectacular real-life example of resigning royal estate during Chaucer's lifetime (Chrimes 112–13). But the phrase "estat roial" was central to discussions of monarchy as early as the 1380s, while Chaucer was working on *Troilus and Criseyde*. The word belonged most prominently to current political discourse, however smoothly it may have been appropriated to suit courtly romance. Troilus does not and can not divest himself of princedom in a private gesture, but he does carry out his resignation by deferring to Criseyde's decisions when the prisoner exchange is proposed. Pandarus would have him exert the claims of his birth-estate to carry Criseyde off: "hadde ich it so hoote, / And thyn estat, she sholde go with me" (IV.583–84), but Troilus counts his own estate less relevant in this matter than hers. The point is that Troilus carries out his promise to Love *not* to rule according to his birthright. But medieval usage and the shape of this story allow the interpretation of Troilus's action as resigning his "man's estate" of free will as well. In Book IV, he gives up on the problem posed philosophically; perhaps this vow has interfered with his independence.

Late in their story, Criseyde claims that Troilus's "moral vertu, grounded upon trouthe" was the source of her love, not "estat roial, / Ne veyn delit, nor only worthinessee / Of yow in werre or torney marcial, / Ne pompe, array, nobleye, or ek richesse" (IV.11642–43, 1667–70). Because of the way Books II and IV are balanced in their emphasis on *estat*, we know that Criseyde did ponder these things "first." In deferring to her, Troilus has let his power over a subject in Troy lapse, but Criseyde never shows that she understands the meaning of his deferral to her as a resignation of his *estat*, regarding it as a birthright inseparable from his being in Troy. What the narrator calls Troilus's "estat real above" in the "epilogue" (V.1830) recasts the frame through which the meaning of this love story can be assessed. This phrase may be taken to devalue Troilus's royalty—"above" it does not matter whether you are royal on earth or not—a reading that fits a *contemptus mundi* sense for the "swich fin..." list. Since Troilus is looking at the earthly from *above*, from the eighth sphere, he may have been restored to a spiritually royal estate as a result of his understanding of the "false worldes brotelnesse." In this second reading, his mistake was not in loving but in resigning his manly free will to a creature. His "sensitivity" to Criseyde's wishes may look emergent from the perspective of the companionate love relationships of a later era, but the "epilogue" recasts Troilus's tragedy (often seen by modern readers as novelistic in its psychological realism), as his confusion of priorities and duties in a medieval hierarchy easily rendered as moral allegory.

The medieval consensus melting into air

In the long logic of social change, the cash nexus and the Protestant Reformation combined to undermine the broad consensus which had sustained the explanatory power of the three estates in the Middle Ages. But a precipitating cause of its demise was probably a quarrel in the 1580s between James VI of Scotland and Presbyterian reformers who had succeeded in undermining the episcopacy in that country. Reformers disputed the existence of a "spiritual estate," claiming government consisted of a new three: King, nobles, and commons. James framed the "Black Acts" of 1584 to prohibit espousal of that position "under the pain of treason," and a temporarily strong Presbyterian party in Parliament stripped the Scottish bishops of most of their power and wealth, "indirectly abolishing" their estate (Mendle 72–73, 89). Some Scots threatened by the "Black Acts" fled to England, and there influenced English Puritans like Job Throckmorton, who is likely to have had a hand in writing the Marprelate tracts (Mendle 76–91). James brought his uncompromising espousal of the traditional three estates when he became James I of England. What he had called the "ancient and lovable custom" of Scotland (quoted in Mendle 73), he also used to give his regime what he regarded as the proper aura of *English* tradition. In *Basilikon Doron*, James writes: "As the whole Subjects of our countrey (by the ancient and fundamentall policie of our Kingdome) are diuided into three estates" (22.33–36) and describes the "nobilitie" as "second in ranke, yet ouer farre first in greatnesse and power" (24.34–36), and the "Burghes" as "Merchants and Craftesmen" (26.13–15). Note the shift in power relations toward the secular and the reinterpretation of the last category from a primarily rural peasantry to an urban trading class. In a speech to Parliament in 1607 James is still referring to "the three Estates" (303.12); he seems to regard *estates* as a current technical term in political discourse. There is evidence, though, that he could not resuscitate the term in its old sense: the Lords petitioned the King's high-handed policy of appropriating goods without fair remuneration, protesting their interest in the

common good as well as of their "own particular estates and possessions," using *estate* in its emergent sense "right to property" (*Select
Statutes* 299). The tradition of three estates was no longer the incon-
testable ground for other social pronouncements it had been in the
Middle Ages; there was legal dispute over how the estates were constituted and broad social focus on money and goods rather than ancient
and lovable status.

In a less specifically governmental discourse, Protestants explicitly
attacked the clerical estate through the doctrine of the priesthood of
all believers and the sanctified nature of all work. According to Luther
and Tyndale, the layperson and the pastor differ only in the offices in
which they serve, not in any essential distinction between their
estates. The difference between washing dishes and preaching the
word of God, writes Tyndale in *Wicked Mammon*, "as touching to
please God" makes no difference at all (quoted in Daniell 167).
Protestant ethics not only denied the priestly claim to a special spiritual estate, but exalted the righteous conduct of daily work as direct
service to God and denied the right to leisure, thereby weakening the
distinction between the second and third estates; in this new social
Eden everybody delves and spins, no idle "gentlemen."[8] Consider how
the term *estate* appears in William Perkins's *Of the Vocations or Callings
of Men, Work*: "Now all societies of men are bodies...and in these
bodies there be several members which are men walking in several callings and offices, the execution whereof must tend to the happy and
good estate of the rest, yea, of all men everywhere, as much as possible
is" (449). The "several callings and offices" refer to people's specific
duties (as the estates did in earlier times) and the "happy and good
estates" to society's general condition as a result of duties properly
carried out. Duties differ from one to another, but not according to an
inborn capacity to exert special powers and enjoy special prerogatives.
As Walzer puts it, "Among Puritans it was behavior rather than being
that determined status" (163).

Perkins wrote near the end of the sixteenth century. His sort of
attack on the three traditional estates was not evident in the Protestant
lexicon immediately. The first generation of English Protestants—
David Lindsay and John Knox, for example—tended to adapt the older
vocabulary for their purposes or use *estate* in its most general sense, as
"condition." In his polemical Protestant Scots play *Ane Satyre of the
Thrie Estaitis*, Lindsay uses the old tripartite division precisely to make
his point that the clerical estate is impoverishing the other two. In no
less than 16 instances of the term (13 of them in Part II), Lindsay

builds first a personification allegory and then a drama in which the characters are social types, but his dramatic logic works against the essential nature of the estates. Especially noteworthy is that Common Thift (theft) includes among his followers covetous kings who are "wrangous conquerours" and non-resident prelates along with low-life sinners (4232–71), placing national conquest and abuse of clerical office on the same scale as ordinary thievery and designating it by the old term for the third estate, "common." Knox addresses his *Appellation to the Nobility*, his defense against the charges of the Scottish bishops, to the "nobility, estates, and commonalty" of Scotland. His usage is medieval when he refers to "estate ecclesiastical" (118.28–29), but when he consistently appeals to the nobility to act against the bishops (118.5–6, 125.34–35), he is both echoing Wycliffite arguments and stressing function over birthright. This appeal is part of Knox's insistence on the duty of every man to act according to his vocation, which for the nobility is to "bridle and repress their [the bishops'] folly and blind rage" (127.27–28). In *The First Blast of the Trumpet*, Knox presents *estate* as a set of powers and responsibilities, rather than possessions, in arguing that, since God has forbidden rule to women, it is "a repugnancy to justice" "to promote her to that estate" (63.10–11). These early Protestants are careful to attack hierarchy only on the religious front, to seem socially conservative with regard to royal and aristocratic claims to power, a strategy which in the long run abetted the rise of the absolutist state.

There was more going on in the late sixteenth century than Protestant reform and political jockeying for position. Inflation caused by the influx of gold from the Americas and the new careers enabled by the vast enlargement of the economic world gradually eroded the connection between birth-estate and the ability to display it. Lawrence Stone's description of the period highlights movement of land ownership out of the hands of the medieval aristocratic families, new "vulgar" wealth rising to titles, less respect for those titles, and lower morals among those who held them (*Crisis* 11, 15, 45, 58). Many old families took up lending at interest, investing in speculative ventures, and allowing marriages which allied them to new money. The Lords began to refer to their financial holdings and control of property as *estates* (rather than to their membership in an *estate*), as we have seen in their petition to James I. Archbishop Aylmer, although a very rich man, often complained publicly of his "poor estate and great charges" (quoted in Pierce 125). So did Ralegh, who in *Discovery* claims he "might have bettered [his] poor estate" in the New World, but for his loyal service to the interests of the Queen (4). In his *View of Ireland*, Spenser discusses English and Irish *estates*, consistently using the term to mean "holdings." Moreover, older and newer titled families were divided by mistrust and envy and no longer seemed a single estate. And "estate" unmodified no longer always meant "high estate"; even ordinary people were said to have estates.[9] We are in the realm of property owned or controlled, the realm of the cash nexus.

By the last two decades of the sixteenth century the residual "three estates" meaning is still intelligible, the general sense "condition" is common, and the emergent sense "holdings" is widely used. Francis Bacon, Edmund Spenser, and Philip Sidney sometimes use that linguistic situation for playful effects. The bifurcation of the term *estate* is clear in the 1597 version of Bacon's *Essays*. "Of Nobility" begins: "We will speak of Nobility first as a portion of an estate; then as a condition of particular persons" (45.1), clearly identifying the second of the medieval estates. But in the brief essay "Of Expense" Bacon makes use of the word in no less than six instances, all of which refer to financial resources, as:

> He that cannot look into his own estate at all, had need both choose well those whom he employeth, and change them often; for new are more timorous and less subtle. He that can look into his estate but seldom, it behoveth him to turn all to certainties.
>
> (84.14–18)

How far from a medieval *sprezzatura* Bacon is in his thinking about money comes through in "It is no baseness for the greatest to descend and look into their own estate" (10–11). Yet the next essay is entitled "Of the True Greatness of Kingdoms and Estates," and in it *estates* slides between the traditional divisions of society and whole societies, called "states."

Although Spenser makes use of *estate* as part of his feudal vocabulary only to shift its valences in subtle ways toward the emerging social gestalt, it is Sidney who makes *estate* a veritable leitmotif for his "medieval" tale. The *New Arcadia* deploys an ample range of feudal and early modern significations for *estate* and apparently initiates a new one: "body politic" (11.21; 124.24; 160.25). The vicissitudes of the love status of Musidorus and Pyrocles (Zelmane) is the backbone of the fiction. Their feudal birth-estates are disguised downward—to stranger and female—and their mental, moral, and socially deserved estates are pursued against a backdrop of political complexity which lacks the stability of the feudal norm (the medieval term promises. As a result, the "obvious" or "natural" signs which bespeak *estate* are occluded during most of the action (King Basilius wants to know Zelmane's "estate," so that he may see "what the nest is out of which such birds do fly" [82.25–26], but he never discovers it), deflecting attention to incidents which highlight the daring, ingenuity, and eloquence of the disguised princes when they appear alone, unaided by their status. In spite of its direct references to medieval estates (always omitting the clerical),[10] the fiction as a whole turns markedly toward the emergent, even novelistic, sense of young individuals confronting an old society. A medieval use of *estate* had referred to one's condition as bond or free, and so it does here as "standing in love" (the lover is bound by love, 128.5; 133.24). In spite of the playfulness of the text with *estate*, the princes *do* deserve their ladies by birthright when all is known; it is the episodic middle that puts a new spin on the quest romance.

The peasants' revolt episode makes *estate* an important focus. The rebellion begins with an attack on the women, for whom the "unruly sort of clowns and other rebels" had no "respect for their estates or pity for their sex" (280.10–11), continuing with an account of the battle in which specific social roles are punished with fitting wounds in a kind of gleeful black humor. The negotiating speech with which Zelmane quiets the crowd is worthy of Machiavelli—inciting them to disagree about their demands, shaming them for the resulting disunity, and finally offering herself as a sacrifice to their now confused wrath. "Imagine, what could your enemies more wish unto you than to see your own estate with your own hands undermined?" (286.15–17), she says, preparing to force them to equate their interests with wise government, and that government with their obedience. The equivocation on *estate* is the key, since taken as "polity" it is theirs and in their interest to protect, but as each person's status within the polity, the value of maintaining the status quo is not so persuasive. Further, the "newness of his estate" may tempt your neighbor who gains power by the revolt to trample on your rights (286.15). As the rebels disperse after further internecine fighting, one Clinias attempts to ingratiate himself with King Basilius by reporting how the revolt came about. Again *estate* is at stake:

> the sum was, you disdained them; and what were the pomps of your estate if their arms maintained you not; who would call you a prince if you had not a people—when certain of them of wretched

estates and worse minds... began to say that your government was
to be looked into...

(291.27–32)

While this argument about mutual obligation between a prince and
his people is bracketed by Clinias's cowardice and treachery, it is
powerfully phrased and resonates with similar arguments by Tyndale,
Hythloday in *Utopia*, and Philippe de Mornay. On the other hand, in
Book III, Pamela constructs an elaborate and technical argument for
the governance of God over chance, during the course of which she
glancingly proves that "this fair estate" cannot be sustained by popular
government (360.34–35). Her ingenious, and in context perhaps even
over-ingenious, speculations suggest some strain within *Arcadia's*
textual sympathies. Moreover, the peasants' revolt section is in some
measure at odds with the emphasis on individual talent and character
elsewhere in the tale. For all its attention to *estate*, the *New Arcadia* is
finally unclear about its implications.

Into the thin air of London

As court circles revisited medieval senses of *estate*, however playfully,
metropolitan writers tended to use the term as either generalized
"condition" or fiscal "holdings." John Stow's *Survey of London* (1598) is
subtitled *containing the Original, Antiquity, Increase, Modern Estate, and
Description of that City* and his address to the reader (xxv) also uses
estate in that general way, but Thomas Greene means "holdings" when
a victim's "estate [is] looked into" and his "lands given over to a
stranger" (*The Black Book's Messenger* 182). Thomas Deloney in *Jacke of
Newberie* uses *estate* for both general "situation" and "available
money"; he produces a pointed comic moment when Jacke first
notices his employer's amorous interest in him and considers that "her
estate was reasonable good" (11.6), registering at the same time sober
self-interest in her money and awe for her social station. On the stage,
estate increasingly involves claims to land and money.

   Christopher Marlowe's *Tamburlaine* plays exhibit a pattern of use for
estate consistent with the overall fable the two plays present. Their
protagonist, the son of a shepherd who becomes the most powerful
potentate of his day, wrests the signs of *estate*—crowns, treasure,
women, and command—from those who inherited their titles. The
Souldane of Egypt claims it to be "a blemish to the Majestie / And high
estate of mightie Emperours, / That such a base usurping vagabond /

Should brave a king" (Part I, IV.iii.19–21). Tamburlaine acknowledges early in Part I that his estate is "meane", "I cal it meane, because being yet obscure, / The Nations far remoov'd admyre me not" (I.ii.203–04). As he moves from victory to victory, unseating those born to rule, attaining *estate* for himself and acquiring the power to give "royall places of estate" (Part I, V.i.525) to faithful supporters, he exhibits military competence, ruthlessness, self-confidence, and resolution— *virtù*, with its full Machiavellian range of meanings. His career challenges the inheritance system whether he is winning *estate* not due him by birth or disinheriting his oldest son for disdaining the arts of war. As he sees his death approaching, though, Tamburlaine pays a small debt to tradition in commanding his second son to be crowned. The Tamburlaine plays place this fable forcefully before the London public and use the word *estate* to phrase it (six of Marlowe's eight instances occur in these plays), acknowledging and impelling the move toward an emergent meaning.

Plays with urban settings, like Thomas Middleton's *A Chaste Maid in Cheapside*, emphasize the erosion of the old sense of *estate* and its slide toward cash.[11] Touchstone Senior tells his wife that "The feast of marriage is not lust but love / And care of the estate" (II.i.50–51), as a reason for their temporarily living apart. His immediate concern is with their financial estate, which is threatened by their large brood. The wittol Allwit complains to his wife that if he had to provide for all her children his "estate [would be] buried in Bucklersbury," the street of the grocers and apothecaries (III.ii.70); here too *estate* is clearly money. The grasping Mrs. Allwit, still hoping for something from their "benefactor" even when he is said to have killed a man, argues that if it was in self-defense "Neither his life nor estate will be touched" by the law (V.i.118), a thoroughly modern use. (Similarly, in *A Trick to Catch the Old One*, Witgood speaks of "some estate that I have either in land or money" [I.iii.44], and later, kissing his mortgage, refers to it as "soul of my estate" [IV.ii.93].) Middleton's ingenious contrivance of ways for children to contribute to family fortunes makes *estate* a key term in *Chaste Maid*, deriving some of its humor from the reversal of the old expectation that *estate* is passed on from parents to offspring. Although all the early modern London playwrights deploy, often with corrosive irony, the emergent sense of *estate*, it is Shakespeare in an early comedy, *Merchant of Venice* and a late tragedy, *Timon of Athens*, who makes the term central to his analyses of social London, in those plays called Venice and Athens. In *Merchant* and *Timon* the erosion of the medieval consensus about estate is writ especially large.

In *Merchant of Venice*, Antonio and Bassanio use *estate* quite frankly to discuss financial holdings, liquid assets and contracts. In the first act, Antonio denies that his melancholy arises from worry over money:

> My ventures are not in one bottom trusted,
> Nor to one place; nor is my whole estate
> Upon the fortune of this present year:
> Therefore my merchandise makes me not sad.
>
> (I.i.42–45)

This is the sophisticated financier Michael Nerlich claims has inherited the aura of "adventure" from the medieval questing knight (see above p. 9). Antonio is very rich, but he is also careful, because he knows he is taking potentially devastating risks. His loan to Bassanio, who has "disabled [his] estate" (I.i.123) with ostentatious outlay in the style of the early renaissance courtier, understands this world too little, as events reveal, to treat its legalities and time constraints with proper respect. In Act III, the scene of Bassanio's winning Portia and the "golden fleece" of her estate is interrupted by Salerio's delivery of the letter that announces Antonio's imperiled *estate* back in Venice (ii.235–36). Antonio's letter also uses the word: "my creditors grow cruel, my estate is very low, my bond to the Jew is forfeit" (ii.316–17).[12]

Portia's financial estate is referred to by other terms—"this fair mansion...these servants, and this same myself" (III.ii.160–70)—when it is handed over to Bassanio. This estate, obviously a more feudal economic entity, is under Portia's direct and immediate control, and its resources are inexhaustible.

> Pay him six thousand, deface the bond;
> Double six thousand, and then treble that,
> Before a friend of this description
> Shall lose a hair through Bassanio's fault.
>
> (III.ii.299–302)

Comparing Portia's description of her resources to Antonio's makes the marked contrast between the economic discourses of Venice and Belmont starkly apparent, even as the plot draws them together. This play acknowledges the mixed nature of the English economy, and the resolution of the dilemma it poses is solved, insofar as it is solved at all, through an idealized feudal (almost magical) female agent.

There are no important female characters in *Timon of Athens* and no last-minute rescues for the plot or the social anxieties it registers. *Timon* may be seen as a kind of answer to *Merchant*, an answer that lets the logic of *estate* taken as money and only money to its end, no *deus* (or *dea*) in the machinery. *Timon* contains more instances of the word *estate* (there are eight) than any other Shakespeare play, and all of them refer to money quite directly, denying the efficacy of other signs of standing, like birth or service. The old man who refuses his daughter's hand to her suitor because his "estate deserves an heir more rais'd / Than one which holds a trencher" (I.i.119–20) eagerly consents to it when Timon offers money. Flavius tries to warn Timon of the "ebb of [his] estate / And [his] great flow of debts" (II.ii.141–42) and later says I told you so: suspicion "still comes when an estate is least" (IV.iii.514). Ventidius "stepp'd / Into a great estate" (II.ii.223–24) when he buried his father. Strangers on the street discuss how Timon's "estate shrinks from him" and how he had supported Lucius's estate (III.ii.7, 69). Sempronius points out others who owe "their estates unto him [Timon]" (III.iii.4). And the Poet tells the Painter: "Then do we sin against our own estate, / When we may profit meet and come too late" (V.i.41–42).

Timon's tragedy is that he misunderstands the social/economic demands of his world, and the play concentrates single-mindedly on that misunderstanding. Timon closes his eyes to what Flavius (and modern readers) see as obvious economic facts. In order to give feasts, rescue imprisoned friends, enable propitious marriages, and patronize the arts and crafts, you must have money. Timon does not attend to the matter of getting; his sources are as occluded as Portia's, but not as inexhaustible. Neither of them is brought to rent-racking, investing in joint-stock companies, or selling land to buy into emerging ventures to shore up diminished *estates*, as some English aristocrats were. Timon's rhetoric eagerly celebrates the discourse of feudal hierarchy, dependent on bonds of blood and friendship among men of established feudal status, and there is scarcely another play in the period, certainly none by Shakespeare, so highly dependent on rhetoric and so little on plot. Timon flaunts the residual medieval virtue of *fredom*, magnanimity, at a time when economic realities no longer register it as a virtue, but he lacks the needed emergent virtues of thrift and timely financial care, of which more will be said in later chapters.

The logic of *Timon of Athens* on *estate* is, of course, too stark to account for the nuanced social changes we have been looking at, although it must, I think, be counted as a reaction to them. Deference paid to birth-estate did not suddenly disappear in the early seventeenth century, but the play's unremitting focus on the cash nexus, which gives Timon his celebrity early in the play and accounts for his banishment later, gestures toward a trend which will not be reversed. Medieval protagonists who fall from Fortune's good graces may lose battles, offend God, fail to win the desired woman, or just die, but they do not do so simply because they have spent their material resources. To London theater-goers, though, that threat may well have seemed quite real, especially to those who came to the city dispossessed of their small freeholds or their duties as retainers in great houses because of the enclosures and who had experienced the unpredictable monetary fluctuations governing wages and prices influenced by international commerce and Spanish gold. Raymond Williams discusses hegemony as "a lived system of meanings and values...in the strongest sense a 'culture,' but a culture which has also to be seen as the lived dominance and subordination of particular classes" (*Marxism and Literature* 110). The case of the London theater displays the mutual reinforcement of "the pressures and limits of simple experience" and the public meanings carried by staged drama. In a relatively short time, a broad "common sense" layer of social thinking about *estate* shifted from adherence to the "ancient and lovable custom" of deference toward the three estates King James belatedly tried to command to a sharp-eyed attention to fortunes (not Fortune) which even James took into account when he awarded new titles. *Estate*, therefore, is heavily freighted with one of the central contradictions of early modern culture.

4
Fre/Free

"Freedom's just another word for nothin' left to lose.
Nothin' don't mean nothin' hon, unless it's free," or
"Nothin' don't mean nothin' honey, but its free."
Kris Kristofferson, "Bobby Magee", as sung by
Janis Joplin

I was never entirely sure which line Janis Joplin was singing, and
maybe she sang both. The first phrasing stresses the importance of
freedom from constraint and suggests that the singer has come to
terms with Bobby's leaving her, that his love was only valuable as long
as it was a free association between them. The second is a cynical
reduction of "freedom" to something too worthless to pay anything
for. *Free* has carried equivocation with it for centuries, although the
particular equivocation in "Bobby Magee" is differently inflected in
the period under discussion here.

In its Germanic and Celtic roots, *fre* means "dear," implying blood
ties and non-servitude. The word entered Middle English in two main
developments from that "dear," on the one hand, "kindred," "noble"
(in its various senses) and on the other "not in bondage," "unconstrained." The connection between "noble" and "unconstrained" both
reflects and buttresses feudal modes of production and social hierarchy, and, like estates theory, can claim an ancient linguistic lineage.
Throughout the Middle Ages, *fre* is seen in honorific salutations, especially "my lady fre," addressed to the chatelaine or the Virgin Mary.
But the word also occurs, in both medieval and early modern
discourse, in expressions which match modern usage, e.g., "free from,"
"free of," "free to." *Fre* also implies various kinds of liberty throughout
the whole period. As "uncoerced," William Thirning tells Richard II

48

that his renunciation of the crown had been "frelich accepted and fullich agreed" by all the States and People concerned (Chrimes 113). John Knox warns in *The First Blast of the Trumpet* that the freedom of the nation must be rescued from the bondage into which it has been brought by women (64.35), and Shakespeare's Prospero agrees to free delicate Ariel. Similarly widespread are instances of *free* to refer to political freedom within a jurisdiction, as in free cities, free marriages, free chapel, and freehold (property held without rent or the obligation of feudal service). What remains constant during this period is this implication of "liberty"; what progressively drops out is the medieval sense "noble," "gracious."

By the early seventeenth century, some instances of *free* hint at an implication of looseness. Thomas Middleton's *A Trick to Catch the Old One* features a character named Freedom, son of Mistress Lucre, and John Marston's *The Dutch Courtesan* features a character named Freeville. "License" is also Gosson's implication in *Playes Confuted*, "choise [in theaters] without shame hath bene as free, as it is for your money in the royale exchaung" (194.21–23). Even so, "forward" or ready to "take liberties" is an emergent rather than a predictable sense until 1635, and the phrase "free and easy" as a pejorative is recorded by the *OED* for the first time in Addison's *Spectator* 119. The trend toward *free* as "loose," though, does mark a complete reversal of its medieval implication of recognized noble bearing. The deference due to birthright can be seen eroding, and the London theaters contributed to the erosion by staging fictions in which the discourse of citizens, sometimes successfully, competes with that of their aristocratic "betters."

Feudal freedoms

Nobility as high birth itself was an important use of "fre" as an adjective or a noun (the free person) throughout the medieval period, and was understood as late as Milton's *L'Allegro*: "But come thou Goddess fair and free, / In Heaven yclept Euphrosyne." This sense turns up most often as salutation, in phrases like "my lady fair and fre," which is often used to address the Virgin Mary. Gawain casually addresses his hostess as "my fre" in *Gawain and the Green Knight* (1545), and the narrator refers to her that way as well (1549): "thus hym frayned that fre." In *William of Palerne*, *fre* is used as a noun: "When the fre was in the forest founde.... In comely clothes was he clad" (505), identifying the protagonist's birthright. Chaucer's Franklin brings his tale to a

close with a striking address to his audience: "Lordlynges, this question, thanne, I aske now, / Which was the mooste fre, as thynketh
yow?" (V.1621–22). Who should be awarded that term of high respect
for his sacrifice—the knight-husband, the squire-suitor, or the clerk-
magician—has not proved to be a rhetorical question. Such
expressions were apparently so familiar that they could be used for
comic effect, as in the *Castle of Perseverance* when Lechery, Sloth, and
Gluttony are said to be "fendys fre" ("noble devils"), Superbia calls
Auaricia "my fader fre," or Mankind calls Spousebreche "a frend ryth
fre" (896, 917, 1195). The theological problem of God's *freedom* is the
crux around which *Castle of Perseverance* builds its climax, two of the
daughters of God arguing that Mankind is unworthy of salvation,
while Misericordia builds her case for his "fre respyth" on God's
eternal mercy (3458–82). Misericordia prevails.

The interesting complication here is that medieval discourse allows
the determining social fact of high birth to be broadened—in two
ways. First, it becomes associated with preciousness in general: the
shape of a handsome man's body is free (*Firumbras* 2823), so is the
medicinal power of an herb (Arderne's *Fistula* 97), or the efficacy of a
holy relic (*Firumbras* 1.64). *Unfreli* means "unbeautifully" in *Morte
Arthure* (780) and in *Octavian* (1443). Secondly, *fre* becomes a key term
in religious thinking. As "unconstrained," *fre* is central, of course, to
the medieval English-language debates over the nature of the will,
registered, for example, in Chaucer's *Boece* and in Book IV of *Troilus*
(where it fuses clerical and courtly discourses). Then too, the graciousness and magnanimity of noble life is appropriated to image the holy
family, especially the Virgin, "that fre" or "our lady free." Jesus is "that
fre" in the striking line from the York Cycle: "There faughte that fre
with feendis feele" (498.35). This sacralization of the term carries more
significance than appears at first, since Mary's standing in her *social*
world was that of a peasant woman in a colonized province of the
Roman Empire, whose son became an itinerant preacher to the poor.
The naturalization of the trappings of feudal nobility for the Holy
Family (in both pictorial and verbal art) serves the interests of social
hegemony, representing God as a member of the ruling class, but it
was also challenged in the Middle Ages, by, for example, the
Franciscan movement and the Peasants' Rising. As a strategy, it had
some unpredicted destabilizing effects.

The frequent appropriation of the social category of high birth as a
religious image enables Julian of Norwich to refer to God's "curtesse"
and "freedom" as if he were an aristocrat dealing mercifully with his

people rather than exacting contractual obligations, thus her differentiation between "gevyng" and "rewardyng" (*Showings* Long Text 58.52–55). The human recipient can also be said to be free, since both texts of the *Showings* stress that the desire to receive the gift of sickness came to her "frely, without any sekyng" (1.28; 2.20–21). In *Cleanness*, Christians are urged to be "frely and fresch fonde in thy lyue" (173) to appear before their Prince and to seek shrift if "folk be defowled by unfre chaunce" (1129). The fourteenth-century translator of Groseteste's *Castle of Love* also gives a decidedly feudal cast to Christ's rescue of humankind. Adam lost his "seysyne" through sin, thus becoming the thrall of the devil. To regain his heritage a free man must be sent: "And that he the kynde haue; / That he beo I-boren fre" (361.58–59). A poet like Langland can downright democratize the term. In several striking images he links *fre* with the nobility of the souls of those of humble birth: "His herte blood he shadde, to maken alle folk free that folwen his lawe" (*Piers Plowman* B Text 19.59) and "Such a frende with so fre an herte" (B.15.147). But Langland can also use "fre" as a status-inflected word: in the C Text, we read that no man marries Meade for her virtue or beauty or "high kinde" (noble blood), but the B Text reads "free kinde" in the same place (C. 3. 82; B. 2. 75; noted by Lewis).

Wyclif makes a point of the Christian's freedom in many venues closed off by clerical authorities, as Tyndale will after him. The English Sermons often chide the friars and bishops who seek to control access to scripture and to forgiveness (Arnold II.206 and 237), "For thes men have distroyed freedom, and pervertid Cristis Chirche, and so, as myche as in hem is, thei have maad Crist unfree, and this unfreedom is worse than al the richessis of this world" (I.363). The early fifteenth-century Wycliffite *Jack Upland* bases much of its anti-fraternal satire on the issue of selling the truths and sacraments of the faith for money and for committing to prison or the fire (Lollard) priests who refused to do so by "prechinge of Cristis lawe freli" (Dean 127.201). This passage and several others in the treatise, fuse the various implications of free, involving all of them in the satire. The Wycliffites offered the gospel *freely,* as "without requiring payment," "unencumbered by rules," and "graciously, generously." The Gospel "biddith thee preie freli for frende and fo" (128.1–2) suggests, "graciously, nobly" even more strongly, as does the admonition to the friars to do spiritual works freely "as God gyveth freeli, as ellis it were cursid symony" (130.280). It is the "fend" himself who refuses to teach God's law, "frely & trewely with-outen flaterynge" (*Satan and His Children* in Matthew 212.29).

The various potential relationships between *fre* as a term marking social class and a term carrying religious weight are explored in *The Parson's Tale*. Its ten instances of *fre* (no other has more than four) encompass the major medieval uses: as markers of social estate and spiritual estate, as "unconstrained," and in constructions like "free from." When the Parson teaches that the degree of sin is determined in part by the situation of the sinner—"male or female yong or oold, gentil or thral, free or servant" (960)—he uses the word in its social sense, but in "thurgh synne ther he was free now is he maked bond" (145–50), the powerful social *fredom* (nobility, membership in the family) is shifted to a spiritual venue. References to high and low status surround this passage, further linking the prestige of *free* to noble standing even while democratizing it by placing it within the grasp of everyone who resists sin. The Parson even says that "in somme contrees, ther they byen thralles, when they han turned hem to the feith, they maken hire thralles free out of thraldom" (770–75), which obliquely suggests that Christian communities must be egalitarian in this "time of grace."

The Parson's best example of an emergent use for *fre* may be his excoriation of wicked priests as

> Belial—that is, the devel. / Belial is to seyn, 'withouten juge.' And so faren they; hem thynketh they been free and han no juge, namoore than hath a free bole that taketh which cow that hym liketh in the town. / So faren they by wommen. For right as a free bole is ynough for al a toun, right so is a wikked preest corrupcioun ynough for al a parisshe, or for al a contree.
>
> (895–900)

What I see here is a negotiation between the old association with nobility—the priest thinks that his estate makes him *free*—and the new meaning of "unfettered" with a tilt toward "licentious"—in what the Parson alleges about him through the analogy with the bull's sexual proclivities.[1] Stressing the importance of voluntary confession, the Parson urges that "he that trespasseth by his free wyl, that by his free wyl he confesse his trespas" (1010–1015). This passage, like so much else in the tale, focuses on the individual Christian's responsibility in accounting for his or her spiritual life.

Four women on freedom

I would like to show how the semantic complications of *fre*—class status shaded toward spiritual status and thereby democratized—play out by examining the stories of four medieval women. Three of these women are presented in Chaucerian fiction and the fourth is Margery Kempe, who presents her own story in her *Book*. I will start with Margery, who as a female and a layperson, was an unlikely contributor to late medieval thinking on free will. She insists that God's "wil may not be constreyned, it is in hys owyn fre disposicyon" as an argument that she had received her visions "not of hir owyn stody ne of hir owyn witte," but of his free and "incomprehensibyl" gift (199.11–15). This is a fairly sophisticated theological point for Margery to make and one she had to keep restating through the many trials of her orthodoxy. It attracts attention among Margery's visions of the Holy Family, which she usually phrased in a more homely idiom. I want to argue that she gives an egalitarian slant to the word *fre*, even though her position here—that God's actions are unconstrained—is perfectly orthodox. While the passage stresses *God's* "fre disposicyon," the effect of his freedom is that a lay woman like Margery herself may become privy to his special intimations, according to *his* incomprehensible wisdom, not through the mediation of the earthly Church. Although her iconic religious imagination links her with orthodoxy in some ways (Aers 114), in this matter her position accords well with Wyclif's "ʒif a lord or a laborer loue betere god than thes veyn religious & proude & lecherous possessioneris, the lewid manys preiere is betere" (*Veritate Sacrae Scripturae* 117). Margery's *Book* stands on both sides of the great controversy of her time, a fascinating hybrid which still attracts us.

A leveling tendency like Margery's is also apparent in frequent late medieval uses of *fre* which stress the meaning "unconstrained," as in freehold property held without feudal obligation and membership in town or guild privileges. That very lack of feudal obligation may be Margery's intended meaning of *fre* when she wins her husband's consent to live with him without sexual contact:

> "Grawntyth me that ye schal not komyn in my bed, & I grawnt yow to qwyte your dettys er I go to Ierusalem & makyth my body fre to God so that ye neuyr make no chalengyng in me to askyn dett of matrimony aftyr this day whyl ye leuyn, & I schal etyn & drynkyn on the Fryday at yowr byddyng."

Than seyd hir husbond a-yen to hir, "As fre mot yowr body ben
to God as it hath ben to me." Thys creatur thankyd God gretly.
                                                              (25.6–14)[2]

If we imagine John allowing his *feudal right* to Margery's body to be
transferred to God, the passage records an almost legal exchange of
power, but another, equally attractive reading is possible: John's *fre* as
"noble" asserts her body has been valued by him and he hopes God
will also find it valuable. She perhaps intended that meaning too, her
body will be noble, even holy, for God's use.

Margery's lay female status and incomplete education did not
prevent her from producing a text in which remakable use is made of
the entwined senses of Middle English *fre:* "nobly born," "gracious as if
noble," "unencumbered with guilt," "endowed with certain unconstrained avenues of choice," "politically enfranchised," or "empowered
with rights of ownership." Some notable Chaucerian instances of *fre*
also make use of both the richness and the porousness between secular
and religious senses of the word. Surely the broadest meaning for *frely*,
"unconstrainedly," suggests itself first in Dame Alisoun's "In wyfhod I
wol use myn instrument / As frely as my Makere hath it sent" (*Wife's
Tale* 149–50). But God is noble as well as unconstrained; perhaps
Alisoun means that He sent her sexual nature to her nobly, and that
she, while she uses it within the sacrament of marriage, uses it nobly.
Or perhaps she is claiming ownership of her person on the grounds
that God has given her her body "frely," without obligation to anyone
else.

A good deal is at stake in how the Wife's "frely" is read; the text does
invite an assessment of Alisoun's character (which Chaucer criticism
has amply supplied). More playful is the lovely leitmotif of praise of
Criseyde as "lady fre," in each of the five books, even including
Troilus's last love-letter to Criseyde in the Greek camp. The instance I
want to look at is the line "And in his armes took his lady free" after
their first night together in Book III (1522). Troilus presumably means
noble, gracious, dear, just as he has and will again. On this particular
morning he has a new reason for praising Criseyde's magnanimity, a
reason which pits the courtly against the clerical implications of the
word. But reading with an eye for playful irony, we might wonder a bit
at whether, so constrained as she is in his arms, she has lost what she
feared to lose in II.771, when she hesitated, being "free," to "put in
jupartie / My sikernesse, and thrallen libertee." Her decision to love
has certainly made her more free, in connecting her with the highest

circles of the Trojan court, albeit secretly; the generosity and delicacy of her behavior in love (to this point, surely) entitle her to be called free, gracious; but is she unconstrained? In her initial debate with herself, she treats the decision to love as a matter of free will, an offer she can accept or reject, but other passages in the poem complicate that construal, most obviously Troilus's more formal scholarly anxiety over the free will question in Book IV.

A darker irony is evident in January's echo from the Song of Solomon, "Rys up, my wyf, my love, my lady free!" (2138). We are watchful for such irony in the tale, since January himself is earlier referred to as "this noble January free" (2069). Technically "noble" because of his knighthood, the extra "free" is clearly inappropriate to both his spiritual and his intellectual state, since he is a bondsman to self-interest and carnality if there ever was one. May, we know by this time in the tale, is neither noble (in birth or behavior) nor unconstrained. She is a thrall both to sin and to January, since his hand is constantly upon her. Here what at first looks like a stock phrase bristles with interpretive clues. January intends his salutation as a polite compliment to his socially non-noble wife and, in his breathtaking blindness to May's feelings, probably would wish to imply the freedom of her choice to share his garden fantasy, perhaps her liberality as well. Interpreters, including the tale's narrator, cannot help seeing the extreme denial of "political" freedoms in this story of a captive girl of the third estate by an aristocrat with a walled garden which becomes in effect a prison (cf., Kolve on the *Knight's Tale*).

For all its complexity in the lexicons of Chaucer and Margery Kempe, what we do not find in this period is the implication "licentious." John Florio, translating Montaigne in 1603, must pair his pejorative use of *free* with "license"—*free* alone seems not to be able to carry that signification ("Raymond Sebond" 224). So we cannot suspect either May or Criseyde (or for that matter any of the men in *The Franklin's Tale* who are nominated for "mooste fre") of cheap or abandoned behavior on the grounds of that lexical choice alone. Instead, the complexities of these instances gesture toward frictions within medieval usages: Criseyde and May become more *fre* in social status only to enjoy less liberty, and Margery (for sexual abstinence) and Alisoun (for sexual activity) present their wish for unconstrained control of their sexuality as nobility.

Freedom re-structured

The changing significances of the word *fre* provide an instructive index for the considerable shifts in political, religious, and erotic discourse which testify to shifts in "structures of feeling...characteristic elements of impulse, restraint, and tone" (Williams, *Marxism and Literature* 132) in the responses of sixteenth-century English men and women. In order to suggest the range of political senses for *fre*, I want to look at *Utopia's* playful engagement with radical new forms of citizenship in Ralph Robinson's 1551 English translation of More's 1516 treatise as it contrasts with Castiglione's idealization of humanist politics in Hoby's translation of *The Courtier*. Then I will examine Tyndale's contribution to the religious nuances of *free*, and finally the role of the sonnet tradition as it figures the relevance of *freedom* to erotic love.

As might be expected in a political treatise, Robinson's translation of *Utopia* uses *fre* very often, almost always to mean political non-constraint. What is so remarkable about the piece (which More himself later tried to disown) is the consistency of its leveling vision; although behavior may be highly constrained by the seamless hegemony of the community, Utopians are equally bound by it. Utopia's citizens are freed not only from princely whims, but from all but the most "basic" legal and religious restrictions as well as from the coercive power of unequal control of property. Even the playful reference to aristocratic hunting rights—the Utopians are said to find "all thys exercyse of huntynge" to be "unworthye to be used of free men [Latin: *liberis*]" (76)—serves the egalitarian agenda, since in More's day the *fre* (in the old sense), and they alone, were accorded the privilege of hunting. My argument is not that this trend represents More's most settled thoughts on good government—I see Hythloday and "More" as contending strains of the author's thought—but that, through Robinson's translation, this inflection for *free* was made available to sixteenth-century English readers.

Thomas Hoby's translation of *The Courtier*, in contrast, exhibits its nuanced appreciation of the medieval range of *fre* through a kind of modulation within the group of conversants called together for "free and honest conversation," "bridled" only by the very great respect in which all of them held the Duchess. This explicit description is offered early (20), and the treatise as a whole and in every part enacts it. This conversation is *free*, unconstrained, open to various stances, and permissive of direct confrontation, yet all is bridled by an ingrained, unopposable graciousness, the *freedom* of the ideal aristocratic house-hold. Hoby calls it a conversation "between brothers"—and we are back to "dear" and "kin." This emphasis is especially strong in "ought the life of a good prince to bee free and safe and as dear to his subjects as their own" (278). *Free* is also noted on the boundaries of impropri-ety in "You would have made this woman of yours somewhat more courteous and free towarde the Courtier than my Lorde Julian hath made his" (314); the subtle shadings here threaten to move freedom toward license, but are bridled by "courteous" and end up suggesting merely gracious generosity. Hoby's interpretation of *The Courtier* looks to residual thought by idealizing the ethos of a "natural" aristocracy obeying unalterable rules because its members were constitutionally noble, *fre*. *Utopia's* thoroughly emergent severance of the link between liberty and status connects it with a more modern mode of thought to which More was attracted early in his career and spent much of his later life attempting to defeat.[3]

William Tyndale's *Obedience of a Christian Man* returns to themes Wycliffite writers had associated with Christian *freedom* in the four-teenth century. A leitmotif for the treatise is developed from Paul's Epistles: "[T]he children of faith are under no law (as thou seest in the epistles to the Romans, to the Galatians, in the first to Timothy), but are free" (297). Human freedom allows service to be given "for love freely," and divine freedom provides the grace—"the free gift of God" (182)—to kindle the desire to perform it. This basic tenet of Tyndale's position—that the new covenant involves God's free (non-necessary, non-rule-bound) grace and the Christian's free (unobstructed, uncon-strained) acceptance of that gift—is continually called upon to subvert the institutionally controlled sacraments and "works" by which Rome defines salvation. Tyndale rhetorically addresses Anti-Christ's false prophets: "A thousand things forbid ye, which Christ made free" (147.28–29). Papists are therefore bond-children, "which will be justi-fied by deeds"; they persecute Sarah's "free children which are justified by faith" (307.19–22).[4] This understanding of spiritual *freedom* modu-lates into a contrast (again reminiscent of Lollardy) between God's grace given freely and Church sacraments sold for money. The pope claims "power to sell that which God gives freely" (271.35), the wise "will not buy of a wily fox that which his father hath given him freely" (294.34), and "[we] are ready to work freely, and not to obtain that which is given us freely and wherof we are heirs already" (*Wicked Mammon,* quoted by Daniell 170).[5] On God's side the freedom with which the gift of grace is bestowed retains a hint of the aristocratic *fre* of the Middle Ages. God gives, he does not sell. The Christian who freely receives this grace is also ennobled—"he that receiveth forgiveness free of Christ, will buy no forgiveness of them" (204.3–4)—and raised above the marketplace to join a noble family through that which "his father hath given him." This structure of feeling acknowledges moral curbs as familial responsibility; although bound by no law, the Christian is enjoined to accept duties "lest thy freedom make thy weak brother grudge and rebel, in that he seeth thee go empty, and he himself more laden" (190.31–191.1–2). In appropriating the aristocratic tenor of the old *freedom* as a description of all believers, Tyndale's usage neatly fuses "membership in a noble family" with "not involving rule-bound payment."

All this is still further complicated by a central conceit of the Petrarchan love sonnet tradition. The lover is figured in this poetic genre as a noble man, free in his birth and free therefore to manage his affections as he is inclined. The beloved, however (or sometimes Cupid), has brought him into subjection, as in Wyatt's Song CCIII, "Tangled was I in love's snare," from which this time the persona "had no hurt, but scaped free" (1, 34). The conceit is so familiar that the delicacy needed to handle it is easy to overlook: the poet's persona must become abject, yet desirable, subject to his cruel mistress, but only to her. Wyatt indulges the contradictions of this plight: "since I it bound where it was free" (XCIII.2, 5), representing the paradox of love by valuing unfreedom as the more honorable state. As a structure of feeling, this paradox of erotic life is not as far as it might seem at first glance from the spiritual commitment, freely made, but emotionally binding, described by Tyndale and other Protestants. Donne, for example, in "Elegie XIX" addresses the lady thus: "To enter in these bonds, is to be free" and in Holy Sonnet 14, implores God: "imprison mee, for I / Except you'enthrall mee, never shall be free." The paradox of chosen unfreedom, ratified by Protestant thought, lends emotional weight to the sonnet lover's plea.

Sidney's valorization of imagination and inwardness is structurally similar to Tyndale's confidence in the believer's direct access to grace and More's (however repudiated later) focus on the citizen. It deepens the seriousness of the sonnet sensibility by making personal states of mind participate in cosmic vision. *Freedom*, one of the most privileged terms in the *Apology for Poetry*, allows the poet to escape bondage to nature, "freely ranging only within the zodiac of his own wit" (100), allowing him to create a golden world. The diction of the passage suggests a geographical and political metaphor, yet a faint resonance from the feudal sense of "grace" may be heard in it too. *Astrophel and Stella* uses the paradox of *freedom* to create some striking effects, for example, in 29 Stella is figured as the weak ruler who yields the hinterlands in order to keep her "chief cities free," barring love from her heart, but admitting it to her outward self (as beauty), and making the poet a slave "upon that coast." The *New Arcadia*, though, puts a darker spin on the love/freedom conceit when Amphialus imprisons Philoclea, claiming her beauty the forger of her bondage (323.14, 31–32), in a scene that calls attention to the constructedness of the convention of the male lover's helplessness.[6]

A major accomplice of the sonnet sensibility was Arthur Golding's translation of *The Metamorphoses*, which exhibits, in addition to a full range of implications for *free*, the striking sense "unviolated." When Phebe was *free*, she was sexually innocent (52.558). During the golden age the "fertile earth as yet was free, untoucht of spade or plough" (23.115), but in the iron age, "men began to bound" it with "dowles and diches" (24.152–53). (Walter Ralegh uses the same trope in writing of Guiana as "a country that hath yet her maidenhead.") That sense of *free* extends to men as well. Hermaphroditus is addressed as a "Maiden free from wedlock bonde" (98.400) and "a childe and free" (90.418) before he is transformed into his "doubleshape." Myrrha is warned to avoid thoughts of incest "whyle thy body yit is free" (208.391). A subtle contradiction reveals itself in these instances: on the one hand, nature is free and valued for giving and allowing, on the other, human freedom consists in virginity and obedience to rules. This contradiction is, in one sense, what the myth of the golden and iron ages seeks to explain, but fails to put to rest, as the various metamorphoses work themselves out through fifteen books of stories. That such a tension might register in people's felt experience is acknowledged as a risk of resusitating texts, genres (like Ovidian love poetry), and ideas from the ancients.

A theater for citizens

Meanwhile streetwise London popular writing uses *free* to suggest unencumbered activity. Christopher Hill has described London as "for the sixteenth-century vagabond what the greenwood had been for the medieval outlaw—an anonymous refuge" (*Upside Down* 33), and quotes Donald Lupton writing in 1632, "Fisherwomen are fre in all places and pay nothing for shop-rent." But there was an older and more regulated sense in which *freedom* was associated with urban living. *Freedom* as a synonym of citizenship in a town or city is important in the Middle Ages, the crafts guilds having won an important victory by the charter of 1319, which required freemen to be "of some mystery or trade" (Rappaport 35), but medieval *fredom*, even in this sense, was associated with the religious community in that excommunication barred one from trading in the marketplace (Agnew 29). Even as London tripled in size in the sixteenth century and came to be home for a tenth of England's population,[7] it retained an aura of public-ness, where witnesses rather than written contracts were often still in use (Agnew 29). Formal procedures, oaths, fees, and records were involved in obtaining "freedom of the city," usually for apprentices. Once granted, the freeman had a certain status to protect. The Merchant Taylors complained in 1518 that,

> A great multitude of strangers and aliens born out of this realm, not being freemen of this city...presume to work and do work in houses, chambers, alleys and in other places...to the great loss, hurt and damage of the freemen of the handicraft or mystery of Merchant Taylors.

> (Quoted in Rappaport 43)

Citizenship was held by three-fourths of the men in London by the middle of the sixteenth century, in contrast with the "privileged minority" who had held it in the Middle Ages (Rappaport 49), and Lord Chancellor Thomas More introduced the legislation that extended the freedom and enlarged the proportion of Londoners who were citizens. Even so, the protection it offered was not complete. In 1587 the Merchant Taylors Company complained about the "great number of freemen of this mystery who are destitute of dwellings" (Rappaport 62).

Citizens were often the subjects for early modern plays, but they were even oftener its audiences. Whether or not Londoners saw the analogy between their conduct and the profession of acting—the Puritan merchant William Scott is quoted by Agnew as claiming that dissimulation was "a thing more tolerable with a Citizen" (80)—they did see the appeal of public theater, and in some measure controlled it by their attendance.[8] I would like to turn now to the ways that *freedom*, with its accumulated mix of political, religious, and erotic implications, is enmeshed in the public discourse of the theaters and how it both registers and encourages new structures of feeling.

In 1605 Thomas Middleton's *Michaelmas Term* and Ben Jonson's

Volpone provided particularly good foci for the political nuances of *free;* both plays use the term as a site on which the contentions between gentlemen and citizens are played out. In *Michaelmas Term*, Richard Easy, the unsuspecting young heir from Essex, is repeatedly called *free* in the sense "generous," pointing to the late medieval link between noble birth and morality (induction 7 and 53, I.i.117, II.ii.171, and III.ii.15). Easy himself makes an unconscious pun in claiming: "you have easily possessed me, I am free" (I.i.47), thinking he is announcing his control of his estate at his father's death, and therefore his self-determination, but predicting how effortlessly the city folk will be able to despoil him of his feudal rights. What the citizens in the play mean by *free* is the legal right of "freedom of the city," which most of them abuse—Quomodo's operatives, disguised as wealthy citizens, claim to have "pitied more gentlemen in distress than any two citizens within the freedom" (III.iv.205–06). Lethe's baud tells her victim that "Virginity's no city trade, / You're out o'th' freedom when you're a maid" (I.ii.44)—that is, if you are not willing to sell what you have, you cannot count yourself a capable member of the working community.[9] But the play also treats the straightforward freedom from restraint in debtor's prison which constantly threatens Easy: in seeming to contrive to "set [Quomodo's] prisoner free" (III.iv.227), those same operatives point up the constraining power of the new economic arrangements, with their confusing commodity scams and legal entanglements sealed by a mere signature on paper. Like the coney-catching pamphlets, the play's intricate plot can serve as warning to the innocent, acknowledgment of the superior sophistication of the street people, and training in the labyrinthine ways of the city.

In *Volpone*, Jonson exploits the possibilities of *free* to produce an equivocation about the nature of his protagonist's project. Volpone's opening soliloquy poses the rhetorical question "What should I do, / But cocker up my genius, and live free / To all delights, my fortune calls me to?" (I.i.70–72), and that question haunts the play. In a sly way, it suggests the early modern fascination with transgressing traditional authority, not unlike the lure of the New World in Jonson's *Eastward Ho*, "And then you shall live freely there, without sergeants, or courtiers, or lawyers, or intelligencers, only a few industrious Scots perhaps" (III.iii.40). But Volpone's discourse is also bound up with an earlier sense of *free*; he is an aristocrat who needs no productive career to justify his wealth and entitled to pamper his "genius," his proper spirit, by living free—open, gracious—to pleasure. Volpone does behave like a nobly-born person, in that he wounds no earth with

ploughshares, and if "nobly" were the only available meaning for *free*,
Jonson's satiric target would be the idleness of the high-born. But
Volpone lacks the *sprezzatura* of the born aristocrat; he manages his
fortune with a capitalist's eye to financial control. His characterization
therefore impels a critique of both feudal and proto-capitalist fiscal
modes. One of his victims, the jealous husband Corvino, becomes
enmeshed in some of these ironies when he prostitutes his wife "Of
[his] own free motion.... Freely, unasked, or unentreated" (II.iii.197;
III.ii.358), registering a neat opposition between *free* as "noble" and as
"unconstrained." Corvino's old-fashioned jealousy is lampooned and
so is the rampant greed that enables him to overcome it. The plot of
the play posits a crisis for Volpone himself and all his dupes that
causes them to abandon an accustomed structure of feeling for a new
one. The free speaking and hearing remarked on in the trial scenes in
Acts IV and V are heavily ironized, since none of the parties, except
Celia and Bonario, can speak unconstrainedly, even in simple self-
interest. Agnew's sense that the trading city demands dissimulation is
pointedly presented, but *Volpone* also undercuts the traditional attitudes toward high estate, marriage, and law which should have
chastened its excesses.[10]

Shakespeare's plays explore the full range of associations for *free*,
combining and reconfiguring its place in the discursive terrain of Early
Modern English, including its older class-inflected uses, its religious
colorings, and hints of an emergent sense. Many of his well over 200
instances of *free* occur in the histories and refer to political freedom, as
do, in a more playfully ironic way, instances in *The Tempest*, where
Ariel's freedom from a sort of feudal servitude, is an insistent issue. In
several plays, though, the ambivalences of *free* are explored in especially complicated ways. *Hamlet* and *The Winter's Tale* focus on its
medieval senses, both class-bound and religious, *Othello* on the emergent border with "license," and *Cymbeline* on all of these senses.

The text of *Hamlet* assumes the medieval senses of *free* and then
undercuts a full acceptance of those senses. Polonius taxes Ophelia
with being "most free and bounteous" in receiving Hamlet's visits
(I.iii.93), which both assumes her to be the aloof lady with bounty to
control and accuses her of an over-generousness which risks the
appearance of license. Hamlet insults Rosencrantz and Guildenstern
by asking if theirs is a "free visitation" (II.ii.275), and their denial of a
gracious, friendly visit implies that their behavior is servile, obligated,
or suborned. They report to Gertrude that Hamlet's replies were "most
free" (III.i.14), unlike his niggard questions, *free* as spontaneous,

comfortable within one's family (Hamlet has fooled them). In a heightened use of the sense of *free* as innocent, Claudius calls Hamlet "Most generous and free from all contriving" (V.i.135), linking him with the idealized, pre-Machiavellian, Denmark the play posits as preceding the fratricide, and damaging the ethical force of the argument Claudius is making to Laertes. (This view of Hamlet, though, is complicated for the audience by the knowledge that he has put an antic disposition on ever since Act I.) "Make mad the guilty and appall the free" (II.ii.564), like "we that have free souls" (III.ii.242), calls up notions of spiritual redemption, as do Claudius's anguished "limed soul...struggling to be free" (III.iii.68), Hamlet's forgiveness of Laertes, "Heaven make thee free of it" (V.ii.332), and his plea for forgiveness "Free me so far in your most generous thoughts" (V.ii.242).

"Innocent" is the key association for *free* in *The Winter's Tale*. Paulina argues that Hermione's baby is blameless: "By law and process of great Nature thence / Freed and enfranchis'd, not a party to / The anger of the King, not guilty of / (If any be) the trespass of the Queen" (II.ii.57–59). This legalism may be construed as either a doctrinal or politcal force of *free*. In the next scene Paulina uses the word in its feudal sense of spiritually noble to describe Hermione as "A gracious, innocent soul / More free than he [Leontes] is jealous" (28–29). The Queen is, as Paulina speaks, imprisoned, nor can Paulina (a very consecutive arguer) be imagined as meaning "liberal," since even that would weaken her case. At her trial Hermione asks not for life, but for the freeing of her honor from taint (III.ii.110–11). Moreover Leontes uses the word with the force of moral innocence when he denies Hermione access to his "free person." He may be claiming that she might try to kill him, so he may mean "freely accessible" (as the *Riverside Shakespeare* glosses it), but I think it more likely registers his fear of moral contamination. He is relieved that Hermione did not nurse Mamillius, which reveals, as some convincing psychoanalytic readings of the play allege, why, thinking of female sexuality itself as sullied, he falls into his jealous rage in the first place (Schwartz 1973, 1975). Leontes would like to think he is "author of himself," like Coriolanus, and sole author of his son as well.

As befits a play about both the deliberate and the unintended misrecognition of words, *Othello* is particularly rich for our purposes. Consider the *free* at the beginning of Act III. Iago offers to occupy Othello so that Cassio may talk with Desdemona alone, "that your converse and business / May be more free" (37–38). More unencumbered, certainly; but also more licentious, as Iago is framing the interview. Later in this scene, Iago is "relieved" to speak "with franker spirit" in order to want Othello's "free and noble nature" against the super-subtle wiles of Venetians and urges him to wait to see if she presses Cassio's case too vehemently, so that we may "hold her free," if she doesn't. Desdemona's is a "frank hand" in Othello's first hint to her of his jealousy (III.iv.44). In this play the difference between male and female *freedoms* is writ large. Montano's "free duty" (I.iii.41) and Othello's "free and open nature" (I.iii.399) as "noble," "gracious," are virtually untouched by equivocation, but Desdemona's description as *free* (II.iii.320, 342) increasingly suggests license through Iago's machinations. Being, in Iago's soliloquy, "as fruitful as the free elements" (II.iii.342) calls attention to her sexuality and links her with untrammeled nature, rather than feudal nobilty (and resonates with an equivocation from Golding's *Metamorphoses*). The positive sense of this naturalness, "generosity," is calculated to remind Othello that Desdemona married him, rather than one of the "curl'd darlings" of her own set, but the undertone of ungoverned license becomes part of the vision of Desdemona and of womanhood generally that Iago is preparing for Othello's consumption. It has the appeal it does for the men in the play (Othello, Iago, Roderigo, Brabantio) because it connects with the ancient and current binary male=culture, female=nature.

In *Cymbeline* a somewhat different set of verbal tensions is played out. Jachimo visits Imogen with Posthumus's commendation for his "free entertainment" (I.iv.155), his gracious reception at court, so Imogen will take him for a nobleman and not a mere churl. But since Jachimo's purpose is to seduce her, his word takes on the sinister cast its counterpart will have when he returns with his gloating "Your lady being so easy" (II.iv.47). On the political stage we have Cymbeline's "we were free" until Julius Caesar exacted tribute and the humbly-reared prince Arviragus's we "sing our bondage freely" (III.iii.44). On the (faintly represented) religious issue of guilt v. freedom, there is Posthumus's desire to expiate his guilt toward Imogen by his death in bonds—this death will be his "freedom" (V.iv.3–29). Sexual, political, and religious venues are all fraught with paradox and tension—the gracious reception Jachimo desires will disgrace either Imogen or him; the bonds the prince complains of keep him from the British court, which is itself a bound tributary to Rome; the freedom from guilt Posthumus might find in death he carelessly bequeaths to the jailer who has no relish of salvation in him. But Cymbeline's unambiguously medieval use of *free*—"We'll learn our freeness of a son-in-law"

(V.v.421)—is what averts the threat of continuing war which would have prevented the play from filling out its romance genre. In a single line, the king has accepted the legality of his daughter's marriage, reconciling his family, and acknowledged his tributary status to Rome, knitting up the civilized world in hierarchical order. As in the other romance visions, the oppressions and obsessions of masculine competition are dissolved by the daughter/wife who calls forth true graciousness from the competing men.

Fre/free displays a remarkable centrality, then, to both medieval and early modern social styles. The "lady fre," either as courtly hostess or interceding Virgin, was unequivocally ennobled by the salutation. "Articulated," in Stuart Hall's sense, supplanted "within the logic of another political discourse," the *freedom* of the urban citizen as a social agent and a practicing Christian was also deeply valued, although at the same time imbued with anxieties about where such liberty might ultimately lead; Thomas More, after all, recoiled from his playful early vision of egalitarian citizenship soon after he sent *Utopia* into the world. Tyndale, had he not been executed in 1536, would have seen many of his hopes for lay Christians' freedom expressed in mainstream discourse. But the "fresh and free" which describes Richard Easy in *Michaelmas Term* takes the term to the brink of "license." London theater-goers were treated to both the old inflections and new, often in ironic and playful juxtapositions which highlighted the history of the term and commented on its social uses: Jonson's harsh critique of both the privilege of the old sense of *freedom* and the crassness of the new and Shakespeare's regret for the loss of unrecoverable gentilities and fear of the momentum of what he sees coming.

5
Gloss

> To clarify what follows I must provide a gloss, for if I do not,
> I will not know where I am either.
>
> Umberto Eco, *The Island of the Day Before*

> [Bridget in *The Last Seduction* is] a lot like Kathleen Turner in
> *Body Heat*, a very similar, far glossier, movie.
>
> Marylynn Uricchio, *Pittsburgh Post-Gazette* (1995)

Augustine was so impressed with the scriptural commentaries Ambrose preached in Milan that they allayed his doubts about Christianity and ultimately led to his conversion. These commentaries, he said, lay open "spiritually what according to the letter, seemed to teach something unsound" (*Confessions* VI.IV.6). The Middle English word *gloss* (from Latin *glossa*, "tongue," through Old French *glosa*) as "explanatory comment, exposition," was primarily a technical term for the use of the clerical estate in scholarly disputation and preaching. Its fortunes are therefore closely tied to those of *estat* and *lewed*. The practice of inserting explanatory material between the lines or in the margins of important texts, especially the Bible, grounded the production and dissemination of knowledge during the Middle Ages. This sense is still current in scholarly circles, *glossing* and seeing other writers as having *glossed* refers to the "unpacking" of dense or historically distant passages or to charting the coherent meaning of a complicated series of events, as in Eco's narrator's gloss to keep him oriented in his telling. In the sixteenth century, a second etymological strand, paralleled by the Middle High German *glos*, *glose*, "to gleam, glow, or shine", complicated the picture, augmenting connotations of sophistry the word had acquired by suggesting a superficial attractiveness masking something less attractive. And we still register the impressiveness of a seamless surface as "glossy," usually hinting that the sheen is "just surface," as Marylynn Uricchio does in her film review. By the sixteenth century, both of those usages were common English parlance.

Wimbledon's sermon at Paul's Cross is merely one example of the most common fourteenth-century use of *gloss* in buttressing its explanation of a biblical text with "thus seith the glose" (657). Even in non-clerical contexts, *gloss* usually appears in connection with books, literally, as when Scrope's *Othea* defines the divisions of a book and its commentaries as "exposicyons or glosis vpon the seyde textys" (4), or metaphorically, as when John Gower's narrator in *Confessio Amantis* claims that he will not teach "Venus bokes . . . nowther text ne glose" (1.271). But occasionally life itself was glossed, as in Lydgate's *Fall of Princes*: "Whan a child is first born . . . Kynde to his dethward anon doth hym dispose; / Ech day a iourne; ther is noon other glose" (1.3463). Although there are a few examples of Wycliffite writing using the sense "learned commentary" respectfully, by the 1380s Wyclif and his followers were well known for their opposition to the extensive scholarly glosses of the orthodox clergy. Although Wyclif was a committed Augustinian in philosophical stance, he witnessed, not the first-fruits of interpretive energy that Augustine had seen in Ambrose's glosses, but the intricacies of ten centuries of accreted exegesis and argument. His objection to the Patristic glossing that made "goddis lawe derk" made it a central term in the Lollard controversy and intensified the negative inflection that came to haunt the word. The medieval bifurcation of the Middle English term, then, resulted from an attempt to reform the *practice* of glossing by the Wycliffite group— forging a new articulation in Stuart Hall's sense.

This new articulation was facilitated by the fact that earlier instances of *gloss* had occasionally carried the implication of speaking smoothly and flatteringly, as in *Le Freine*: "With his fair bihest & with his gloseing atte lest hye graunted him do don his wille" (290). Thomas Hoccleve uses *glose* to describe political flatterers: "Yet canst thou glose in contenance & cheere . . . Thy lordes wordes in eche mateere" ("La Male Regele," 266–68). And Margery Kempe acquits herself of evasion: "Sche seyde many scharp wordys on-to hym wyth-owtyn any glosyng er flateryng" (108.35), this trend blending easily with Wycliffite suspicion of biblical glossing. Later influence from the Germanic *glos*, *glose*, "sheen" could be used to register positive luster, as in *The Tempest*

when Gonzalo notes the miraculous "freshness and glosses" of the
clothes which had been drenched in sea water (II.i.62–64), but it could
also reinforce suspicions of the deceptiveness of surfaces, as in
Nicholas Udall's *Paraphrases of Erasmus*: "Beware ye that all your life
bee void of all cloking or countrefaicte glosse" (Luke 12.1–7).
The history of the word *gloss* in this period flip-flops twice. The prestige of *glossing* was attacked by Wycliffites in the late medieval period
as a protest against clerical control of the scripture and therefore proto-
Protestant in effect. But sixteenth-century Protestant translators used
glosses to re-configure the meanings of many scriptural passages, and
both Catholic and Anglican authorities inveighed against the glosses
in translations like the Tyndale New Testament and the Geneva Bible,
as well as the translations themselves. There are, therefore, two movements which attempt to capture *glossing*, as a practice and as a term,
and "supplant it within the logic of another political [and in this case
religious] discourse." Late medieval distrust of Patristic glosses as
scholarly, usually allegorical, annotation undermined the sense "reli-
able interpretation" in favor of "self-serving obfuscation"; early
modern Anglican authorities made a similar attack on glossing to
discredit Lutheran and Calvinist commentaries. In the second wave of
controversy it was the establishment which condemned glossing and
claimed to champion the "plain text."

Wyclif, Langland, Chaucer

As part of his increasingly radical vision for the reform of Christian
life, Wyclif defended the adequacy of scripture to guide individual
conduct and ecclesiastical governance. These views appear throughout
his scholarly disputes and his sermons, both in Latin and in English.
The English Wycliffite sermons (whether written by Wyclif himself or
a follower makes little difference to this argument) consist of the Latin
text with a translation and commentary in idiomatic Middle English—
Wyclif opposed both the preaching tactic of including non-biblical
stories like those in the *Gesta Romanorum* in sermons, and that of over-
loading the scriptural text with learned and potentially distracting
allegorical senses. Rebukes like these are not uncommon in the English
sermons: "bastard dyvynes seien algates that this wordis of Crist ben
false, and so no wordis of Crist bynden, but to the witt that gloseris
tellen" (I.367); these priests do not teach "bot flatren hom and glosen
and norischen hom in synne" (III.377); and "her Anticristis tirauntis
[the official Church] speken a,en the newe lawe, and seien that literal

witte of it shulde never be takun, but goostli witt; and thei feynen this goostli witt after shrewid wille that thei han" (II.343).[1] In "The Clergy May Not Hold Property," Wyclif uses *gloss* seven times in four sentences, explaining the difference between official glosses and Christ's own:

> as thu maist not undo for euer suche textis nor ʒit thu wilt do aftir the letter of siche textis; therfore thu saist thu most haue a gloss. Wel than for goddis loue, If thu wilt glose the textis of the gospelle that ben so euen aʒens thi lordeschip, glose hem as criste did and commaundid the to ʒeue fulle credence to his gloss, whan he saide: "ʒif ʒe leue not me for my wordis, leue ʒe the dedis." And if thu bileue effectualy this glose, thu schalt not oonly forsake the lordeschip that thu occupiest, but also, rather than thu schuldist be ocupied therwith, thu schalt renne awai ther-fro & hyde the, as cristis glose saith that he did. And if thu wilt not bileue effectualy cristis wordis nether his glose, than thu wilfully & obstynatly forsakist crist utterly.
>
> (Matthew 376.7–19)

Lollardy's disdain for the warped exegetical tradition is sometimes conflated with this sense of the word as "flattering," as in "clerkis and religious folke that louen unkyndely thes lordlynes, willen glose here" (Matthew 384), and both Wycliffite translations of the Bible into English use *gloss* to translate the Latin *blandire*: "Thei seiden to the wijf of Sampson, 'Glose thin hosebonde, and counseile hym'" (Judges 14.15, Early Version) and "The king...with these wordis gloside, 'What hast thou, Ester?'" (Esther 15.11, Later Version).

The fictitious debaters in the one-sided "dialogue" which structures the Lollard *Plowman's Tale* —the Gryffon who represents the argument for the papacy and the Pellycan who speaks for the Wycliffites—accuse one another of misinterpreting the Bible, each using *glose* to carry his points. The Gryffon says, "Wyth glosynge gettest thou thy mete; / So fareth the devell that wonneth in hell" (94.1139–40), "Thou woldest other people dystry / Wyth your glose, and your heresy" (1144–45), and "Therfore ye glose Goddes hestes, / And begyle the people yonge and olde" (1155–56). The Pellycan replies that the established Church has misrepresented the Ten Commandments and "by glose wrechedlyche / Selleth any of the sacramentes" (96.1203–04). *Piers Plowman's Creed* also accuses the friars of flattering, telling fables, and "gabbynge of glose" (16.275), of scratching kings' backs and deceiving them by glossing to the peril of their soule (19.367), and of blunting Christian preaching by glossing the gospel "in gladding tales" (23.515). *Jack Upland* calls attention to the human ingenuity required for glossing: "a glos feyned of youre wittis" (132.331). *Upland's Rejoinder* tasks his opponent "Friar Daw," with beguiling simple hearts with "thi gildyn glose and with thi costly houses" (206.72), and lets the misinterpretation of scripture, "glasen glose" slip into sitting at the high table to "glosen lordes and ladies" (214.357, 359).

Glossing had its defenders against such charges, of course, but Langland does not seem to have been one of them. Notwithstanding the importance he places on interpretation,[2] *Piers Plowman* has little good to say about the glossing practices he envisions in his fiction. The B Version has: "I fond there Freris... Prechynge the peple for profit of the wombe; / Glosed the gospel as hem good liked" (prol. 58–60), "I wiste neuere freke that as a frere ȝede bifore men on englissh / Taken it for his teme, and telle it withouten glosyng" (13.74–75), "And fals prophetes fele, flatereris & gloseris / Shullen come" (19.221–22). So when we see the gloss in B 17.15 "glosiousely writen with a gilte penne," we suspect that the quest for moral instruction is not going to be completed here (cf., 5.281 and 10.175). In one of the last actions of the narrative, a limiter offers to send a friar (for "a litel siluer") who "gooth and gadereth and gloseth there he shryueth / Til Contricion hadde clene foryeten to crye and to wepe" (20.368–69). This outrageous gloss is the immediate cause of the vow of Conscience to become a pilgrim seeking Piers with which the final dream ends.

In his translation of Boethius's *The Consolation of Philosophy*, *Boece*, Chaucer both translates glosses from Nicholas Trivet and perhaps other commentators and provides glosses of his own, some based on his concurrent use of Jean de Meun's French translation.[3] This exegetical tradition becomes the Wife of Bath's comic target in all three of the instances of *glose* in her Prologue. "Men may devyne and glosen, up and doun" (26) and "Glose whoso wole, and seye bothe up and doun" (119) suggest that the technique of showing extended or allegorical ("up and doun") senses for a scriptural passage or natural phenomenon could be used to evade common sense and misstate God's intentions. The third instance chronicles a success at glossing. Alisoun's fifth husband could entreat her to a peace even after beating her, "so wel koude he me glose" (509). In this case, the suggestion of elaborate reading (though here apparently accurate reading) is combined with that of flattering and of "getting around" someone with seductive verbal maneuvers. The Wife's skepticism about glossing is matched by the Summoner's, whose Friar John is an inaccurate reader of scripture, of *exempla*, and even of his intended mark, Thomas. He arrogantly refuses to base his sermons or his private counsel on scripture, but skips immediately to teaching "al the glose. / Glosynge is a glorious thyng, certeyne, / For lettre sleeth, so as we clerkes seyn" (1792–94), claiming the special insights of the clergy trained in Latin and disdaining simple parish priests. He disclaims the text a second time, finding "in a maner glose" (1920) his theme for the sermon he preaches for Thomas. Friar John demonstrates every error and vice Wyclif had charged the fraternal orders with in his writings after 1376. The Summoner cleverly includes enough scripture (for example, the letter slays, the poor in spirit are blessed) to condemn his friar out of his own mouth.[4]

Chaucer's most direct reference to the Wycliffite controversies, though, occurs in two widely separated passages in which the Shipman (or perhaps the Wife, see *Riverside* notes) objects to the Parson as the next teller because he has scolded the pilgrims for swearing. The Host smells "a Lollere in the wynd":

> "This Lollere heer wil prechen us somwhat."
>   "Nay, by my fader soule, that schal he nat!"
> Seyde the Shipman, "Heer schal he nat preche;
> "He schal no gospel glosen here ne teche"
> We leven alle in the grete God," quod he.
> He wolde sowen som difficulte ,
> Or springen cokkel in our clene corn."
>
> (II.1172–73, 77–81)

The Parson "answers," (but much later) "I wol nat glose— / I wol yow telle a myrie tale in prose / To knytte up al this feeste and make an ende" (X.45–47). My reading of this exchange is that the Shipman or Wife objects to the Puritanical tone he or she hears in the Parson's objection to swearing and takes his somber manner as evidence of Lollard leanings. The "gospel gloss" referred to in the first passage was a common way of identifying Wycliffite preachers because their sermons stayed so close to the Bible, reading the text line by line.[5] Although his "tale" is not a Wycliffite "gospel glose," the Parson's "I wol nat glose" does, I think, disclaim elaborate scholarly glosses and explain his being "nat textueel." And Chaucer does allow it to "knytte up al this feeste."

As the fifteenth century goes on, casual usage tilts the sense of *gloss* quite strongly toward distortion, flattery, and general unreliability. The *Medula Grammatice* defines "adulator" as *gloser*, and a story from 1500 in the *Gesta Romanorum* contains this claim: "My systers han seide to you words of glosyng, but I say to you trouthe" (Add. 49). A late medieval poem called "Lerne say wele," which warns against indiscreet gossiping, begins, "What a glosere here or see, / Thou3 it shulde to shame falle, / He knoweth in chambre preuytee, / Telleth his felow in the halle; / And felow to felow, tyl they knowe alle, / ffro toun to toun, in all contray." In sum, by 1500 scholarly *glossing* refers either to the interpretive efforts of one's own group or the self-interested misreadings exhibited by one's rivals, but the unmodified common use implies flattery and deceit. Reformation controversies over the English Bible also revolved around the *gloss*.

Déjà vu all over again

The Authorized Version was, as Christopher Hill asserts in *The English Bible and the Seventeenth-Century Revolution*, "consciously political" (63). It was undertaken to counteract the enormous influence of the Geneva Bible of 1560, a cheap book widely available, often in handy quarto form. Geneva provided a scholarly and polemical introduction to scripture with maps, concordances, and, above all, glosses. It was out of official favor long before 1611; one of Archbishop Whitgift's first acts was to prohibit all translations and annotations not authorized by him or the Bishop of London (Pierce 70). Its glosses, especially those that seemed to James I insufficiently deferential to royal power, occasioned his calling it the "worst translation" (60) and authorizing the 1611 Version to drive it out—by 1615, it was illegal to import Geneva Bibles. James even gave instructions to the scholars who were to produce the Authorized Version to avoid translating *ecclesia* as "congregation," recalling a dispute that goes back to Thomas More and William Tyndale (see above, pp. 11–12). Yet for all the official standing accorded the Authorized Version, ninety percent of its phrasings of the New Testament coincide with Tyndale's, a translation so loathsome to the establishment in its time that Cuthbert Tunstall commanded copies of it to be confiscated on the grounds that they profaned the "majesty of scripture" by printing "in the English tongue that pestiferous and pernicious poison" (quoted in Daniell 190). It is not clear, since Tunstall cites books both with and without glosses, whether it is Tyndale's phrasing that is "pestiferous" or the project of using English to convey sacred truths. If the latter, Tunstall is making the argument that the Latin of scripture participates in its sacredness, as in Benedict Anderson's characterization of the pre-modern "transcontinental sodalities of Christianity" (40).

The charges traded by More and Tyndale over biblical interpretation in turn recall the debates of Wyclif's time. In More's *Dialogue Concerning Heresies*, Lutherans are said to prefer "theyr owne fonde gloses agaynste the olde connynge and blessyd fathers interpret-acyons" (123.15–17). The term is used here, modified by "fond," to refer to the interpretive matter of the Lollard-like Protestants of More's day, but avoids it when referring to the glosses of the Catholic Fathers. (More called the Bible-as-sole-authority assertion a "pestilential heresy" [Hill, *English Bible* 15].) In *A Supplication of Souls*, the souls in purgatory claim that the Bible plainly declares their need for the prayers of the living, and heretics "can fynd neyther glose nor colour to the contrary" (180.2–3). The implication is that a gloss is normally an authoritative aid to interpretation. What "heretics" must do to advance their case, then, is to "set some false glose to the text that is layed agaynst theym / and deny the ryght sense" (186.7–9). The possi-bility of a false gloss signals the presence of competing schemes for biblical interpretation and re-opens the questions raised by the Lollards. In one passage in *A Dialogue of Comfort*, More uses the term in its plainest sense of interpretation: "I will not dispute vpon any glosyng of that prohibicion" (136.17), but others recall the sense of flattery Alisoun of Bath associates with *gloss* (perhaps even its rela-tionship to *glaze*) as he commends King Ladislaus for rejecting any retelling of his deeds which "set a glose vpon" the story in order to flatter him (218.17). The hollow heart which flatters itself with "so gay a glose of good and graciouse purpose" (228.24) that it cannot examine itself deeply, shows a yet clearer link with *glaze*.

Tyndale always uses the word *gloss* in connection with biblical gloss-ing, and it always implies a popish avoidance of the direct meaning of scripture.[6] In *The Obedience of a Christian Man* he accuses contem-porary priests of being like the lawyers Christ castigates for not seeking knowledge themselves and denying it to others "with glosses and traditions" (205.23). On the doctrine of contrition, he writes, "with such glosses corrupt they God's word, to sit in the consciences of the people, to lead them captive, and to make a prey of them; buying and selling their sins" (265.20–23). In this way he links the issue of vernac-ular scripture with the central concern of *Obedience*, the freedom Christians enjoy under God's properly understood dispensation.

Tyndale's rejection of the glossing tradition is even more centrally based on his tenet that the Bible alone ought to be decisive for Christian belief and that therefore every Christian must have access to it in a language he or she understands. Yet he recognized the need for interpretive aids and produced his own marginal glosses, often very controversial. A gloss for Matthew interpreted the *confession* of Peter, rather than the specific person, as the rock on which Christ's Church is to be built, directly countering the Catholic position that the bishopric of Rome retained secrets of the faith not recorded in scripture ("Peter in greek signifieth a stone in English. This confession is the rock"—quoted in Daniell 119). Such glosses were, of course, deeply offensive to the powers that be, but they were not openly accusatory, like Wycliffites calling the Pope anti-Christ, or "salty," as some later commentators have maintained. Tyndale's recent biographer, David Daniell, calls his glosses on Matthew, "Lutheran, but not sensational," mainly expository (117). But they were glosses.

In secular venues, early modern writers seem to imply something like "gloss over" or "misstate." Spenser's *View of Ireland* describes the Irish as giving lewdness itself "a goodly gloss and painted show" which makes it look like virtue (74.23–24). "To lye, faine, gloze, to steale, pry, and accuse," describes what ill "a miser state doth breed," for Sidney, and he advises destruction of "that fancy glosse" ("First Eclogue" 8.22–23, 9.117). Greene's Lucanio is warned that it is as easy "to weigh the wind, as to diue into the thoughtes of worldlye glosers" (*Groatsworth* 13), with the implication perhaps of both worldly interpreters and worldly liars. And in Middleton's *Father Hubbard*, "soothing glosers oil the son" whom they hated while his father lived (60–61). Something of that sense of obfuscating sophistication is evident in Thomas Wyatt's epigram LXIX:

> Nor in my heart sank never such disdain
> To be a forger, faults for to disclose.
> Nor I cannot endure the truth to gloze,
> To set a gloss upon an earnest pain.

The poem generally urges the poet's frankness and depth of feeling; he will neither start rumors nor "gloss over" unpleasant truths, and in CLXXIX *gloze* appears in the list "feign, flatter, or gloze."[7]

John Florio's translation of Montaigne's "Of the Cannibals" provides a notable instance of *gloss*: "For subtle people may indeed mark more curiously and observe things more exactly, but they amplify and gloss them; and, the better to persuade and make their interpretations of more validity, they cannot choose but somewhat alter the story." Here the *gloss* is seen as imbedded in the report of the "story." It is both interpretive and rhetorical, and the essay's case for the "natural" argues that it is all but inevitable for subtle intelligencers. Montaigne relies on impressions of the New World he had received from "a simple and rough-hewn fellow, a condition fit to yield a true testimony" (220.23), employing *gloss* to represent European sophistication, even sophistry, which cannot but prejudice a just assessment of New World cultures, and thus makes it part of his argument for the world of the "cannibals."[8]

Theatrical performance was often attacked as inherently deceitful because it produced (and sold) the mere semblances of events. Stephen Gosson thinks of all stage performance as chicanery, referring to "that glosing plaie at the *Theater*" in *Playes Confuted* (171.1). John Earle likened the way actors put "a false glosse upon his [God's] creatures" to the way tradesman adulterated their wares (quoted in Agnew 118). The accused theater often targeted showy court life, also using *gloss* to distinguish appearance from depth. John of Gaunt predicts in *Richard II* that the young king will perhaps credit the terse words of a dying man more than those "whom youth and ease have taught to glose" (II.i.10). Chapman's *Bussy D'Ambois* also uses *gloss* to discredit courtly flattery and deceit when Bussy claims that "brave barks and outward gloss / Attract court loves, be in-parts ne'er so gross," and Monsieur accepts his allegation, promising him gloss enough (I.i.109–11). Protestant reformers had successfully elevated literal plainness to the moral status of probity and sincerity in venues far from the insistence on an unadorned scriptural text.

Appropriating the residual gloss

Yet the old sense "scholarly commentary" persisted into the early modern period as one strand of the meaning of *gloss*. Philemon Holland in *Plutarch's Morals* thought it had to be explained to general audiences: "The interpretation of obscure terms, which we call Glosses" (28).[9] Edmund Spenser, or Gabriel Harvey, or whoever provided the framing material of *The Shepheardes Calender* under the signature "E.K.," treated glossing as a serious, scholarly unfolding of linguistic, historical, and interpretive issues in the main text, something like a secularized version of medieval patristic glosses. E.K.'s Dedicatory Epistle explains his tactic as a facet of the enhancement of serious *English* learning.

Hereunto have I added a certain glosse or scholion for the exposition of old wordes and harder phrases: which manner of glossing
and commenting, well I wote, wil seeme straunge and rare in our
tongue: yet for somuch as I knew many excellent and proper
devises, both in wordes and matter, would passe in the speedy
course of reading, either as unknowen, or as not marked, and that
in this kind, as in other, we might be equal to the learned of other
nations, I thought good to take the paines upon me.

(240–52)

Although one might see a slightly parodic tone in E.K.'s over-careful
explanations—"the Glosse (running continually in maner of a
Paraphrase)" is, as the postscript to Spenser's first letter to Harvey
claims, as big as the *Calender* itself—its educative, clarifying goal seems
for the most part quite straightforward. The glosses themselves explain
the classical and biblical imagery of the poem and call up its moral
implications, but they do not run counter to the "plain sense" of the
text, as Protestant critiques had alleged of Catholic glosses. It might
even be said that *The Shepheardes Calender* aims to reinterpret and
reform the practice of glossing as well as bring it into English letters,
just as *The Faerie Queene* reinterprets medieval English history.
References to *glossing* in *The Faerie Queene* make the point that it needs
to be reformed.[10] Two instances are cast in metaphors of metal-
working: the "glistring glosse" of good old armor is hidden by rust in
II.vii.4.3, and a "guileful Goldsmith" coats vulgar metal with a "goodly
glosse" in IV.v.15.5. These metaphors owe something to the Germanic
sense of *gloss* as "gleam," but the second particularly suggests the
Protestant sense of false exterior semblance. Trompart's seductive
"glozing speaches" to "Florimel" combine the sense of "dazzling" with
that of dissembling true motives, but there is a nice irony in the
passage, since the "lady" being seduced is herself a simulacrum, a false
Florimel constructed by a witch (III.vii.144). Braggadocchio's attempts
at seduction are also referred to as "glozing speaches" (III.viii.14.4).

Christopher Marlowe's *Edward II* relates the story of a monarch who
is offered what Protestants would call "outward gloss" by Gaveston and
then by the Spencers, whose flattery he mistakes for counsel. Lancaster
warns Edward to renounce Gaveston or "see the throne, where you
should sit, / To float in blood; and at thy wanton head, / The glosing
head of thy base minion thrown" (I.i.131–33). *Glossing* in another
sense of the term, though, is *enacted* in *Edward II*. The play seems to be
about reading, interpreting; consider its dense concentration of

classical imagery, introduced not only by the king and his minion who like to pose as figures from Ovid, but by the politically focused rebels as well. The sprinkling of untranslated Latin in the play (in the mouths of Mortimer Junior and Senior, Lancaster, Leicester, and even Matrevis) makes the same point. This is a court in which momentous truths, solemn orders, and the mottoes for the "stately triumph" Edward planned for the return of Gaveston are phrased in the old sacred language. Thus, when Young Mortimer, acting as regent with Queen Isabel during Edward's imprisonment, decides that Edward will have to be killed to avoid the risk of his being restored, he issues the orders for Edward's murder, in an "unpointed letter" one which must be interpreted, glossed in the old sense, to be obeyed.

> "*Edwardum occidere nolite timere bonum est:*
> *Fear not to kill the king, 'tis good he die.*"
> But read it thus, and that's another sense:
> *Edwardum occidere nolite, timere bonum est:*
> *Kill not the king, 'tis good to fear the worst.*
> Unpointed as it is, thus shall it go,
> That, being dead, if it chance to be found,
> Matrevis and the rest may bear the blame,
> And we be quit that caused it to be done.
>
> (V.iv.8–16)

The unpointed letter does present Gurney with a problem of interpretation: "What's here? I know not how to conster it" (V.v.15), but Matrevis concludes that the significantly absent comma comes after *timere,* enjoining him to kill Edward without fear, as Mortimer had expected (16–17). Gurney's word *conster* (or "construe") is the technical term for producing word-for-word English translations of Latin in the Middle Ages, like Wyclif's Early Version of scripture. This ruse does not, in the end, protect Mortimer from the resolve of young Edward III to behead *him* for tyranny. For the newly crowned Edward III, the fact that the letter is in Mortimer's hand is enough to convict him.

Gloss and *gloze* in Shakespeare's plays combine (sometimes in separate passages and sometimes layered in a single instance) the medieval sense of interpretive commentary with implications of distortion and superficial sheen. The tradition of glossing as disclosing deep, hidden meaning is registered, but somewhat suspiciously, in Canterbury's claim that the French "unjustly gloze" the "Salique land" to be France (*Henry V*) and Hector's rebuttal to Paris and Troilus's argument for keeping Helen that they have "gloz'd, but superficially" like young men "whom Aristotle thought unfit to hear moral philosophy" (*Troilus*). Other instances of *gloss* emphasize the MHG *glos*, to glow or shine. Virtues, honors, deeds, fortunes, and marriages may be said to have a gloss on them, but such glosses, for example the freshness of the shipwrecked Europeans' garments unspoiled by the storm in *The Tempest*, are appearances, fair but fragile. Although the claim that certain glosses are superficial or unjust involves the assumption that a deep and honest gloss is still possible to imagine, the bulk of Shakespeare's usage falls on the pejorative side: Tamora compliments herself that she, "high-witted," can fool everyone—"gloze with all"— and Antiochus tries to cheat—"but I will gloze with him"—Pericles out his reward for properly glossing the riddle (*Titus* IV.iv.35; *Pericles* I.i.110).

Love's Labors Lost, though, provides one of the richest instances of the term. The emphasis throughout the play is on scholarly overingenuity or even impropriety (if some references allude to the Marprelate controversy or the "School of Night"). The play seems to have been "a battle in a private war between court factions" written for private performance (David's *Introduction* to the Arden edition i). In an early scene, Maria concludes her elaborate praise of Longaville as having too sharp a wit and blunt a will, "The only soil of his fair virtue's gloss, / If virtue's gloss will stain with any soil" (II.i.47–48), implying his splendid presence. Boyet's equally elaborate figure of Navarre's senses being "lock'd in his eye, / As jewels in crystal," "glass'd" (encased in glass) to induce their sale (242–44) also suggests visual sheen, playfully, but not altogether dismissively. The older sense "elaboration, exegesis," though, also runs through the play, for example, in Costard's verbal quibble over explications of the terms *wench*, *damsel*, *virgin*, *maid*, *girl* (I.i.272–95), in Holofernes's untranslated Latin and self-conscious linguistic argument, and in the Princess's mention that her love-letter was "Writ o' both sides the leaf, margent and all" (V.ii.8). This last instance may contain a very precise topical allusion; although writing in the margins is an obvious reference to glossing, it was apparently also a habit of the historical Henri of Navarre (David xxxiv). Katherine refers to "Text B in a copy-book" (V.ii.42), continuing the scholarly vocabulary.

The comic crisis of the play—the men's abandonment of their vow eschewing women—is marked by an allusion to glossing, in keeping with the scholarly project they are about to forego. Longaville's "Now to plain-dealing, lay these glozes by" (IV.iii.367), identifies Berowne's

77-line speech with over-elaborate medieval commentaries. Only a few lines later, Berowne delivers an enigmatic little quatrain beginning "Sowed cockle reaped no corn" (380), which echoes the Shipman's fear that Chaucer's Parson will sow cokles [Wycliffite glosses] in "oure clene corn." His point does not complete his own line of reasoning in praise of the power of love (since it warns that the women may prove "plagues" to the men later), nor does it make a graceful ending to Act IV. What it does do is suggest that the serious focus of the play, and perhaps its topical subtext no longer fully available to us, is attentive to the history of the glossing tradition.

The chronicle of *gloss* exhibits with particular force Gadamer's dictum that culture always "bears the imprint of its historical tradition." *Gloss* as searching, detailed scholarly interpretation persisted in usage from the 1380s to 1611, particularly in the realm of biblical exegesis, but also in attempts by writers like Chaucer in *Boece* and later Spenser to raise English-language texts to the level of scholarly thoroughness associated with Latin and continental writing. Yet from the decades of the Wycliffite controversies onward that meaning was always stalked by the almost completely contradictory sense of surface glitz which distracts from understanding, what we now call "glossing over." Wycliffites at first tried to taint Patristic glossing with the second meaning, but soon found their opponents referring pejoratively to their simple, expository sermon style as "gospel glossing." This dense tapestry of charge and counter-charge was re-enacted in Anglican denunciations of the glosses in the Tyndale New Testament and the Geneva Bible. Both the proto-Protestant Wycliffites and Protestants of the sixteenth century set out to reform structures of religious feeling, including attitudes toward language and languages, and, despite their considerable success, found themselves enmeshed in broad, continuing controversies.

6
Kynde/Kind

He never offer'd me the least kindness that way, after our marriage.

Moll, in *Moll Flanders*

Pity this Busy Monster Manunkind.

e e cummings

The force of e e cummings's title lies in the way it summons up the history of *kind* from its earliest to its surviving uses. The modern word "mankind" is a fossilized trace from the Old English noun ȝecynde, "nature," a noun closely linked literally or metaphorically to "kindred," just as *fre* was linked to birth into a family. In Middle English the word is usually spelled *kynde*, and its associations as a noun are with nature in the sense of birth, progeny, or racial stock (ȝecynd-limu or "kind-limbs" for the genitals in "Phoenix," *kynde* for offspring in *Piers Plowman*, and semen in Mirk's *Festial*). This close association of natural processes with birth and birthright impart a sort of anthropomorphic coloration to Middle English natural history, which phrased as "inborn" or "related" what would later be regarded as "systemic." "Pity this Busy Monster" fuses the current sense of *kind*, "beneficent," with the Middle English suggestion of human membership in a common lineage, playing up the anomalies embedded in the history of the word.

The most common force of the Middle English *kynde* is "nature" as "inherent." When late fourteenth- and fifteenth-century translators chose *kynde* to render Latin "naturam" and "naturae," some suggested by it "inborn" and some a broader system of causes and effects.[1]

Adjectivally, *kynde* has the force "inherently" or "by right of birth." The "birthright" strand leads to OE and ME *kynde king, kynde land,* and *kynde speech.* Such usages resonate strongly with a feudal social emphasis on birth privileges. "Inherent" sometimes shades into "well-born" (C.S. Lewis suggests the familiar ellipses which gives us to understand "of high birth" from "of birth" or "of high quality" for "of quality"), which provides one bridge to the Modern English "well disposed," "generous," "benevolent." Another is the frequent use of *kynde* as "beneficent" for actions within kin or other close-knit groups, linking *kindness* to a conception of natural duty. The Wycliffite tract *Concord* defines *kynde* in a way that recognizes its two facets, but does not try to fuse them: "As, this word kynde bitokeneth nature, and also such a man clepen we kynde which is a fre-hertid man & that gladly wole rewarde what that men don for hym" (5b). This "fre-hertid" sense has only two examples in the *Middle English Dictionary* before 1375, but its use increases after that, and it is found quite frequently in Malory.[2] Even so, there are at least ten times as many citations in the *MED* in which the adjective *kynde* means "nature" or "natural" as for its meaning "beneficent." By 1600, it will be hard to find an adjectival instance in which "beneficent" is *not* the first or surface meaning. Yet the kin and kind pun must be seen as a possibility, although residual, as late as *Moll Flanders,* where we read of Moll's disappointment that her first lover, who had married her off to his younger brother, stopped making love to her after her marriage, stopped offering her "the least kindness that way." The comic effect of this wordplay rests on dissonance between the dangers of adultery and the mutual pleasure ("love of kynde") Moll had shared with the older brother. A continued sexual liaison between them would be a kindness in one moral universe and a guilty perversion in another.

Between 1380 and 1611, *kynde* also gradually takes on a grammatical function almost devoid of its lexical meanings as either "nature" or "beneficent." The linguistic process is called "grammaticalization," a feature of linguistic change only recently explored in detail, which describes "changes through which a lexical [content] item in certain uses becomes a grammatical [function-indicating] term" (Hopper and Traugott 2–4). Paul Hopper describes what he calls the "Principle of Divergence," which I think fits the case of *kynde* quite well. Divergence "results in pairs or multiples of forms having a common etymology, but diverging functionally. The grammaticalized form may be phonologically identical with the autonomous lexical form" or not (Hopper [1991] 24). In *kynde* we have a multiple, which splits in the years before 1600 into two lexical items, meaning "nature" or "genre" and "beneficent," and a grammaticalized form with the same pronunciation and spelling, which increasingly becomes a non-meaning-bearing marker of class or sort. (Later still, the *kind* in "He feels kind of sick" has lost even more of its lexical force and in colloquial speech becomes "kinda.") The grammaticalization of *kynde* is clearly observable at least as early as the sixteenth century. This history is not marked by dramatic gestures by persons (like James I's attempt to control the meaning of *estate* by calling new definitions seditious) or by groups (like Protestant redefinitions of Christian *freedom*), who set out to maintain or supplant the particular articulations of words with ideologies. It consists rather in the slow erosion of a shared conception of the natural and human worlds as dominated by a nature linked to birth and birthright.

Medieval kyndes

In Middle English, the strong implication of *kynde* is inherence, and its etymological link with *kin* results in an association with sex, and specifically semen. In *Wars of Alexander*, we find: "I kan noȝt supose it [the child] be consayued of my kynde ne come of my-selfe" (578) and *Assembly of Gods* has Sensualyte sewing the field "with hys vnkynde seed" (1023). "Love of kynde" is sexual desire. The "natural" claims of blood are, of course, needed for inheritance, as in *William of Palerne*, in which a character says, "Myn elder son min eritage schul haue... as kinde skil it wold" (4098). It adds force to the assertion that "Cornelius was cald to his kynde name" (70)—his birth name but not his legal name—in *Destruction of Troy*. A few instances of the biological nexus are found in the sixteenth century, as in Thomas Elyot's *Defence of Good Women*, which forbids judgments of the "hole kinde [or kynde] of women" (18.15, 26.8, 50.2) and John Knox's *First Blast of the Trumpet*, which insists that the female lives under God's sentence for "her kind" (49.7, cf. 44.33).[3]

The contention that blood relations determine what is natural in human communities results in a strong emphasis on kinship loyalties, and that is what medieval instances of *kynde* consistently show. In relations between parents and children, *unkind* carries the weight of unnaturalness as well as moral failure. A loyal son will oppose his father's enemies, "ȝif that ye be kynde" (Lydgate's *Troy Book* 2.1154, and *passim*). The lack of care by parents is also called *unkynd*, as when a story in the *Gesta Romanorum* treats a "fadir so vnkynde that he woll not pay my raunsom for me" (306; 307 treats an *vnkynde* daughter). Sexual perversions are also called *unkynde* by Wyclif (*Apology for Lollard Doctrines* 87), and the word is defined by the *Catholicon Anglicum* as *adultervius, ingratus,* and *degener.* Incest with one's sister (Gower) and fratricide (Lydgate) are particularly unnatural. Trevisa's *Bartholomeus* tells the story of the weakened mother bird, some of whose children feed her and some "vnkynde" do not. *Robert of Glocester's Chronicle* tells how Lier "playnede of the vnkynde dede of hys doȝter Gornorille" (32). Duties to kin can be generalized to larger groups. The *Mirror of St. Edmund* refers to the "twelf kuyndes of Israel" (1088) and the *Conquest of Ireland* to the "kynde of troy" (23.26). Lydagte frequently uses *unkynde* to characterize traitors to country like Judas, Ganelon, and Humfrey (4.6446). *Unkyndness* is also unnaturalness toward friends, as in *Dives & Pauper,* "Leue frend...Y haue ben to the wol vnkende and lytil loue schewyd to the" (*MED* Library, 2.282). Gower's *Confessio Amantis* tags many as *unkinde* for disloyalty in love (4.849, 5.535, 5.5424), and Lydgate's *Troy Book* charges Jason (1.3611) and Aeneas (5.1451) for that "unnatural" behavior. Disloyalty to family, lovers, and country fall into the general category of ungratefulness. Particularly striking is this comment from *Body Politic*: "Symple labourers of the erthe....It is pyte that any man shulde be vnkynde to theim, seing the notable seruyce that they doo to euery creatur" (190.5). Ingratitude is also involved in *unkyndness* toward God. Julian of Norwich, for example, laments, "Than were it a grete vnkyndenesse of me to blame or wondyr of god for my synnes, syn he blames not me for synne" (61.2).[4] Notwithstanding, of the relatively few instances of *unkynde* as "cruel," many more have to do with weather than with human actions.

Many instances of *kynde* deal with the world of animals and physical properties. In connection with animals, *kynde* often means "species," as in the phrasing of Genesis 1.20 from the Early Version of the Wycliffite Bible: "God also seide waters bryng they forth the creping kynd of the lyuyng soul & the fleing kynd vp on the erth" and *Ludus Coventry*: "Noe...Of euery kyndys best a cowpyl thou take" (39.120). Trevisa's *Bartholomeus* makes *unkindness* a veritable motif: kites reveal that their "owne kynde is vnkynde," certain foods produce *unkinde* moisture, "salt flewme" is an *vnkynde* humour, leprosy produces "unkynde blode," and rotting comes from "vnkynde hete." Sometimes nature is imagined as an orderly process or system, hence the many examples of the phrase "aȝens kynde" (as when Chaucer's Dorigen sees the removal of the rocks as "agayns the proces of nature" [5.1345]).[5]

For the adjective *unkynde*, citations are about equally divided between
"unnatural" in physical phenomena and in family relations.[6]
Writers like the *Pearl*-poet, Chaucer, the members of the Wycliffite
group, and Malory made use of this range of meanings for *kynde* for
double implication and verbal play. The *Pearl*-poet uses *kynde* as
"species" or "sort" in phrases that keep it very close to "nature," as in
the description of the pearl, "so cler of kynde," and "by kynde . . . clerer"
when washed in wine (*Pearl*, 74, *Cleanness*, 1128), "of vche clene comly
kynde" (*Cleanness*, 334), and "the worthyest of the worldes kynde"
(*Gawain*, 261). But most often, *kynde* implies "nature" in its strongest
sense, underwritten by God in the act of creation: Adam was at first
given no law except to "loke to kynde, / And kepe to hit, and alle hit
cors clanly fulfylle" and the fall meant contriving "agayn kynde
contraré werkez" (*Cleanness*, 263, 266). Without losing the sense
"naturally," *Pearl* has the father asking the maiden to make known to
him "kyndely your coumforde" which seems to imply "beneficently"
as well (369), and in *Cleanness* the window of the ark is enjoined to be
"a cubit kyndelt sware"—exactly a cubit square (319).

Chaucer plays with the oldest as well as its emergent associations of
kynde. The Parson warns against polluting the church by spilling
"kynde [semen] inwith that place" (X.965). The birds in the *Parliament
of Fowls* came from "every kynde" (311) that men can imagine, every
species. The Wife of Bath alleges that God himself gives "wommen
kyndely" deceit, weeping and spinning, presumably "by nature," and
the Loathly Lady in her tale is accused by her new high born husband
of coming "of so lough a kynde" (III.101), by which he means her
inherited status. The narrator in the *Book of the Duchess* locates the
book he is reading as an old one from a time when "men loved the
lawe of kynde" (56), the natural rather than the revealed dispensation,
and *The Second Nun's Tale* asserts that God had "no desdeyne" of
kynde (VIII.41). When complex effects are produced with the term,
especially in *Troilus and Criseyde*, it is within the medieval sense
"natural," in an attempt, I think, to organize natural and theological
duties. The comic treatment of Troilus's struggle against love as a
horse in the trays ends with "may no man fordon the lawe of kynde"
(I.238). Criseyde's situation is similarly, if somewhat more soberly,
described, in that no one escapes the heat of some sort of love, either
"celestial, or elles love of kynde" (I.979). Having chosen *kynde*
Criseyde avows she can no more live without it than any other
"plaunte or lyves creature" can live "withouten his kynde noriture"
(IV.767–68). Having posited sexual love as nature, the lovers'

separation forces new accommodations: Criseyde moves quickly to another sexual liaison and Troilus eventually to a comprehensive contempt for the world of *kynde*.

Malory's practice hints at things to come. *Morte D'Arthur* refers to the inherent trait of Bretons "braggars of kynde" (207.25) and to Lancelot's need to sleep "by course of kynde" (805.14), but the most interesting instances in the tale are intimations that lordship is natural, as in the frequently used pattern "Cause youre lyege men to know you as for their kynde lord" (245.17 and many similar phrasings). (The "kynde words," frequently accompanying truces, though, are conciliatory, and make the point that political bargains depend on tactful, not natural, locutions.) Malory's negative instances include several that make use of the fully emergent sense. Elaine says, "the unkyndenes of sir Lancelot sleyth myne harte nere!" (803.23), the narrator, "at laste there befelle a jolesy and an unkyndenesse betwyxte kyng Marke and sir Trystrames, for they loved bothe one lady" (393.14), and Lancelot, to a knight who had taken his horse, "thou deddist me grete unkyndnes" (929.9). But the strongest (in spite of its probably unintended irony) occurs in Sir Ector's lament for Lancelot's death, "thou were the kyndest man that ever strake wyth swerde" (XXI.13; 725.20–21).

Nature and revelation: William Langland and Dame Julian

The implications of *kynde* for the argument of *Piers Plowman* appear as well in the *Pearl*-poet's emphasis on God's role in creation, and in Chaucer's play with Boethian subtexts for sexual longings in *Troilus and Criseyde*. But no other medieval text examines the term so tenaciously. *Kynde*, with its wide range of implications, is an issue in *Piers Plowman* from the Prologue, in which Kynde Wit helps shape the estates into which civil life will be organized (118–22), to the last moment of the poem, in which Conscience asks Kynde for aid. Will the Dreamer seeks "kynde knowing" throughout the poem, but he understands it differently as the poem progresses. At first he looks for propositions he can examine through experience or logic, but he comes to the point of realizing that God cannot be known in that way (Harwood 9). One of the movements of the poem is toward a sort of spiritual insight which surpasses the kynde knowing Will originally wanted, but, looked at another way, the practical intelligence of the early passages is not repudiated but re-positioned within a larger field of vision. *Piers Plowman* is both an allegorical poem about the longings of the soul and a satire on the practices of Middle Earth, and *kynde* is a key term in both of these schemes.[7] *Kynde Wit* is associated with the physical world and the human need to sustain life economically and to continue to people the earth. In the Prologue, *Kynde Wit* is the arbiter who justifies the work of the common estate "to tilie and to trauaille as trewe lif asketh" to support both themselves and the other estates (120–22). It is also *Kynde* who takes the dreamer to the mountain Middle Earth to show him the beauty and variety of the created world and the untaught ways the birds and beasts obey the behests of reason (11.321–68). Instead of providing the dreamer with comfort or confidence, this fair vision reinstates the problem he has had with *Kynde Knowyng* all along: why does the rest of the created world know right behavior instinctively while human hearts suffer the painful divisions and uncertainties which are the poem's subject? The natural world needs "wedded libbynge folk" to work and procreate in order to sustain it (9.110–11)— Anima, after all, lives in "a castel that kynde made" of earth and air, wind and water (9.2–4). The duty implied by our living in the castle *caro* (9.50) is work in a craft and a family, yet that imperative often seems to conflict with the law enjoined by the fraternal orders. Then again, *kynde* is also the destroyer of the good things in castle *caro* through old age, and in the end *Kynde* tells Will to give up all crafts but that of love. *Kynde* and *Kynde Wit* are seen as Will's wise advisors throughout, but never supply a direct answer to the nagging abyss between the created world and the revealed law. Yet the vision of a world in which nature and moral law coincide is presented in Passus 3, when Conscience and *Kind Love* make "of lawe a laborer" instead of a lord (299–300). And, tantalizingly, "contricion, feith and conscience is *kyndeliche* dowel" (14.88), the first of the moral levels granted by grace.

In yet another sense, *kynde* is specifically *human* nature. Will's first request of Holy Church is that she pray for his sins and "kenne me kyndely on crist to beleue" (1.81); what he seeks is a knowledge proper to human intellect, what Harwood links to the tradition of *notitia intuitiva* ("Langland's *Kynde Knowing*" 245–46). Holy Church wants to shift the catechism to ethical matters, but Will remains insistent on knowing the grounds of ethical standards, on knowing Dowel "kyndely" (10.151; 15.2). Even on the ethical plane, *Kynde Wit*, though a near cousin to the Lord and a mirror for confronting our faults (12.93–95), sometimes offers temptations to pride and folly (12.41–56). Yet the lack of *kyndnesse* is even more serious: Christians who allow their fellows to suffer want are *vnkynde*, worse than Jews, Judas's fellows (9.87). Scattered hints that nature may provide moral standards are brought together in the impressive instruction of the Samaritan in Passus 17. In the Samaritan's teaching, it is *vnkynde* to harm what God has created (119) or deny sustenance to the poor (269), because these acts are contrary to the nature of "goddes owne kynde. / For that kynde dooth vnkynde fordooth" (275–76) and "vnkyndenesse is the contrarie of alle kynnes reson" (349). Here *kynde* action is directly linked with God's extra-natural plan and the two medieval meanings of *kynde* are also linked, since *kyndenesse* as "beneficence" is also obedience to the imperatives of nature. Immediately after the Samaritan's instruction, the dreamer wakes and falls into another dream, this one potentially the answer to his dilemma over human nature. In Passus 18 and 19 the passion and incarnation are presented through a kaleidoscopic overlay of Christ and Piers, at first "spakliche" ("sprightly," 18.12) and later "so blody" (19.13). These passages are not about the human search for God, but God's quest to know human *kynde*.[8] In the incarnation, God "took Adam's kynde / To se what he hath suffred" (18.222–23), and therefore Christ is of one nature with us: "For I were an vnkynde kyng but I my kynde helpe" (398). This remarkable logic reunites the poem's salvific story with its civil one by stressing the duties of kings and calling on all the senses of *kynde*. The burden of Passus 19 is that Do-Best is the human vision of God's love which flows "from a point he shares with humanity," as Harwood puts it (*Problems of Belief* 137). The consequence of this vision is, once again, a spiritual lesson which coincides with the building of a good earthly society: a life of patience, humility, and work.

The *Showings* of Julian of Norwich also carries on a nuanced discussion of the theological standing of *kynde*. Julian may have read one or another text of *Piers Plowman*, and her use of *kynde* (but not her conclusions about it) point to speculations shared with Langland (I.305, n. 24). The Short Text and early chapters in the Long Text use *kynde* rather unproblematically as "nature," sometimes to contrast human knowledge and value with divine, as in the phrase "both by kynde and by grace" (47.7). When God's nature is discussed, *kynde* fuses implications of "nature" with those of "beneficence." (*Vnkyndness* often performs that fusion; to be ungenerous is to be unnatural, since God created nature.) In chapters 56 to 63 of the Long Text, during her discussion of the way Christ's incarnation has rescued nature for God, the word *kynde* turns up in almost every sentence (more than 63 times). This section is a celebration of a sort of basic trust humankind (Julian frequently—22 instances—uses *mankind* for all human beings) may have in the workings of a God-created and saved world:

> it is growndyd in kynde, that is to say: oure reson is groundyd in god, whych is substanncyally knydnesse. Of this substancyall kyndnesse mercy and grace spryngyth and spredyth in to vs, werkyng all thynges in fulfyllyng of oure joy.
>
> (56.39–41)

"Substancyall" here seems to have its full force as a technical term in theology, as the Augustinian "real," opposed to the accidental or contingent. This passage—and there are many reinforcing it—seems to redeem the world of sense and "natural reason" without reservation and instate God as seamlessly both lawgiving father and nurturing mother.

Perhaps this serene understanding is the purchase of her long meditation on her vision of the servant who fell in his lord's service:

> The lorde lokyth vppon his seruannt full louely and swetly and mekely. He sendyth hym in to a certeyne place to do his wyll. The sevannt nott onely he goyth, but sodenly he stertyth and rynnyth in grett hast for loue to do his lordes wylle. And anon he fallyth in a slade, and takyth grett sorow ... and I behelde with avysement to wytt yf I culde perceyve in hym ony defaute, or yf the lorde shuld assigne in hym ony maner of blame; and verely there was none seen.
>
> (51.514–16)

Although not exactly heterodox, Julian's emphasis in this section—the lord's reaction to his servant Adam's fall assigned him no blame—contrasts strongly with sin-obsessed devotional tracts like Nicholas Love's *Mirror*, with its praise of the disciples, who, in order to receive the Last Supper, had to take leave of "their kyndely resoun of man" to believe in Christ (204) and with the relegation of the "tyme of the lawe of kynde" to the first of three scriptural ages—the others being the old law and grace. Julian's steady assurance about *kynde* also contrasts with Langland's uneasy vacillations over *kynde* and *Kynde Knowing* in *Piers Plowman*. Her vision of Christ is richly concrete as well as spiritually generative: "sodenly I saw the reed bloud rynnyng downe from vnder the garlande, hote and freyshely, / plentuously and liuely, right as it was in the tyme that the garland of thornes was pressed on his blessed head" (4.294). The vivid sight of Jesus' blood flowing, as it had and as ours (perhaps even hers) does, seems to have provided Julian with an existential *notitia intuitiva*, or grounded intuition, in which the nagging breach between human intellection and divine revelation is bridged.

These two searching records of late medieval thought situate the term *kynde* at the intersection of human struggles in the material world and divinely revealed truths, with *kynde* as the lower, though not despised, member of the dyad. When the term is deployed in the equally passionate inquiries of Shylock and Lear two centuries later, the questions have shifted from theological to social venues. Perhaps as a result of broader public (written) discourse on physical and legal issues, *kynde/kind* as "nature" lost ground to the word *nature*, which gradually could come to be seen as a rule-governed system rather than a field full of folk supervised by the female deity Natura. *Kind* then became available for the weaker sense "sort" or "category," which propelled it toward grammaticalization. Simultaneously adjectival *kind* split off toward its modern implication, "beneficent," in only a few interesting cases resonating with its residual element "natural."

Universal laws and cruel ladies

In early modern writing, the noun *kind* as "nature" blends with, and eventually disappears into, the noun "sort," impelling it toward grammaticalization, although occasional instances in the sixteenth century must be read as "nature" unequivocally, as in Surrey's praise of the lady's "beauty of kind, her virtues from above" ("Geraldine"). The feudal way of organizing experience had kept the idea of family, sometimes literally, sometimes as metaphor, close to the idea of nature and fixed in "common sense" by the closeness of the words *kyn* and *kynde*. The more urban life of many early modern citizens thrust other social relations into that picture, to some extent displacing dynastic loyalties with new allegiances to nation, guild, and/or religious sect. The new usage may reflect the shift from a polity governed personally by family clans to a conception of the state as monarchs, parliaments, and bishops governing according to established rules. Richard Hooker's diction in *The Laws of Ecclesiastical Polity* is noteworthy in registering and impelling *kind* toward "category" or "sort," and away from a nature imagined as the personal, the engendered. In the First Book of the *Laws* alone, Hooker uses *kind* to mean "sort" or "category" over 80 times, and it figures in that book's title: "Concerning Laws and their several kinds in general." The force of Hooker's argument rests on the premise of a stable, impersonal natural law divisible into various *kinds*, and separating out the *kinds* (making legal, philosophical, and theological distinctions) is the achievement of the book.[9] The sense of system Hooker invoked in the realm of ecclesiastical governance, Philip Sidney's *Apology for Poetry* and Richard Puttenham's *The Arte of English Poesie* offered for thinking about imaginative writing as poetic genre. Sidney establishes first the "three several kinds," divine, natural, and delight/instruction (101–02) and later the Renaissance genres moving downward from epic (119). This system of categories suggests the weight and complication Sidney ascribes to the poetic tradition English poetry will now join.

Thomas Hoby's translation of *The Courtier* also evokes the sense "genre" (on the sub-genres of witty jests, we read, "in both kindes the chief matter is to deceive opinion, to answere otherwise than the hearer looketh for" [168]), but it is particularly notable for its playful use of *unkind* for female sexual coolness seen as both cruel and unnatural—an equivocation which depends on active senses of both "beneficent" and "nature" for *kind*.[10] In Hoby's translation beautiful women are charged with *unkindnesse* toward men who serve them and deserve their favors (243); are they cruel or unnatural or both? Hoby makes playful use of this equivocation (it is a major theme in Castiglione's treatise) when Emilia charges Unico with indirection: "But these your continuall complaintes and accusing of the women whom you have served, of unkindnesse...is a certain kinde of discretion, to cloke the favours...you have received in love" (244). The unkind lady appears most prominently, of course, in the sonnet sequences, beginning with those based on Petrarch's. The strategy behind the frequent use of *kind* in the cruel-fair sonnets is to play off that primary sense "beneficent" against the older "nature," allowing some remarkable effects with emergent and residual meanings of *kind*, as a few examples will demonstrate.

Straightforward examples of the Petrarchan equivocation are found in Wyatt's Songs 98 and 99, where the lover imagines his death and the lady's continued unkindness, with the refrain "I die! I die! and you regard it not" in the first and the concluding lines "Therefore when ye hear tell, / Believe it not although ye see my grave. / Cruel, unkind! I say, 'Farewell, farewell!'" in the second (cf. Songs 139 and 144). In Sonnet 35, the poet plays with the convention, feigning a serious tone in commending the infidelity of the lady who has abandoned him:

> And if ye were to me as ye are not
> I would be loath to see you so unkind
> But since your faith must need be so by kind
> Though I hate it, I pray you leave it not.
>
> (5–8)

The point rests, of course, on the pun: if she really loved him, he would be hurt at her unkind (ungenerous, unnatural) behavior, but since it is her natural bent to be untrue, he hopes her next lover(s) will be subjected to it as he was. Song 109 was entitled "The lover complaineth of the unkindness of his love" in *Tottle's Miscellany*, and the "unkind" in it seems almost casual; the emphasis is on the inevitable vengeance to be visited on the lady when *she* feels unrequited love. The conclusion of "They flee from me" contains the best known of Wyatt's instances: "But since that I so kindly am served / I would fain know what she hath deserved" (80.20). Here the lady is accused ironically of beneficence and straightforwardly of a natural inclination toward unfaithful forsaking, here "naturalness" in women is fickle carnality.[11]

A particularly fine equivocation between "unnatural" and "cruel" is the last line of Philip Sidney's Sonnet 38 in the *Astrophel* sequence. Stella's face visited the poet in sleep, but when waking he tried to woo sleep again "Him her host that unkind guest had slain" (14). Stella's image here is both unnatural to slay that on which its being depended and cruel to prevent the poet's sleep when she has also deserted him in "opend sense." In Sonnet 44 the poet plays with the nature/culture opposition, describing her "sweet heart" as "of no Tygre's kind" and accusing "Nobleness it selfe" of making the lady "thus unkind" (4, 8; cf. 47, 57, 62, and 65). Spenser's Sonnets, too, suggest "nature" (love can "alter all the course of kynd," 30), or melt it unobtrusively with "sort" (6), except when his playful attribution of body, fortune and mind to his three Elizabeths rhymes *kind* "nature" (5) with *kind* "beneficent" (7), as though they were separate words:

> The first my being to me gave by kind,
> From mothers womb deriv'd by dew descent:
> The second is my sovereigne Queene most kind,
> That honour and large richesse to me lent.
>
> (74.5–8)

Shakespeare's Sonnet 105 "Let not my love be called idolatry" is
based on a clever inversion of the cruel–fair conceit. It concludes:

> Kind is my love today, tomorrow kind
> Still constant in a wondrous excellence,
> Therefore my verse, to constancy confin'd
> One thing expressing, leaves out difference.
> "Fair," "kind," and "true" is all my argument,
> "Fair," "kind," and "true" varying to other words,
> And in this change is my invention spent,
> Three themes in one, which wondrous scope affords.
> "Fair," "kind," and "true" have often liv'd alone,
> Which three till now never kept seat in one.
>
> (5–14)

This poem throws itself violently against the cruel/fair tradition. Its
force lies in the reader's expectation that it will revert to type and
chide the lady, or at least hint (as lines 9–11 begin to do, perhaps to
balance the unmixed praise that might be taken for idolatry [see
Booth's edition 336]) at a lament that it is harder to write about a
gererous and faithful lover than a disdainful or disloyal one. In line 12
"scope" restores the elegiac tone, and leads to the creation of the royal
or holy "seat" in which the ideal beloved is finally ensconced.

Shepherds, Shylock, and Lear

When so much discourse in the last two decades of the sixteenth
century (except in the cruel/fair sonnet tradition) had lost the sense
"nature, natural" to its rivals "sort" and "beneficent," Sidney and
Shakespeare involved *kind* in their attempts to reinterpret residual
notions.[12] Sidney's *New Arcadia* looks to the Middle Ages with one
auspicious and one dropping eye, as retrospective in its vocabulary as
it is in its generic models, the romances and epics of late antiquity and
medieval Europe. But the nostalgia is employed for distinctively
contemporary uses: key terms, especially *virtue, courage, estate,* and
kind, are appropriated for new ends and subtly manipulated to produce
new linguistic effects and invoke new mind-sets. To put the case of
kind baldly, Sidney moves from the medieval emphasis on an unalterable nature, given in the original creation and acquired by humans at
birth, to an achieved nature won through choice, learning, and resolution. His instances include all the familiar meanings of *kind,* the

rather neutral "category": "by such kind of speeches" (429.14), "nature," as when the lion "contrary to her own kind would have wronged the prince's blood" (113.13); and "benevolent," "kind mercifulness" as the band that ought to hold together the other virtues (130.29). But far oftener these three strands of potential meaning are fused to produce effects of either intensification or irony.

Consider, for example, the complex intensification in Cecropia's (brilliant, but malevolent) attempt to persuade Philoclea to marry her son by painting to her the joys of motherhood. "If you could conceive what a heart-tickling joy it is to see your own little ones with awful love come running to your lap ... you would think unkindness in your own thoughts that they ever did rebel against the mean unto it" ("conceive" and "awful" also deserve comment for their richly calculated designs in the argument). *Unkindness* here takes on the full effect of both "unnaturalness," since the propagation of the species must be a chief aim of nature, and (perfectly blended with it) the full effect of "lack of generosity or tenderness" toward the helpless babies whose very existence is being prevented by cruel chastity (332.24–28). Or, again, "a pretty fear came up to endamask her [Philoclea's] rose cheeks, but it was such a fear as rather seemed a kindly child to her innate humbleness than any other dismayedness" (415.11–12). In this case the fear that causes her to blush is natural, because Philoclea is modest and unassertive by constitution, and yet the next lines indicate that her fear is more "for Zelmane than for herself," and therefore the force of tenderness or magnanimity is just as strong.[13]

An even more striking irony in the use of *kind* is Cecropia's coming into Philoclea's prison-room "haling kindness into her countenance" (330.2). She brings herself by force to counterfeit benevolence—that much is clear from the Machiavellianism of her plan—and readers know it fully and Philoclea seems to guess it too. But if we think of Cecropia as bringing "naturalness" into her demeanor, we have a more interesting narrative moment. Cecropia is not shown as obedient to nature here (for example to the "natural pity" one woman might be expected to feel for another) but taming it, bending it to her unnatural purposes. This reading fits with the many instances of disguise on which this narrative repeatedly depends: knights are expected to display their *kind*, their kinship, their inherent estates and natures, but more often than not they display someone else's by using the emblems and furniture of others or of unknown fighters, often with tragic effects, as when Parthenia rides to meet Amphialus as the Knight of the Tomb.

The first thing to say about Shakespeare's use of *kind* is that it is predominantly modern: of roughly 280 instances in the plays and poems, only 26 or so can be read as "nature" at a first level, although a few others can be seen to have some lurking suggestiveness in that direction. The remaining instances are divided about evenly between a more or less grammaticalized "sort" and "beneficent." Hamlet's pun "A little more than kin and less than kind" (I.ii.65) takes up all available strands of implication at once. As in his use of "thrift" for the funeral baked meats, Hamlet avoids committing open treason, since he might be taken to mean merely "You are now more than uncle to me, but not benevolent." Lurking in that "kind," though, is surely the charge that Claudius's marriage is incestuous and therefore unnatural (later he calls Claudius a "kindless villain"), as well as in violation of Hamlet's rightful (natural) succession to the Danish throne as his birthright. Hamlet also may be remarking Claudius's difference from his father and himself in category or sort; they are royal Danes, he a thing of shreds and patches, of a lesser *kind* than Hamlet's father. There are many such complicated passages in Shakespeare's plays, but the sharpest focus for historical change can be seen in *The Merchant of Venice*, with its image of early capitalist Venice (London) and idealized feudal Belmont and in *King Lear*, with its contest between a very old and a very new English body politic.

Kind is the keyword in Act I, scene iii of *The Merchant of Venice*. The dual possibilities in the word are differently understood by Antonio and Bassanio seeking the loan and Shylock laying down its stipulations. Audiences alert to the older sense of *kind* feel a mounting tension as potentially disputed instances of *kind* as "beneficence" or "nature" pile up. Shylock begins this strained language by describing a loan with no doit of interest taken—"This is kind I offer," and Bassanio takes him to mean generosity—"This were kindness," the subjunctive mood of which questions Shylock's intent to follow through, but not the meaning of the deed if it were done. Shylock offers to go immediately to a notary to prove his resolve, and elicits Antonio's "I'll seal to such a bond, / And say there is much kindness in the Jew" as a result. It is tempting to think that Shylock means by kind "nature," in which case this exchange is linked to the "Hath not a Jew eyes" speech (III.i.50–69) and refers to a vengeful human nature demonstrated by an intolerant Christian community over the centuries. Shylock's bargain is "natural" because it carries out the need for vengeance which is inherent in human nature just as laughter follows tickling or bleeding pricking. Bassanio and Antonio take the same word to mean "generous" and proceed on that assumption, perhaps even to the point of allowing Bassanio's strange forgetfulness once he has left for Belmont. Shylock may be imagined as seeing and using the equivocation or not, but it is available to the audience in either case. This scene is witness to the anxiety of early modern culture over the substitution of written notes and contracts for the witnessed personal exchanges of a generation or two earlier (Agnew, Ch. 1). This unsettled social understanding also causes Bassanio to misread Shylock's comment that Antonio is "good"—Bassanio would have meant that he knows and trusts the man, Shylock that his credit as a legal holder of commodities is sound.

Lear's problem touches on even deeper anxieties. The archaic setting for *King Lear* is as striking as Venice's modernity is in *Merchant*. But, although the topicality of the earlier play is more obvious, *Lear*'s address to the problems of its generation is just as pointed, though perhaps more generalized, more metaphysical. No one would dispute that the play generates tensions around the idea of nature; I want to show how the word *kind* contributes to that tension. Lear initiates the action of the play by making some assumptions about nature within his family and the body politic. He assumes *kind* to be both nature and beneficent—within the kin-group, nature endows heirs, as feudal ideology insists, with generosity and gentility. Lear staged the praise contest because he thought Cordelia would win it and ratify publicly his decision to set his rest on "her kind nursery" (I.i.124). Ironically, although Lear's stubborn linkage between kin and kindliness accounts for a good part of his tragic blindness, he is proved right in this instance of it: Cordelia does eventually offer "kind nursery," although by Act V, the signified of "nature" is thoroughly problematized and Cordelia's love for Lear has surpassed beneficence into something like sanctified grace.

Many of the instances of *kind* in the play occur in a running dispute between Lear and the Fool. The Fool marvels "what kin thou and thy daughters are" for threatening him with whipping whatever he does; "I had rather be any kind o' thing than a Fool, and yet I would not be thee, nuncle" (I.iv.182, 185–87). This speech links *kin* with *kind* by suggesting that Lear himself is flawed in the same way Goneril and Regan are, and he persists with that genealogical notion in predicting that Regan will "use [Lear] as kindly" as her sister has (I.v.14–15). Both the knight and Lear have noted Goneril's "great abatement of kindness" (I.iv.60, 71). The Fool sees "nature" as self-preserving greed, as his little song in Act II makes clear: "fathers that bear bags / Shall see

their children kind" (II.iv.51). Lear has known very little about nature
that was not inscribed in the patriarchal ideology which benefited him
so much when he actually held power, but he learns, perforce, on the
heath. His mistaken idea that he had behaved kindly—as *either* generously or naturally—is too dear to him to part with (I.v.32; III.iv.20;
Kent persists in it too—III.i.28), but after his enlightenment on the
heath, he does let it go. The next time he uses the word *kind* it is in a
very pointed relation to the raw "nature" the Fool had insisted on:
"Why dost thou lash that whore? Strip thy own back, / Thou hotly
lusts to use her in that kind / For which thou whip'st her"
(IV.vi.161–64). Even more than the Fool's elusive logic, Lear's imagination links "kind" with sex, invoking yet another medieval echo.

  The Gloucester plot follows a similar pattern in relation to the "kind
gods" Gloucester invokes during his torture—gods who never deliver
him. His reversal—"As flies to wanton boys are we to th' gods"
(IV.i.36)—must then be modified once again by Edgar's enigmatic
ministrations on the Dover cliffs. Edmund never uses the retrospective
word *kind*, with its drag backward toward *kin* and birthright. His
goddess is the Nature who executes an automatic rule-governed world
of self interest devoid of superstitious loyalties and taboos. Goneril and
Regan avoid the word too; it belongs, late in the play, to Cordelia, who
calls the gods kind for letting Lear sleep and to Kent who calls Cordelia
kind for coming to her father's aid (IV.vii.13, 28). Even in so minute a
matter as the distribution of this word, *King Lear* has carried out a fully
coherent contrast between the residual, but now damaged and
outdated, mind-set of the old fathers and a worst-case scenario of the
emergent.

  What this feature of *King Lear* demonstrates is that the "obviousness"
of the bonds and obligations of kinship has blurred and faded, *kynde*
has transmogrified into "nature," an impersonal, even mechanical,
effect of general laws, far from Langland's puzzling but benign *Kynde*,
kin to God Himself through the incarnation, and the motherly *kynde*
of Dame Julian. This trend is by no means complete by 1611—enlightenment hegemonies will distance the natural world still more sharply
from explanations like "God's providence," which, as we shall see in
Chapter 8, accomplish a good deal of cultural work. None the less, the
shift in the meaning of *kynde/kind* amounts to a major shift in what we
might call (by analogy to Benedict Anderson's phrase "imagined
communities") "imagined cosmologies." The Golden Chain linking
God's   superintendence   of   nature   with   the   feudal   baron's

superintendence of society is still called upon, but it does not always present itself to social imagination when called.

7
Lewid/Lewd

> She raised the muddy hem of her skirts some inches and
> spread her knees and the gesture was slight but very lewd, a
> whore's gesture.
>
> <div align="right">Barry Unsworth, <i>Morality Play</i></div>

The semantic path traced from *lewid* to *lewd* is clear. Very early, as early
as Bede's *Historia* (890), *laewde* meant "lay" as opposed to "clerical."
This distinction in estate was, in theory at least, based on learning, so
that an equally good definition of *lewed* in the Middle Ages is
"untaught in Latin."[1] The celebrated Latin "neck verse" saved a man
from hanging as a felon, taking him out of the jurisdiction of local
secular authorities. The privilege granted to Latin is enforced in scholarly circles as late as 1564 in the stipulation that "nothing might be
said openly to the University [Cambridge] in English," even by the
Queen.[2] Sometimes the distinction between *lerned* and *lewed* was
marked in obvious ways, as Mandeville's *Travels* has it, "Thai hafe
thaire crownes shauen, the clerkes rownde and the lawed men foure
cornerd" (13.60). Middle English translators use *lewed* to render Latin
"laicus" (*Medulla*), "illitteratus," "agramatus," "inscius," "ignarus,"
and "inscientia" (*Promptorium Parvulorum*). *Lewed* in this sense turns up
as a medieval modesty topos: Thomas Usk's *Testament of Love* has
"Though my book be leude, the cause with which I am stered, and for
whom I ought it doon, noble...ben bothe" (49.110), and one of the
Paston letters reads: "Hold me escused of my lewde, rude wrytyng"
(2.147). Medical treatises refer to outsiders in their field as *lewed*.
Lanfranc, Arderne's *Fistula*, and *Chauliac* all speak of the inadvisability
of saying too much about their mystery before *lewed* (inexpert) men.
But the most frequent usage simply distinguishes the first estate from

the other two, the initiate in Latin from the unlearned outsider, often in the phrase "the lernyde and the lewyde." Everyone is therefore either *lerned* or *lewed*.[3] No disapproval attached to *lewedness* in Middle English when it indicated an uneducated layperson—Trevisa's *Higden* refers to Constantine as "a lewed man" (6.247)—a priest or monk called *lewed*, though, was being insulted.

Occasionally, Latin literacy and clerical estate do not coincide: Pope Formosus was not only denied the papacy after holding it for some years, he was degraded to the status of "a lewid man" (*A Lollard Chronicle of the Papacy* 177.58), one who had lost the public recognition of his Latin learning. The *Speculum Sacerdotale* tells of the embarrassment of the other monks when a knight joined their monastery "but letter cowde he noon; Therefore alle his brethren schamyd that so noble a persoun schulde be putt with lewde-men" (48.4). Such a passage is a reminder that the aristocracy, especially the first-born who were expected to inherit, were not necessarily literate—a verse from *Political Poems and Songs* and chides the inappropriate literacy as well as the dubious orthodoxy of the so-called Wycliffite knights, who "babel the Bibel day and night in resting time when they should sleep" (II.244). The embarrassment of the monks, though, suggests that status in general as well as estate proper and Latin literacy are implicated in the use of *lewed*. The association between undistinguished birth and lack of learning eventually led to an evaluative sense: "ignorant, foolish, coarse" for people and "worthless" for things, but these senses do not turn up until the late Middle Ages.[4] In Spenser's *View of Ireland*, *lewd* is a contemptuous leit motif for the Irish (but never for their English occupiers, unless they are being accused of having "gone native," like those wards who are brought up by Irish lords "lewdly and Irish like" [29.7]), a complete reversal of the medieval meaning, since the Catholic Irish were more likely to know Latin than the English Protestants.

The use of *lewed* to designate a lay person was rendered outmoded by the Reformation on two fronts. First, the division of society into three estates was eclipsed by Protestant ways of construing divinely sanctioned callings as available to all Christians, denying that the clergy inhabited an elevated sphere. Second, the necessity of Latin learning was nullified by Protestant insistence on the importance of vernacular Bible reading.[5] In this matter, what Raymond Williams calls an "authentic break" with hegemonic cultural practice is clearly visible (*Marxism and Literature* 114). *Lewd* was still a very frequently used word, though, and its association with common birth allowed it to signal a general affront to propriety. General disapprobation spilled over into "wickedness," and then into "sexual license"—as in William Warner's *Albions England*: "Lewde Ammon, thou didst lust in deed" (x.lix.259)—quite rare in medieval usage, but of course the surviving sense.[6] The most prominent Middle English sense of *lewed*—untaught in Latin—is absent, not merely subordinated, in today's lexicon. The *lewed* man of the Middle Ages was someone who *did not know,* while Barry Unsworth's character makes a gesture which betrays her *know-ingness.* The weekly "Crime and Incident" column in our student newspaper reports instances of "Public Lewdness," which may include acts like those Alisoun of Bath confided to her friend when her husband "pissed on a wall," but they never mention the inability of anyone on campus to construe the Latin Vulgate or deliver an appropriate neck verse.

Wyclif and Chaucer

John Wyclif and Geoffrey Chaucer were the two writers who most influenced England's dramatic appropriation of the English language for serious written discourse in the fourteenth century, the one in theological, the other in literary matters. As perhaps the most learned and intellectually aggressive scholar of his generation at Oxford, Wyclif left a distinctively English mark on the Christianity of his countrymen. It is widely held that Wycliffite beliefs and phrases from his English translation of the Bible were passed on in some communities until the Reformation, and it is certain that copies of his vernacular translation survived in many of them. Chaucer, of course, exerted a major influence on the language, due in part to his tireless energies as a translator. In a different venue from Wyclif, he helped raise the status of London English to a serious and sophisticated level, flexible and subtle enough for previously unattempted literary effects. Both writers influenced the history of the word *lewed.*

Wyclif used *lewed* both for non-judgmental reference to the lay estate and for strong disapproval of certain clerics. These are dominant medieval senses, but his position on *lewedness* in both his senses stirred up controversy. His group tirelessly defended lay people and designed English sermons and the Later Version of the English Bible translation for them. "Therfore this prayere, declared en Englyssche, may edify the lewede peple, as it doth clerkes in Latyn" (*Pater Noster* in Matthew 2.98). If an understanding of sacred truth gained through the English language were held to be the key to salvation, the Wycliffite stand would effectively undermine the sacredness of Latinity, which is "an inseparable part of that truth" for "the great transcontinental sodalities of Christendom," as Benedict Anderson puts it (40).[7] Wycliffite thought does go that far. If the people were taught the Bible in their mother tongue, the first estate would lose some of its special duties and prerogatives, weakening its unchallenged control over the means to salvation. *De Veritate Sacrae Scripturae* dignifies the third estate without dismantling estates theory: "ȝif a lord or a laborer loue betere god than thes veyn religious & proude & lecherous possessioneris, the lewid manys preiere is betere" (117). Christ's disciples Peter and James astonished the scribes and elders by their eloquence, although "Thei weren men vnlettrid, and lewid men," as the Later Version puts it in Deeds (Acts) 4.13. Wycliffite enclaves were noted for their practice of committing scripture to memory, a practice which Reginald Pecock claimed had persisted into the fifteenth century (quoted by Coleman 209). Her quick *verbatim* recall of biblical teaching in English was doubtless one of the reasons Margery Kempe was so often subjected to examination for Lollardy.

   In addition to its non-pejorative use to refer to the laity, Wycliffite discourse often uses *lewed* to dispraise the clergy who disputed his tenets. The clerical estate is a high calling, and undeserved by many who pretend to it: "This chirche . . . whanne it is tauȝt, it is the lewidar" (*Lanterne* 133.10) and "This is the lewiderste fendis skile that euere cam out of his leesingis [lyings]" (*Officio Pastorale* in Matthew 409). Wyclif inveighed against the dictum that "seculer men schulde noȝt juge of clerkis" because such a belief showed that the author knew "but lewdydly goddis lawe" (*Wyclifs Dominion* in Matthew 289). Behind this inflammatory language is Wyclif's vision of the Apostolic Church, which he sees betrayed by the priesthood, monks, and especially friars. The friars live "lustli in this world" eschewing the life of labor, where they would dwell "in lewid strait," i.e. like working men (Arnold I.292). "Bishopis that shulden be clerkis and pore men as apostlis weren, ben moost lordis of this world. . . . Sum tyme weren mounkes lewede men as saintis in Jerusalem . . . but now monkes ben turned unto lordis of this worlde" (I.40). This strand of Wyclif's use begins with the sense "unlearned," but takes on the meaning of simply "reprehensible" through its many repetitions in the writing of his group.

   Of course such strong opinions did not go unnoticed or unopposed. Nicholas Love causally refers to "lewde lollardes" (*Mirrour* 208), to refer, oddly enough, to the learning Wycliffites brought to their understandings of the sacraments, an inappropriate intellectualization of what ought to depend on simple faith. A treatise called *Against Lollards* also targets their learning, accusing them of jangling "of Iob or Ieremye, that construen hit after her entente for lewde lust of lollardie" (24). These two detractors have turned a word that usually implies a lack of learning into one intended to insult *because of* learning. Thomas Hoccleve acknowledges *lewd* as "ignorant" in "To Sir John Oldcastle" ("lewd as is an asse," 352), but his more interesting use indicts women who teach scripture as "lewde calates [whores]":

> Some wommen eeke, thogh hir wit be thynne,
> Wele argumentes make in holy writ!
> Lewde calates! sitteth down and spynne,
> And kakele of sumwhat elles, for your wit
> Is al to feeble to despute of it!
>
> (145–49)

There were active women in the Lollard movement; several of them were tried for heresy in the Norwich trials in the 1430s. They were clearly invited to read the English Bible and meditate on it by John Purvey's introduction to the Later Version as being "for lay people and women who could read." Hoccleve's "lewde calates" glancingly registers a link between the vernacular, the feminine, and the sexually transgressive which seems to hover around the Wycliffite controversies.

In some obvious ways Chaucer's deployment of *lewed* resembles Wyclif's closely. The description of the simple Parson in the *General Prologue* stresses his respect for lay people in his parish, though he himself is "a lerned man, a clerk," and contempt for unworthy priests:

> For if a priest be foul, on whom we truste,
> No wonder is a lewed man to ruste;
> And shame it is, if a prest take keep [is involved],
> A shiten shepherde and a clene sheep.
>
> (501–04)

His long journeys "upon his feet and in his hand a staff" (495) suggest (though by no means unequivocally) one of Wyclif's "Poor Priests," as do his plainness of speech and lack of absolute reverence for institutional authority. His tale, the penitential manual, is not markedly Lollard, but it does attack simony by saying that "lewed men" respect the sacraments less when they are administered by the unworthy (790), barely hinting at a Lollard distrust of priestly efficacy. *The Friar's Tale* unmasks the practices of the corrupt summoner who claims to have a writ in order to scare "a lewed man" (who of course cannot read the Latin "summons") into bribing him (III.1346). The Summoner replies in kind with his character Friar John, a would-be despoiler of the lewed who uses his Latin and his clerical status only to mystify and defraud, defying monks for their "lewednesse" and disdaining clear instruction as available from "every lewed viker or person [parson]" in favor of muddled *exempla* (III.1928, 2008–09). Predatory as they are, the summoner and friar in these tales cannot rival the pilgrim Pardoner as a victimizer of the common people. His frank prologue discloses how he stands "lik a clerk in my pulpet, / And when the lewed peple is doun yset" and tell them "an hundred false japes moore," for "lewed peple loven tales olde" (VI.391–94, 437). This kind of preaching—its whimsy and sensationalism—was what Wycliffite tracts and sermons tirelessly inveighed against. One might even hear a faint Lollard accent in *The Second Nun's Tale*, when Saint Cecile fearlessly disputes doctrinal issues with the prefect Almachius, charging him with questioning "lewedly" and being "a lewed officer" (VIII.430, 497)—a woman debating doctrine with a man, indicting *him* as the unlearned one.

This line of social commentary is only a part of Chaucer's deployment of the word *lewed*. He uses it, in a sly way, for the modesty topos, when the Man of Law says he can think of no stories because Chaucer, although "he kan but lewedly / On metres and on rymyng craftily" (II.47–48), has told them all, letting one of his created characters mention his reputation. He uses it repeatedly in *The Canon's Yeoman's Tale* to display the contempt of the adept alchemists for the *lewed* outside their mystery (VIII.647, 787, 844, 925, 1445). He uses it straightforwardly as "untaught" to lament that nobody had been able to predict Custance's trials—all were "to lewed or to slowe" (*Man of Law* 315). Proserpine's opinion that women can make men "as lewed as gees" in *The Merchant's Tale* is also straightforward, but when the Merchant refers to January's "old lewed wordes" inviting May to the garden, he refers to the *Song of Songs*, a sacred text, here put to a *lewed* use in both old and emergent senses (V, 2275, 2149). The Reeve means both unlearned and unchaste when he predicts that the Miller's story will be a "lewed dronken harlotrye" (I.3145), but the Miller comes up with a complicated joke when he uses the word. His John the Carpenter's "Men sholde nat knowe of Goddes pryvetee, / Ye, blessed

he alwey a lewed man / That noght but only his bileve kan!"
(I.3454–56) expresses his pity for Nicholas, whose studies seem to have
rendered him comatose. The comic effects here are layered: at first
John the *lewed* man is the target, since he will be cuckolded on account
of his simplicity, and later it will be Nicholas the *lerned*, since he
outsmarts himself in designing his jest. In managing *lewed*, Chaucer's
discourse exhibits Bakhtinian polyvocality in one of its broadest and
earliest English manifestations.

"That old popish term of laymen"

The confluence of three historical and discursive trends spelled the
end for the time-honored term *lewed* for "lay" and "unlearned,"
current since the days of the Venerable Bede, and turned it toward a
term of censure, especially for sexual transgression. The first two are
driven by theological and social shifts in thinking about status similar
to those which turned *estate* from indicating someone's location in a
social hierarchy (Troilus's "estat royale") toward someone's material
holdings (the ebb of Timon's *estate*). Protestant suspicion of the clerical estate and its monopoly on Latin scripture are exemplified in the
controversy between William Tyndale and Thomas More. The third
trend is the revolution in linguistic taste that characterized the emer-
gence of literary English in the latter decades of the sixteenth century;
it will be discussed in the next section on *The Faerie Queene* and in
Chapter 9 ("Queynte/Quaint").

The medieval clerical estate had in some sense always been international rather than local, founded on the premise that "ecclesiastically,
society was one, greater than any political divisions" (Powicke 2). The
assent of Parliament and most of the people to Henry VIII's Act of
Supremacy, which established the authority of the King and his heirs
as the only supreme head on earth of the Church of England, called
Anglicana Ecclesia, put the clergy on a different footing, even in cases
where the same men retained office. They were henceforth English,
acting within a national system of duties and rights. Two years later,
Parliament acted against the authority of the Pope in England, attacking diverse persons who attempt to "instill into the ears and heads of
the poor, simple, and unlettered people" continued belief in his
pretended authority. Note that the old word *lewd* is bypassed for
"unlettered." One Harry Barrow made no distinction at all between
cleric and lay, referring to "that old popish term laymen" (Powicke
99). All believers are priests, said Luther, and all callings are from God.

A second and related trend is concerned with the English vernacular. Benedict Anderson argues, I think persuasively, that the Christendom imagined as the community to which medieval people looked for their ontological sense of belonging was related to the sacredness of Latin: "the sacred silent languages were the media through which the great global communities of the past were imagined"(21). William Tyndale's scholarly, often clandestine, labor to produce a readily available English Bible translated directly from the Hebrew and Greek became a reality in 1537, when the "Matthew's Bible" or "Great Bible" was "set forth with the king's most gracious licence," and the power of Latin to define the community of the learned was broken, although Tyndale did not live to see it. According to Foxe's account in *Acts and Monuments*, his dying words on the scaffold were "Lord, open the king of England's eyes." When the English Bible was ordered to be placed in every parish church, literacy in the vernacular (of which there was more, even in the Middle Ages, than scholars used to think) confused the issue of who deserved to be called *lerned* and not *lewed*. At the same time, the necessity for using English for the discussion of faith and morals previously carried out in Latin made it necessary to add Latinate words to the language, increasing its variety and sophistication, as had the earlier attempt at reform in Wyclif's era. Wide dissemination of vernacular Bibles, *The Book of Common Prayer*, and Foxe's *Acts and Monuments* connected the provinces of the realm, inviting literacy in a common language. A further implication of Tyndale's insistence on an English Bible, even more directly corrosive of the division of men and women into lay and clerical estates is his consistent denial that God has appointed some callings above others:

> Thou art a kitchen page and washest thy master's dishes, another is an Apostle and preacheth the word of God. . . . Now if thou compare deed to deed there is a difference betwixt washing of dishes and preaching the word of God. But as touching to please God none at all. . . . Let every man of whatsoever craft or occupation he be of . . . refer his craft and occupation unto the common wealth, and serve his brethren as he would do Christ himself.
>
> (*Wicked Mammon*, quoted in Daniell 167–68)

Thomas More was Tyndale's strongest opponent in the controversy over clerical estate. An instructive equivocation appears in his *Dialogue concerning Heresies*. His subject is traditionally one in which *lewde* plays a part: the availability of the Bible to lay people.

Nowe yf it so be that it wolde happely be thought not a thynge
metely to be adventured / to set all on a flushe at ones / and dashe
rashly out holy scrypture in every lewde felowes tethe / yet thynketh me there myght suche a moderacyon be taken therin / as
neyther good vertuous ley folke sholde lacke it / nor rude & rashe
braynes abuse it.

(341)

As More argues the imprudence of making scripture available without
restriction, his use of *lewde* at first seems to indicate the unlearned,
those who cannot approach the Bible because they have no Latin. But
late in this balanced sentence, moderation urges that *some* lay people
("good vertuous" ones) should be allowed to study it in English, and
this clause shifts the meaning of *lewde* retrospectively toward "wicked"
rather than merely untrained in Latin. Note, though, that More substitutes "ley" for "lewde" when he invokes the good vertuous folk. The
term must already have some moral overtones for More.

Similarly, in *The Supplication of Souls*, deniers of purgatory are "men
of such vertew wysdome and lerning as theyre lewd wrytynge and
mych more theyre lewd lyuyng shewyth" (208.18–20). This clever
wording begins by accusing the "heretics" of unlearned discourse
—"lewd wrytynge"—and ends by accusing them of moral wickedness—"lewd lyuyng." This strategy is of course nicely meshed with
More's overall position, which defends the institutional church's
learned commentary against the reformers' avidity for the "plain scripture." The zeal of the unlearned is quickly turned toward disobedience,
lawlessness, and eventually treason. Elsewhere in the *Supplication*
"lewd" tends to mean wicked generally, referring to the lewd fellows
who want license to rail against priests (117.15) or the "lewde galand"
who became the butt of a joke he intended to play on a "poore frere"
(207.17–24). But sometimes a connection with specifically sexual
transgression is suggested, as in his admission of the "lewdnes of
parte" of the clergy (141.26), his rehearsal of Simon Fish's charge of
clerical lewdness (156.26), or his allegation that easy remission of sin
would draw men "lustely" to lewdness (199.29–30). Not so, however,
with the "lewd lyberte" predicted as the result of anti-sacramental
faith (159.30), for that is an intellectual sin rather than a bodily one;
and similarly the "lewd pleasure" More attributes to the "felyshype" of
the heretics (178.7) is that of unlearned, but gleeful participation.
More is perhaps the last English writer to use *lewd* as "unlettered" with
so much rhetorical force.

Lewd was fast becoming an all-purpose pejorative. Ralph Robinson's translation of *Utopia* uses *lewd* in a much more modern way. There prefabricated "inticementes of lewde and unhonest desyres [Latin: improbi]" (75) and the "perverse and lewde custome" that causes people to enjoy pastimes like hunting, are *lewd* as "morally improper"; the argument against them is precisely that they are not natural or unlearned, but the perverse amusements (including tennis [25]) of misguided culture. Custom is highlighted in an interesting passage in Book I of Hooker's *Laws*: "I deny not but lewd and wicked custom... may be of force even in plain things to smother the light of natural understanding" (83.19–22). Here it seems that *lewd* might take its force from both the wickedness of custom and the unlearned state in which the people are kept, which the old word may be chosen to convey. In his translation of Ovid's *Metamorphoses*, Arthur Golding never suggests mere simplicity or lack of learning with *lewd*. To be lewd is to be wicked, usually in a sexually marked or motivated way. Sexual interest must be somehow bent to qualify as lewd, as in Circe's enticements to "leawdnesse of a forreine lust" (283.435), but it is also used to describe acts of violence (178.955), greed (180.1052), disloyalty (253.81), guile (277.108), and cannibalism (305.516). In Book Fifteen, the progress of civilization, with its increase in ritualized killing and eating of animals, is itself "a leawdnesse" (297.120). Each side in the Marprelate controversy imputes improper theological learning and dissolute life to the other, using the word *lewd*.[8] In the coney-catching pamphlets *lewd* means "licentious," especially sexually. It seems to be a favorite term of Thomas Harmon in *A Caveat for Common Cursitors*. "Leaud songs" distracted audiences while cutpurses did their work, according to Henry Chettle in 1592, and "lewde wandring people" waste the grain of the land by drinking in taverns (Kinney's edition of *Rouges, Vagabonds* 30, 50).

Historical records too use *lewd* to carry a generalized sense of dissolution or license. John Dee was imprisoned in England on suspicion of "lewde and vayne practices of calculing and conjuring" in 1555, probably for casting a horoscope for Elizabeth during Mary's reign and may have aided Mary in finding heretics in order to secure his release (Shumaker 16). Middlesex magistrates use *lewde* to characterize both the jigs performed in theaters and predators and disturbers of the peace who attend the performances (quoted in Gurr 175). Stephen Gosson's *Apologie* calls the pagan gods "lewde liuers" (125.17), and his criticism of theater repeatedly charges the plays themselves with *lewdness* (Kinney's edition *passim*). General disapproval connected with civil disturbance turns up in W. Fleetwood's report on the men taken in an apprentice rebellion in 1584: "four or five of the chief conspirators, who are in Newgate, and stand indicted of their lewd demeanors" (quoted in Kegl 135). The Merchant Taylors' Court Minute Book records that the mayor of London in 1601 ordered arrests of "the great numbers of idle, lewd, and wicked persons flocking and resorting hither from all parts of this realm" (Rappaport 65). Both Elizabeth and James I used the term to mean transgressive: in a speech in 1569 about the northern rebellion Elizabeth links "lewd practices" to sedition (Rice's edition 125.8, 132.32), and James in 1607 admits that some in Scotland are "seditious and discontented," and "talke lewdly enough" (McIlwain's edition 301.15–16), though none discredits England in Parliament. In many registers, then, the charge of lewdness was being leveled, and the non-clerical reference "layperson," "the old popish term of layman," has disappeared from them entirely.

The country and the city: Spenser

A third early modern trend which influenced the linguistic fortunes of *lewd* was the gentrification of manners and language. Norbert Elias, summing up the state of *politesse* in medieval Europe, writes: "The feelings of the medieval upper class do not yet demand that everything vulgar should be suppressed from life and therefore from pictures" (*Civilizing Process* 210), and we might add, from literature. Compared with the medieval master in his own castle, the renaissance courtier must "learn to adjust his gestures exactly to the different ranks and standings of the people at court, to measure his language exactly, and even to control his eyes exactly." A new and stronger self-imposed reserve is required by this new social environment, and "people mold themselves and others more deliberately than in the Middle Ages." The simple medieval distinctions were being lost; people "see things with more differentiation, i.e. with a stronger restraint of their emotions" (Elias 217, 79, 71). A contemporary witness to just such changes is provided by Caxton's blunt observation in his *Book of Curtesye*, "Thingis somtyme alowed is now repreuid" (4). People know things which it is lewd to talk about; lewdness is hinting that you know them even though they are now "repreuid." The more national character of writing in early modern England and the concentration of printing facilities in London exposed written discourse to scrutiny for religious and political transgression, but also for breaches of propriety and taste. To compare Spenser's or Harvey's diction with the full-bodied English of Chaucer's (idealized) Parson talking of "shiten sheep" is to see a language under pressure to become "refined," partly from a kind of self-surveillance.

George Puttenham's pronouncements on the rules of taste in *The Arte of English Poesie* display a consistent self-consciousness about the proprieties of expression in an English he regarded as only just becoming a literary language. He uses *lewd* casually in its surviving sense, but shows his awareness of its history as a pair with "learned" in his first chapter, which praises the Queen as the best poet, who can make "the lewd well learned" (5.1). A later instance shows the connections between lack of learning and undisciplined behavior: one who praises the pagan gods by belying them "had been a signe not onely of an vnskilfull Poet, but also of a very impudent and leude man" (28.22). *Lewdness* in language violates decorum. In the most telling instance of *lewd* in the treatise, a bad rhymer uses the lowly term *pelfe* "a lewd terme to be given to a Princes treasure" (259.23)—the impropriety was great enough for Puttenham to mention it again (274.26), and signal the class-related inflection the term *pelfe* carried for him. Puttenham's version suggests an ear very finely tuned and a sensiblity Chaucer's Miller would call "squaymous" and "daungerous" of speech.

Lewd was available for its newer suggestion of social and moral lowness because it was already associated with a rural peasantry, on account of the largely agricultural make-up of the third estate in medieval England. *Churl, knabe* (knave), *boor,* and *villain* (all formerly neutral terms for peasants) were also becoming terms of moral disapprobation. London—court and city—became the major point of dissemination for the newly enfranchised English language. The rural scene, in courtly discourse, became the setting for a nostalgia that signalled national purity and folk origins on the one hand and backwardness and irrelevance on the other. Shakespeare's green world comedies make the point that serious people enjoy "rustic revelry" (like that of the dance at the end of *As You Like It*) as pleasant temporary diversion from the duties and customs of their real lives. As appealing as Corin's simple moral code is—earning what he eats, getting what he wears, owing no man hate—Touchstone's "if thou never wast at court, thou never saw'st good manners" (III.ii.40) exerts the fascination in the scene and provides its comedy. For Londoners, even at a modest social level, the country is where you come *from*, and on London stages, *lewd* quickly comes to suggest the opposite of sophisticated reserve: sexual license. In John Marston's *The Malcontent* we read: "the thaw of her delight / Flows from lewd heat of apprehension, / Only from strange imagination's rankness" (I.iii.125–27) and in Beaumont and Fletcher's *A King and No King*, Arbaces declares: "I would desire her love / Lasciviously, lewdly, incestuously, / To do a sin that needs must damn us both / And thee too" (III.iii.77–80).

But it is the discourse of Edmund Spenser, especially in *The Faerie Queene*, in which the response to reconfigured linguistic manners is most conspicuous. Spenser uses *lewd* as a moral rather than an educational or class marker, and nearly always with the sense of erotic licentiousness. As "sexually loose," *lewd* becomes a general euphemism which allows him to escape mention of specific body parts ("lily paps" and "nether parts" are as far as he goes) and acts of dalliance. In spite of countless episodes which involve flirtation, rape, or attempted rape, nobody ever held anybody "harde by the haunchbones" in *The Faerie Queene* the way Nicholas had Alisoun in Chaucer's *Miller's Tale*. (The comparison with Chaucer is invited by Spenser's unrestrained praise for Chaucer's "skill in making" at the beginning of *Shepheardes Calender*.) Moreover, Spenser uses *lewd* in a great many instances: 52 (including *lewdly* and *lewdness*), as compared with only 18 in Shakespeare's much larger corpus and only one in Sidney's, that in a chapter heading in *New Arcadia*.

Spenser is a scholar of English as well as classical learning, and he does reach back to a somewhat broadened medieval sense in accusing love as the "lewd Pilot" of Britomart's bark in her lament—that pilot is "illiterate" as a poor reader of the course and hazards of the voyage (3.4.9.6). The witch's son who lusts after Florimell is so lazy that he has become "both lewd and poore" (3.7.12.9), a formulation which nicely fuses old and newer meanings. A good deal of the peculiar sexiness of *The Faerie Queene* is bound up in Spenser's pervasive use of *lewd*. It solves two problems for him, preserving linguistic proprieties and castigating "license" without trashing physical love itself. Both problems were newly posed by Protestant thinking. There is some truth in John Ciardi's comment in his introduction to the *Divine Comedy* that in Catholic countries swearing is blasphemous, while in Protestant countries body parts and functions are the swear words. Spenser deliberately crafted chaste language in *The Faerie Queene*, in that many of his instances of *lewd* concern improper speech: Phaedria's "lewd words" (2.12.16.4), Paridell's understanding of Satyrane's "lewd lore" (3.9.28.5), Blandamour's "lewd terms" dispraising ladies' lovers (4.4.4.5), Pastorell's resistance to the Captain's "lewd lay" (6.11.5.3), and the like. All these instances call up the idea of indecent knowledge. Referring to the words, lore, terms, and lays, *lewd* avoids the necessity of reporting what was actually said, in contrast to Nicholas's pun in *The Miller's Tale*, "For deerne love of thee, lemman, I spille" (I.3278).

As his dynastic romance concerns sexual conduct, Spenser is concerned to draw the sharpest possible contrast between his virtuous and his vicious characters, between those who love and will found families (and allegorically unite ideas) and those who lust. Medieval sexual ideology frequently denigrated all sexual feeling, especially in women, yet commanded husbands and wives to "pay the marriage debt." Protestant thinking elevated marriage and saw the family as founded on *mutual* love, including sexual intimacy, respect, and companionability (Archbishop Cranmer, quoted in Stone, *Family* 101). Spenser does not present his female characters as mere emblems of what noble warriors set out to win (like Emelye in *The Knight's Tale*); he produces a whole gallery of willful, ingenious women who seek sexual union with the right knight. The most important discursive strategy for keeping those independent, affectionate women discursively distinct from their morally loose sisters was the word *lewd*. In what Geoffrey Hughes calls, in another connection, "legerdemot" (114) Spenser creates a dichotomy where, even in his own fiction (not to mention in life) it would be easier to see a continuum. Take the case of Pastorell's resistance to the Captain's "lewd lay," for example. Pastorell loves somebody else, so she might well resist, but the Captain's refusal to allow her to be taken by the brigands for a "store of gold" and his fierce and ultimately fatal defense of her person (6.11.14 and 19) might have entitled him to be treated as an heroic protector. What prevents it is the word *lewd*. Again, Poeana, once married, lived with her husband in "peace and ioyous bliss" whereas her earlier life had been "defaste" with "lewd loues and lust intemperate" and Claribel is "lewd Claribel" because she "loued out of measure" (4.9.16.7 and 20.8). Temperance and *measura* are posited as the defining feature in this passage, but it is hard to see Britomart's fervent quest as "measured." Tastes are being created here, structures of feeling are being formed to meet the material and ideological conditions of the Protestant English nation-state—a central terrain for this is verbal, and *lewd* operates as an important counter.

A contrast with Shakespeare's very different use of the range of possibilities for *lewd* will suggest how purposeful Spenser's usage is. Shakespeare uses *lewd* in the residual sense "worthless" to stress Petruchio's outrageous language when he stomps on Kate's new hat (*Taming*, IV.iii.65), and as "common, base" in *Richard II* (I.i.90). But in the Henriad, *lewd* is put to an earlier use as "low-born." In *I Henry IV*, the king, worried about improper class-identified behavior—Hal's "low desires, / Such poor, such bare, such lewd, such mean attempts" could "accompany the greatness of thy blood" (III.ii.13–14,16). Poins also misreads Hal, surprised that he can weep for his father because he has been "so lewd and so much engraff'd to Falstaff" (Part II, II.ii.62–63). The "engraff'd" is telling, as if Hal's nature had been severed from its genetic line and grafted onto the Falstaffian trunk. Falstaff's own semantic contribution is his hilarious defense of himself as he responds to the King in the playlet in Part I. Acting as Prince Hal, he says, of "sweet Jack Falstaff, kind Jack Falstaff, true Jack Falstaff, valiant Jack Falstaff," "if that man should be lewdly given, he deceiveth me" (II.iv.468–69). This instance neatly conflates the class-inflected meaning of *lewd* that precede and follow it with the sense "sexually transgressive"; some texts have "that he is a whoremaster...that I utterly deny" in the place of "lewdly given." In Shakespeare's best known instance, an agonized Othello cries out "Damn her, lewd minx" (III.iii.475). Othello's tragic error is that (unlike Spenser) he does not know when to use the word. Desdemona's sturdy sexual interest in Othello himself makes it hard for him to believe in what he would call her innocence (her unknowingness), and therefore her non-sexual loyalty to Cassio. By giving us an old-fashioned protagonist with a chaste but sexually willful young wife, this play renders the tensions involved in early modern attempts to redeem sexuality within marriage tragically explicit.

What this contrast with Shakespeare's practice reveals is the single-mindedness with which Spenser makes use of the word *lewd* in *The Faerie Queene* to further his aim: "to fashion a gentleman or noble person." This aim is explicitly moral, but it is also explicitly discursive; the poem instructs on how to represent the erotic in chaste language. Shakespeare's more varied uses for *lewd* register the difficulties people encounter in reforming the structures of their feelings and their languages. Early modern instances of *lewd* also carry a class inflection, no longer a straightforward reference to the non-clerical estates, but a more complex allusion to people who cannot or will not monitor their behavior and language (or design their hats) according to the new rules.

8
Providence

Can ye wisely adore a Providence, and not think it wisdom to provide?

Herman Melville, *The Confidence Man*

In this way Roberto's story would not inspire any lesson...concluding that in life things happen because they happen, and it is only in the land of Romances that they seem to happen for some purpose or providence.

Umberto Eco, *The Island of the Day Before*

Providence comes to English rather unproblematically from the Latin *providentia* (foresight), itself from *providere* (to provide). The Middle English term may suggest either human "preparation for the future; timely care" (Samuel Johnson's dictionary definition of 1755) or divine foreknowledge and its effects. In the fourteenth and fifteenth centuries it often describes amassing supplies, the supplies themselves, and good management of resources in the broader sense (as in Gower's "and thus be [by] providence / Of alle thinges wel begon / He tok his leve" [*Confessio* II.1322]). It shares most of this territory with the somewhat older Middle English term *purveyance*. Sometimes *providence* refers to God's providing: in Wyclif's English translation of *Wisdom* (Solomon) 14.3, God's providence is a way in the sea and a steadfast path among the floods, and *Saint Erkenwald* calls God's power "the prouidens of the prince that paradis weldes" (*Pearl*-poet 160). Trevisa's *Higden* alleges that political hierarchies are divinely ordered: "Whiche thynge was not doen with owte the prouidence of God, that somme scholde be gouernoures in realmes and somme subiectes" (2.253).

113

Although usually positive in its connection with prudence, Lydgate's *providence* can veer over into sneakiness, as when Artaxerses is said to "bamaner prouydence / Put pryueli his brother in prisoun" (*Fall of Princes*, 3.4894). Human work is also stressed in the second part, the "domus providencie," of Edward IV's household account-book, the *Liber Niger*. There the image of the court as chivalric magnificence is explained through its elaborate assignment of duties and responsibilities in the king's household to *supply* whatever is needed to produce the image. *Providence* and *purveyance* are used interchangeably to describe this feature of court life which, when properly done, will produce the *estate* of the court and of the king.

These instances all specify who is providing, whether a human agent or God, since the Middle English term does not, by itself, signal the supernatural or inevitable, and those that credit the deity account for only about one-third of the total. But by the late sixteenth century events outside human control are widely represented, not as the duplicitous gifts of medieval Fortune, but as the minutely calibrated workings of benign, though inscrutable, divine providence. English Calvinism provides the leading edge of this transformation in mental habits and emotional structures. The history of *providence* presents an interesting variation on Hall's proposed pattern in which a social group chooses a highly valued term from dominant ideology in which to couch a new idea or emphasis: Calvinists chose a homely, though positive, word and invested it with cosmic significances. The new usage was by no means limited to them, and rather quickly became a key term in consolidating national loyalties. Many early modern domains were touched by the new sense; it reconfigured political, medical, and economic, as well as religious discourses. The elevation of the term *providence* displays a discursive shift within English cosmology from a universe imagined as producing some merely fortuitous events, which good Christians may allowably "grutch" against, to one in which God's providence, as William Perkins puts it, "ordained and disposed all callings, and...designed the persons to bear them" (449).

"Science of presence" or "timely care"

Although the fourteenth-century word-hoard offered *providence*, Chaucer refused it in his translation of the *Consolation of Philosophy*. In his *Boece*, he presents Boethius's case that *providence* misstates the relationship between history and God's knowledge: "thou ne schalt naught demen it as prescience of thinges to comen, but thou schalt demen more ryghtfully that it is science of presence or of instaunce that nevere faileth. For which it nis nat ycleped 'previdence,' but it sholde rathir ben clepid 'purveaunce,' that is establisshed ful fer fro ryght lowe thinges, and byholdeth fro afer alle thingis, right as it were fro the heye heighte of thinges" (V. pr. 6.110–20). Chaucer is translating "unde non praeuidentia sed prouidentia potius dicitur," where the point of the distinction is between that which is distant from immediate sight because it is in the future, and that which is present to divine sight directly because for God there is no time. John Gower also uses this sense, and defends it in the same way: "The hyhe almyhti pourveance / In whos eterne remembrance / Fro ferst was every thing present, / He hath his prophesie send" (*Confessio Amantis*, prologue 585). Julian of Norwich avoids both *providence* and *purveyance*, referring to "the foreseing wysdom of god" which knows from the beginning and anticipates the "best ende" (*Showings* Long Text 11.9–14). But *purveyance* had more homely uses as well. Some suggest a rather positive "timely care," as when the narrator of *Jack Upland* finds it odious to misname covetousness "wise purvyaunce" (120.41). Most instances are ethically neutral, concerned with the supplies amassed for households or military campaigns, or supplies of troops.[1]

What is odd is Chaucer's choice of *purveaunce* as the better term for his *non*-Boethian purposes. Everywhere in his corpus *purveaunce* is used for both time bound human foresight and divine presence/knowledge. It is easy to see the logic of its use in *Boece*, where the largest number of instances (44 of 68) turn up, since the *Consolation of Philosophy* is a book precisely about the intersection of human freedom and divine prescience. Eleven more occurrences are in *Troilus and Criseyde*, where sexual love is discussed in what sometimes seem Boethian terms. The three instances of *purveaunce* in *The Knight's Tale* also point to an extra-human plan: Arcite's allegation that purveaunce gives us better conditions than we choose for ourselves (1251–54), the narrator's claim that his plot is controlled by purveaunce (1663–72), and of course Theseus's justification, in a speech echoing Boethius, of the final movement of events as providential (3011–15). Throughout the tale, the stately providence evoked by Theseus and the narrator is contrasted with complaints against Fortune offered by the adolescent cousins in their time-bound troubles. The strong providential aura of the tale, with its slowly unfolding historical ironies, is an important focus for the Knight's conservative piety—a piety interrogated by the relation of the tale to the Canterbury frame, especially its juxtaposition with the Miller's performance. The remarkable balance of the Knight's mode with the Miller's is apparent even in a matter like the use of the term *purveiaunce*, which occurs in *The Miller's Tale* to refer to the provisioning of the kneading tubs against the flood Nicholas has predicted (3566).[2] At issue is the control of the outcomes of stories, and these contrasts amount to the Miller's miniaturized ideological critique of the Knight's philosophical and social creed.

The voices of Robyn the Miller and his character Nicholas insist on narrative outcomes determined by the clash and/or confluence of human designs. So does the voice of the arche-wife Alisoun of Bath. She takes Jankyn walking in the fields listening to her dream as part of *her* elaborate plan to plant the idea of their marrying: "of my purveiance / I spak to hym" (566–67). Not only does she credit herself with that plan, but with the planning of her sexual career in general: "Yet was I nevere withouten purveiance / Of mariage, n'of othere thynges eek" (570–71). Her ironic nod to piety in thanking "God that is eterne on lyve" for her adventures at the beginning of her prologue makes a glancing and conventional link with the tradition of God's *purveiance* (argued in *Boece* in terms of his eternal-ness) only to tell a story which vigorously insists on her own. *The Man of Law's Tale* contains a neat contrast pair: early the narrator refers to the purveiance of the Emperor preparing for Custance's marriage—preparations which would ultimately go awry—and later to God's "prudent purveiance," which saved Custance just as it had so many biblical figures (II.247, 283). In that tale the contrast points unequivocally to the "real" power as divine, but *The Franklin's Tale* exhibits an equally neat contrast which is much harder to read. Dorigen prays to "Eterne God, that thurgh thy purveiaunce / Ledest the world," although the burden of her prayer is that she does not understand his purposes. Only a few lines later, her friends lay out food and other "purveiaunce" to tempt her to a life-affirming leisure. Although their provisions indirectly lead to her dilemma, it is not clear whose design produces the ultimately happy ending. The blurred focus of power in this tale is, I think, an effect which demarcates the Franklin's genial liberalism—human-centered, but not irreverent—a secular, but still an authorized, voice in medieval discourse.

In texts which distinguish between the terms, uses of *purveyance* fall into two sets. "Science of presence" is implied for a small, sharply defined, group of instances (most of them by Chaucer and Gower), and "timely care" acccounts for most others. In early modern writing, the term is scantily represented compared with its vogue in Middle

English, except as "procuring supplies." It does, however, turn up as a technical term in complaints that Elizabeth used unfair practices to procure goods for the royal court; she answers these charges in 1589 with a promise of reform (Prothero 124, 298, 340). James had insisted on the crown's right of purveyance "at reasonable prices," but the outcry against the practice was even more strident in his reign, the Lords calling for the an end to all abitrary pricing in recompence for royally purveyed goods, including "servants, labourers, and all other provisions, as also for carts, horses and carriages...and generally all purveyances and takings" (June 26, 1610). Notwithstanding the terrain shared by the two words before 1450, *providence*, desirable human foresight (lacked by red haired people, according the *Secreta Secretorum* continuation 2580) emerges as the more clearly positive term on the eve of the Reformation.

Providential England

Providence is not a key biblical term in any of the medieval or early modern translations—Wyclif used it in his first translation, but not in his more idiomatic and widely disseminated second version, nor does it occur (except in the apocryphal *Wisdom*) in the Coverdale, Tyndale, Geneva, or Authorized translations. Yet English Reformation thinkers brought the word in the sense Chaucer and Gower had given *purveyance*, the deity's timeless ordering of events, to theological *and* secular prominence. The positive valence of the word *providence* in Middle English rendered it suitable for takeover by the English follow-ers of Luther and particularly Calvin. Its closeness to the literal provisioning of troops or households offered advantages for discussing a present God who, in Calvin's thought, "nourishes and cares for every creature, even for the little birds" (*Institutes, I.16.1*). The homely, literal idiom held great appeal for English reformers, whose language in the mid-sixteenth century was still "redolent" (as William Haller puts it) "of the household, the farmstead, the sheepfold, the market town and the sea" (51). The vernacular Bibles, tracts, and sermons so central to the reform movement appropriated the earthy richness of the mother tongue while simultaneously pushing English to accom-modate the Latinate abstractions of theological controversy—a process begun by Wycliffites. *Providence*, its value in part depending on its homely connotations, began to be "implicated in the logic of a new political discourse" (in Hall's sense "articulated"); without obscuring its local associations, reformation writers broadened its range and

made it a cornerstone in their reading of sacred and secular history—
or rather in their particular meshing of the sacred and the secular. As
a new "mode of civic consciousness," in J.G.A. Pocock's phrase, it
posited a "public realm, at once secular and godly, in which the individual, at once saint and Englishman, is to act" (337).

Calvin's unequivocal emphasis on God's providence (a result of his
Old Testament and Augustinian emphasis on His power) was used in
England to underwrite both natural and political history. On the one
hand, Calvin's *Institutes* links the governance of the world more
directly to divine providence than did medieval thought, with its
allowance of Fortune as a mediating figure:

> At the outset, then, let my readers grasp that providence means not
> that by which God idly observes from heaven what takes place on
> earth, but that by which, as keeper of the keys, he governs all
> events.
>
> (II.xvi.4; I.201–02)

> God's providence as taught in Scripture is opposed to fortune and
> fortuitous happenings. Now it has been commonly accepted in all
> ages, and almost all mortals hold the same opinion today, that all
> things come about through chance. What we ought to believe
> concerning providence is by this depraved opinion most certainly
> not only beclouded, but almost buried.
>
> (I.xvi.2; I.198)

Calvin implies here that providence is at once more intimate and more
irresistible than instances of *providence* in Middle English suggested—
the middlewoman, Lady Fortune, against whom it was acceptable for
medieval Christians to repine, is eliminated. As Thomas Blundeville
put it in 1574, "nothing is done by chaunce, but all thinges by his foresight, counsell, and diuine prouidence."[3] The Geneva translation was
so insistent on this reading of *providence* that (among the many
instances of *providence* in its glosses) it came close to taking the side of
Job's detractors in the headnote to the Book of Job: "the adversaries
maintaine with manie goodlie arguments, that God punisheth continually according to the trespas, grounding vpon Gods prouidence, his
iustice, and mans sinnes." The detractors were not wrong to hold these
opinions, but to use these goodly arguments in the evil cause of
driving Job to despair. The ethical imperative involved in this move
was to urge a believer's grateful acceptance of whatever comes as an

evidence of "a singular providence watch[ing] over the welfare of believers" (*Institutes* I.xvii.6; I.218).

But in England, Calvinist providentialism could also be appropriated to undergird an interpretation of history like the "Tudor myth." By figuring Henry VII as the union of the ancestral lines of York and Lancaster (not to mention vaguer claims of descent from Arthur through his Welsh blood), the English could be taught their history as a political allegory promising internal stability and international greatness. The coronation of Elizabeth allowed English Protestants to read their national history as providential in yet another sense and their place in world history as God's chosen people delivered like the Old Testament Israelites from the captivity and exile imposed by Rome. I will call the combined force of the "Tudor myth" and the trope of the "Elect Nation" "providential England" for short. It depended on a line of thought widely available through the printed and spoken (often preached) word, and both the Queen and the reform pastorate made use of it, though for different ends. *Acts and Monuments* posited the early roots of English Protestant attitudes toward the Bible and the church in Wycliffism, and, of course, gave the nation the stories of "its" martyrs, ancient and recent. It was ordered to be placed (with the English Bible and the Book of Common Prayer) in churches across the country, quickly becoming a force for establishing its revised ecclesiastical history and standardizing written English (Womack 104–05). And the bishops Elizabeth appointed on her accession were predominantly exiles driven out of the country during Mary's reign, many voices to exult in their nation's timely deliverance from religious tyranny and error. The sense of a vitalized English language and a providential English state which would deliver Europe from the papacy worked together to reshape medieval structures of feeling.

The trope of a providential English people could be used to induce a siege mentality about the nation's survival, a factor in the consolidation of feudal fiefdoms into an absolutist state with centralized powers of surveillance and coercion. Providential England may be read, therefore, as the narrative of an emergent "totalizing society," that, as Stephen Greenblatt defines it, "posits an occult network linking all human, natural, and cosmic powers and that claims on behalf of its ruling elite a privileged place in this network" (*Negotiations* 2). It may be argued that the English appropriation of Calvin's thought posits just such a network, and very openly. If God has indeed directed the course of English history, paying minute attention to the care of his people, resistance to any regime in power is faced with almost insurmountable difficulties. My argument is not that this confluence of material and ideological forces actually produced a seamless social fabric (as E.M.W. Tillyard's presentation of the "Tudor myth" seems to imply), but that it became the hegemonic discourse in which civic debate was to a large extent carried out. Elizabeth played to it, conspicuously kissing the English Bible—the dissemination of which her father had resolutely forbidden until late in his reign—on her coronation day appearance before her London public (Haller 86). Court corridors, city streets, and countryside pulpits sounded the themes, often relying on the word *providence*.

The line taken for public consumption stressed the severity of the threat from outside attack and inside subversion, but it also created a pressure enabling Anglicans, Puritans, and Catholics to subscribe together to a "holy pretense" by which Machiavelli's "reason of state" was yoked together with Christian politics.[4] While acknowledging the overarching providence of God in preserving and guiding the nation, many writers, preachers, and parliamentarians insisted on a version of human prudence in political matters that veered toward *policy*, a term closely associated in England with Machiavelli. Thus, in large measure, debates on the conduct of public affairs tended to circle around the two meanings of *providence:* the control of history by God's immutable plan—Calvin's stated position—and the timely care with which governing bodies protect the polity—the position of Calvinists (and others) who saw the necessity of policy for defending their providentially elect nation. Consider George Puttenham's tactful praise of Queen Elizabeth: "This immeasurable ambition of the Spaniards, if her maiestie by God's prouidence, had not with her forces, prouidently stayed and retranched, no man knoweth what inconuenience might in time haue insued to all the Princes and common wealthes in Christendome" (105). This interpretation of recent history registers the enormity of the threat and gracefully balances the Queen's personal claim to prudence with the Almighty's plan that England be Europe's savior.[5]

England's special mission in the New World was ratified by the many escapes from danger reported in Richard Hakluyt's *Voyages and Discoveries* displaying God's providence. According to Howe's *Annals*, the desperate crew of the *Admiral* on its mission to relieve the Virginia colony was driven to the coast of Bermuda by a violent storm and almost wrecked on dangerous rocks when the ship "by God's divine providence at a high water ran right between two strong rocks, where it stuck fast without breaking." They were sustained on the island for ten months "by the special mercy and Divine Providence of Almighty God," and "by diligence and industry" salvaged enough from their disabled ship to make their way to Virginia. "The ground of all those miseries was the permissive Providence of God," according to the *True Declaration of the State of the Colonie in Virginia*, but the "next Fountaine of woes was the secure negligence, and improvidence, when every man sharked for his present bootie, but was altogether carelesse of succeeding penurie" and "our mutinous Loyterers would not sow with providence, and therefore they reaped the fruits of too deere bought Repentance" (140)—divine and human agency.

Providentialism is posited in many tones, from self justification and even frank celebration, to marked unease, and in many cultural arenas. John Knox in *The First Blast of the Trumpet* quotes Chrysostom that men should have dominion over women "according to providence" (55.7). John Foxe recounts in the *Acts and Monuments* that *providence* protected John Wyclif from persecution and that Pope Gregory XI, "a stirrer up of all this trouble against him, turned up his heels and died" (III.17) at a propitious moment. Arthur Golding's translation of Ovid's *Metamorphoses* attempts to reread history in order to reconcile classical poetry with Christian cosmology, using *providence* as a key term in his introductory epsitle: humankind was formerly unable to receive God's truths directly, but now it is clear that everything we presently know, including "Ovid's scantlings," was "decreed by his providence" from the beginning (378).[6] The theme of providential guidance is never far from the events of Edmund Spenser's *Faerie Queene* either; its links between abstractions like Truth, biblical reference, world history, and local allusion are intricately forged, but it contains only two instances of the word itself. The "woodgods" rescue Una from Sansloy in Book I by "eternall providence" (1.4.7.1), stressing intervention in a local crisis, "special providence." Later Merlin explains as "eternall providence" the magic looking-glass which shows Britomart her destined lover Arthegall and their dynastic role (3.3.24), stressing the providentiality of England's long history.[7] King James attributes the discovery of the Gunpowder Plot to "the wonderfull prouidence of God" (284.8) and argues that divine *providence* had ordained the union with Scotland (271.38).

Richard Hooker's explanation of natural law in *Laws of Ecclesiastical Polity* is derived soberly from the identification of *providence* with orderly process (unlike Foxe's image of God's particular plan for a specific series of events). In the First Book, he writes that:

the natural generation and process of all things receiveth order of proceeding from the settled stability of divine understanding. This appointeth unto them their kinds of working, the disposition whereof in the purity of God's own knowledge and will is rightly termed by the name of *Providence*. The same being referred unto things themselves here disposed by it, was wont by the ancients to be called *natural destiny*.

(62)

Divine *providence* in this sense is attested to by universal history, but a more specific sense of his plan is contained in the Bible—God's providence "hath made principle choice of this way to deliver" his law (110.20). Establishing writing as the most dependable and profound record and linking this authority directly with God's providence (111.21) distinguishes Hooker's view from the Catholic stance that scripture and ecclesiastical tradition are of equal authority. *Laws* also notes human providence; certain civil statutes were given by their founders "with singular providence" (39.19–20). Both of these usages appropriate the term for a calm, rational eliding of the natural order with contemporary scripturalism. Golding's translation of Phillippe de Mornay's tract on kingship and citizenship also presents a providence in nature and history consonant with human rationality. "What else is Prouidence, than the will of God vttered foorth with Reason, and orderly disposed by vnderstanding?" asks Mornay. Hooker and Mornay yoke together the two forces which drive protestant readings of history—God's will and man's capacity for understanding—but those forces can also be made to pull in opposite directions.

Providence and the individual talent

In Calvin's thinking, God's providential care was usually posited for individual believers. It both isolates them by emphasizing inner states rather than outward sacraments and sacralizes the whole world in which they live—every act is opened to pious scrutiny. The ethical thought of all factions of Protestants, though—not just Calvinists —emphasized individual understanding and diligence over institutionalized ceremonies, and made service to God in secular callings as important to his plan as clerical office. The result was a religious sense of the duty of daily work. This development dovetailed nicely with economic shifts toward an urbanized, artisanal England with increasing opportunities for social mobility. Together with Protestant prohibitions against ostentation and self-indulgence, it made a sober *providence* for one's family an ethical duty and a likely result of rightly directed labor. But that very duty threatened to dilute people's trust in the overarching providence which God always exercises *for them*. As with the "providential England," which must be provided for through the "holy pretenses" of her governors, individual Christians, although worth infinitely more than sparrows, must look to their provisions.

Bubonic plague raised the issue of providence in both public and private arenas. As Paul Slack has argued, it is not surprising that divine providence was universally assumed to have a hand in its outbreaks, never losing its currency as an explanation of the plague, even for "the most determined advocates of quarantine measures at the end of the seventeenth century" (48). For some writers, this providence was regarded as a direct intervention in the orderly process of nature, so various and unpredictable were the manifestations of the disease, the marks which sometimes appeared on the sufferer's chest or back being colloquially called "God's tokens." This strand of thought noted the especially high incidence of plague in cities, and especially London's suburbs, "'most polluted' by spiritual 'filthiness' as well as by pestilence" (26) with their overcrowding, poverty, prostitution, and playgoing, and recommended the antidote of moral reform. A 1578 regulation isolating the sick was vigorously attacked by those who felt it to be "a denial of God's pre-eminent role" in plague and a release from the obligation of charity (230). For Henoch Clapham, writing in 1603, plague was a direct intervention of providence into English life (quoted in Slack 247). Robert Abbot (brother to the Archbishop of Canterbury) argued that God would protect those who ministered to the sick by his "extraordinary providence" (236). The "search for providences" in the sins and errors of government and individuals would last into the Interregnum (243).

For other writers, divine providence was administered indirectly, through unusual alignments of the stars and planets which caused the noxious "miasmas" which spread the plague. Miasmas, which just missed engendering theories of contagion (27), suggested measures to enhance public health, since they were also noted—whatever the position of the stars—in the vicinity of graveyards, unburied corpses, and unsanitary poverty. Early attempts at restricting public gatherings, quarantine of the already ill, and destruction of sickbed linens did have some effect in slowing the spread of the disease, and at the same time fed the notion that England was becoming more regulated and orderly, less deserving of providential punishment. To some, these practical measures were both intelligent and godly and constituted a challenge to outworn ideas of providence: "If we make a mock of all preservatives of Art... and trust in God's providence, saying: 'If he will save me, he will save me, and if I die, I die'—this is not faith in God but a gross, ignorant and foolhardy...presumption" (*Certaine Prayers...to be used in the present Visitation*, 1603; quoted in Slack 227). Around the plague, then, developed a discourse which fed both considerations of natural disaster as divine retribution and the beginnings of epidemiology and urban planning.

Plague discourses dramatically point up the contradictions involved in a providential view of England as saved by God to save Europe in turn, and a more intimate providence which operated on more local or individual deserts. These contradictions are both logical and emotional, and they place serious strains on emerging Protestant structures of feeling. Critics of Puritanism castigated the strain as moral hypocrisy, as in Ben Jonson's characterization of Dame Purecraft in *Bartholomew Fair*. Personal hypocrisy of course is one possible result of such ideological pressure, but more interesting is the variety of unstable solutions, public and private, people fashioned to disguise or endure it. Those language games played in early modern discourse, and especially in the London theaters, are the subject of the rest of this chapter.

Staging the language game

Early modern drama enacts both fervent belief in and opportunistic detachment from providentialism's religious and social aura. In 1599 a character named Prouidence appears on stage in *Clyomon and Clamydes*. Just when the faithful Neronis is about to commit suicide upon her belief that her beloved Clyomon has been killed, Providence descends with a message from the seat of Jove, assuring her that her knight lives. Neronis reads, takes heart, and declaims:

> And for their prouidence diuine, the Gods aboue ile praise,
> And shew their works so wonderfull, vnto their laud alwaies.
>
> (1565–66)

The character Providence is a *deus ex machina* in plain sight. Similarly, Shakespeare's Brutus openly states the stoic position in recoiling from Cato's suicide on account of a providence which belongs to "high powers" (*Julius Caesar* V.i.106). And in the most famous instance of *providence* in Shakespeare, Hamlet's own reading is a straightforward Calvinist echo: "There is special providence ["predestinate providence" in Q1 is even more strongly Calvinist] in the fall of a sparrow" (V.ii.220).[8]

Ben Jonson's comedies, in contrast, treat Calvinist versions of providence with unrelenting satire. In *Epicoene*, Truewit, having rashly intervened in his friend Dauphine's affairs, finds that things have turned out well after all. Cleremont ascribes the result to "mere fortune," but Truewit replies: "Fortune! mere providence. Fortune had not a finger in't. I saw it must necessarily in nature fall out so" (II.ii.190–92). Truewit substitutes his own watchful omniscience for the workings of Lady Fortune in witty repartee, but Subtle in *The Alchemist* directly accuses the Puritan Tribulation Wholesome of exploiting belief in providence to conceal his sleazy financial deals. With the possession of the philosopher's stone, Wholesome will no longer need:

> to win widows
> To give you legacies; or make zealous wives
> To rob their husbands, for the common cause:
> Nor take the start of bonds, broke but one day,
> And say they were forfeited, by providence.
>
> (III.ii.69–73)

Jonson not only demystifies the idea of providence by displaying its manipulations, he pointedly accuses Puritanism for mystifying it in the first place.

A similar demystification may be seen in Shakespeare's *The Tempest*, in which the providential implications of Prospero's powers are exactly what is at stake in the plot. Prospero tells Miranda that twelve years earlier they were "blessedly holp hither," coming ashore on their island by "Providence divine" (I.ii.62 and 159), and earlier criticism serenely took him at his word in linking God's purposes and powers with his own. When Ferdinand tells his father about his engagement, he alleges that Miranda is mortal but "by immortal Providence she's mine" (V.i.189). We know, but Ferdinand does not, that the Providence he refers to is largely Prospero's. Reading these passages together discloses the irony with which the play as a whole treats Prospero's pretensions to deity as he virtually scripts its events and predisposes its language (e.g., teaching Caliban to name the greater and lesser lights as God did Adam in Genesis). He might be seen as

self-deluded and his story read as a fable of hubris humbled by imped
ing mortality (by the end, every third thought shall be his grave), or
he might be regarded as the malign prototype of the European colo-
nizer who takes on the role of Providence deliberately to serve his
massive ego and begin to fulfill his manifest destiny. Whichever of
these or the many variations of them we espouse, *The Tempest* presents
a remarkable image of early modern skepticism about the alignment
between God's providence and human rule, but not Shakespeare's first
or only such image.

Ulysses in *Troilus and Cressida* and Vincentio in *Measure for Measure*
are obvious portraits of timely provision presenting itself as divine
foreknowledge, and reception of the plays, until recently, accepted
their "holy pretense." Ulysses accounts for his knowledge of Achilles's
private affairs thus:

> The providence that's in a watchful state
> Knows almost every grain of Pluto's gold,
> Finds bottom in the uncomprehensive depth,
> Keeps place with thought and almost, like the gods,
> Do thoughts unveil in their dumb cradles.
>
> (III.iii.196–200)

Ulysses begins by identifying the providence that has uncovered his
secret with the circumspection he has advocated for Greek military
policy all along, but raises it here to a claim for a mysterious divinity
at the "soul of state" (202). The result is a model of power from the
ruler's point of view so perfect that one might imagine its author to
have been Francis Walsingham himself, the consummate watcher,
who almost seemed to unveil thoughts "in their dumb cradles." Duke
Vincentio, although he never uses the word *providence*, has been
widely seen as its embodiment, and seems to see himself that way as
he sets up his scheme to find out "what our seemers be" (I.iii.54).
Measure for Measure both connects its "ruling elite" with the "occult
powers" that run things (Greenblatt) and allows the connection to be
seen as suspect.

Cyril Tourneur's *Atheist's Tragedy* is perhaps the early modern play
most pointedly and sustainedly *about* providence. Long recognized as
a *"drame à thèse"* (Bradbrook 184), the thesis being worked out is often
taken to be the ethics of natural reason or of the revenge duty, but it
might better be seen as a debate over providence. The word itself
occurs often—nine times—and at strategic points. (Marlowe, treating

similar themes in several plays, never uses the word; in Shakespeare it does not occur more than twice in any play.) The action pits D'Amville—a younger brother who attempts to inherit by killing his brother and arranging the death of his nephew in order to command wealth and bequeath it—against the trusting nephew Charlemont. The play opens with D'Amville's pseudo-Platonic exercise—Borachio as his pupil—on the reason and understanding through which he will bring to pass the events of the play (in this he is a stage manager who speaks candidly to the audience, like Iago and Edmund). D'Amville asserts the absolute control of bold individual persons over their destinies—he is, like Machiavelli, ready to seize Lady Fortune's fore-lock, whether it takes outrageous assertiveness or covert, long-term circumspection. He seems in tune with the aggressive capitalism of his time, and he uses its vocabulary: *increase, substance, industry, increase of substance, provide and add, bond.*[9] Yet he also aims to establish a dynasty, to found a *house*. D'Amville's dynastic goals are clearly invoked in the image of children as branches, nourished by the parent tree which provides the "sap / Whereby they live and flourish" (57–58), a particularly familiar medieval trope.

Both the debate and the action of Act I, scene i are focused on D'Amville's attempt to commandeer the meaning and workings of *providence*. Charlemont, the embodiment of feudal, chivalric values, provides the foil in his unassertive role as believer. Borachio calls Charlemont's departure for war a "commodious providence" for his patron, but Charlemont, too, might have said that, since it was his destined occupation as an aristocratic son only temporarily constrained from trying his mettle by a protective parent (like Perceval at the beginning of his story). Just before D'Amville claims that provi-dence dwells in his reason (126), he calls his sons his "eternity," recalling the link between providence and eternity posited since Boethius. Death is so surely fated that our providence cannot prevent it, he duplicitously tells his brother Montferrers, as he is setting his death-trap (I.ii.51). *The Atheist's Tragedy* pulls the two strands of Mornay's argument apart, presenting the believer in God's providence as honorable passivity and the believer in man's power to provide as clever ruthlessness.

In Act One, the issue of what constitutes providence is openly debated, and the word itself occurs often; in the middle acts, the issue is plotted rather than argued. Act Five opens with a return to direct debate, this time by a protagonist who believes that his plan, and his philosophy, have proved themselves. (This fifth-act return to the "big issues" and the high rhetorical style of the early scenes is reminiscent of *Doctor Faustus*.) "Unpursing" the gold he has inherited from his fratricide, he sighs over it:

> These are the stars, the ministers of fate,
> And man's high wisdom the superior power
> To which their forces are subordinate.

(V.i.24–26)

The serene enjoyment of his triumph, practical and philosophical, is interrupted by the ghost of his murdered brother, who refers to his plot as a "project," accusing him of a specific and nefarious economic practice in early modern England, rather than the older and more general sin of greed. His response to this ghostly visitation is D'Amville's restatement of his success in a speech filled with markers to capitalism—*prosperous judgements, success, instrument, interest, absolute possession, law,* and *real* (perhaps as in the emergent term "real estate"). He makes a point of contrasting himself with Charlemont, now under sentence of death:

> Thus while the simple, honest worshipper
> Of fantastic providence groans under
> The burden of neglected misery,
> My real wisdom has raised up a state
> That shall eternize my posterity.

(44–48)

Here he points out his role as demystifier of the fantastic idea that God is in charge of history. Yet, as he raises an executioner's axe to dispatch his innocent enemies with his own hands, he strikes himself instead and accepts the judge's verdict that "eternal providence" has frustrated his projects.

The Atheist's Tragedy (again like *Doctor Faustus*) can be read simply as a morality play, in which a prideful man constructs his own map of the cosmos, using cool, instrumental reason that eschews any checks on its exercise by piety and tradition. Yet an equally coherent reading can be based on its insistence on the contradictions between English Calvinist notions of providence and early capitalist admonitions to self-reliance which both deconstruct it and are built upon it. D'Amville is not apprehended by his opponents, betrayed by his confederates, or unmasked by the law—it is his resolve that fails. This fable suggests that the structure of feeling that would allow intelligent, amoral human providence to control the plot to the end is not, in 1611, yet firmly in place.

It seems a long way from Neronis's complete and automatic trust in Providence to the sophisticated and ambivalent meditations on it by Jonson, Shakespeare, and Tourneur. The variety of accents in which the word was spoken on London stages discomfits any lingering images of a universally shared "world picture" we might be tempted to ascribe to early modern culture. Yet that variety also testifies to the importance of what we might call a "discourse of providence." It suggests both the attempts (largely successful) of English Calvinists to reform language to reflect new doctrinal positions and shape new structures of religious feeling and the counter-pressures exerted by a linguistically subtle and energetic popular stage.

9
Queynte/Quaint

[Antiquarianism] is the objectification of the peasant classes, the aestheticization of rural life which makes that life "quaint," a survival of an elusive and purer, yet diminished, past.

Susan Stewart, *On Longing*

Susan Stewart is commenting on a poem by H.R. Wadmore, "Time's Footsteps," printed in the *Antiquarian Magazine* in 1882. She uses the emphasized word *quaint* to evoke the antiquarian's desire to posit authenticity, "purity," in the venerated object and his sense of its unbridgeable distance from current life, the solid material object which is none the less uncanny. *Queynte* derives, on the one hand, from Old French *cointe*, and ultimately Latin *cogitum*, found frequently in early Middle English texts in a variety of spellings, with meanings which range from wise and crafty to mysterious and sophistical. In Middle English, *queynte* collides with the Germanic *cunte* (female genitals) as in *Lanfranc's Science of Cirurgie*: "In wymmen the necke of the bladdre is schort & is maad fast to the cunte" (172.12). The word is spelled with a *u* or *ow* for this meaning in some instances: *Proverbs of Hending*: "ȝeve thi cunte to cunning / And crave affetir wedding" (st 42), and *Lyarde*: "Bete the cownte with ȝour neffes, when ȝe may do no more" (282). A still earlier manuscript (*Sir Tristrem* 1300) does too: "Hir queynte abouen his kne, / Naked the kniȝtes knewe" (2254). But Middle English spelling varies widely from dialect to dialect, and Chaucer's scribes write *queynte*.[1]

The arbitrary nature of the link between signifier and signified must be called in to explain how the two etymological strands fell together in the fourteenth century—Hans Henrich Hock's *Principles of Historical*

Linguistics refers to similar events as "semantic merger" (301)—but cultural uses for the coincidence are open to inquiry. The anatomical sense of the word probably had greater currency in oral than in written discourse, as its descendant still does, but in an era when most people read, even silently, by forming the words as they came to them, the oral associations must have colored the more learned term. Such reading could not distinguish the noun signifying the female body part from the adjective "wise, crafty" without the work of interpretation. The potential for wordplay was acknowledged early—"ʒeve thi cunte to cunning"—and also later in the century by John Gower's call for simplicity in love-talking: "I trowe that ther is no beste, / If he with love scholde aqueinte... / That he ne wolde make it queinte / As for the while that it lasts" (*Confessio Amantis* 4.2314). In addition, the two meanings are related through their concern with the unknown, unknowable, or secret. This linguistic terrain enables both punning and a subtler form of wordplay that sexualizes references to knowledge, wisdom, skill, and intricacy with female-inflected forbiddenness. This chapter will investigate how the merger of the two etymological strands which become *queynte* enables paronomasia in Middle English and then splits into the taboo *cunt* and the innocent *quaint* of Early Modern English (which nonetheless retained a whiff of its residual coloring). Even Susan Stewart's sentence is phrased to make that which is *quaint* the object of ever-receding longing, like the sonnet lady of renaissance poetry.

Women and other enigmas

Middle English instances in which *queynte* signals the difficulty of knowing or finding out something sometimes use it to mean hidden from view, as in *William of Palerne*: "The hert & the hinde... hem hed sone... vnder a coynte crag" (2850) or just exotic, as in *The Wars of Alexander*: "Vile neddirs [adders] ... ware crokid & coynnt with corouns on hede" (5423) and *Mandeville's Travels*: "And there beth also in that cuntre / The queintist beestis that man may se" (2378). Not every exotic, elusive state ought to be sought, as in Hilton's warning in *On Mixed Life* against "gapyng aftur sum queynte sturyng" (291). But sometimes intricacy is posited without the hint of threat, as in the ingeniousness described in Mannyng's *Story of England*: "Tonnes of bras with queynte thinges... / That make the water euere hot" (Part I.2246), and in "Piers of Fulham": "A queynt ys vsyd, a quayle pype... / Yn somer, or the corne ys wex rype"(129). *The Castle of Perseverance* is "of so qweynt a gynne / That whoso euere holde hym therinne, / He schal neuere fallyn in dedly synne" (1702)—this is a *queynt* trap but a desirable one.

Queynte learning ranges from wisdom to craft (more often craft), frequently associated with the clergy perhaps for sound—"queintis of clergy"—as well as critique of the estate. In the *Mirror St. Edmunds*, *qweyntise* is the term used for prudence (the eagle), one of the four virtues. But by the last decade of the fourteenth century, its implications for intellectual life are usually negative, associated with verbal adornment and pride. In the religious lyric "Who says Sooth," we read: "Thus is the sothe I-kept in close, / And vche mon maketh touh and queynte; / To leue the tixt and take the glose, / Eueri word thei coloure and peynte" (14) and in *Pauline Epistles*, I Corinthians 1.19 is translated: "I schal lose the wisdam of the wyse; and the queyntyse of the queynte I scal reproue"—not that *wisdam* or *queyntyse* is here evil in itself, but that attainment of them awaits God's judgment. The Lambeth *Secretum Secretorum* provides a positive instance: "It nedys that he be qweynte and warre yn his werkys" (107.1), and so does *Castle of Love*: "The kyngys son, both wyse and queynt, / Herd the iiij systeres pleynt" (419).

This positive use is never found in Wycliffite writing. For Lollards, *queyntise* is always a danger, a sin, and an attempt by antichrist and his minions in the institutionalized Church to befool God's simple people. The Wycliffite *Faith Hope Charity* accuses the powers of evil of being "moo & more koynte in ther dedis by wylis" (in Matthew 347); so do *Antichrist* and *How Satan and His Children*. *Piers the Plowman's Creed* (in Dean) makes *queyntnesse* a kind of leitmotif. In its unremitting attack on the misuses of friar's clerical privileges, an important focus is on the deviousness, the lack of clarity the narrator imputes to their preaching and their living. He finds the very pillars in their houses "queynteli icorven with curiouse knottes" (13.161) and a few lines later mentions the house's "postern in pryvytie, to pasen when hem liste," which seems vaguely sexy, even as it stresses costliness and pride of possessions. So does the description of the elaborate habit "queyntly ybotend, / Lest any spirituall man aspie that gile" (17.296–97) and the scapular "ysewed with whight silk, and semes full queynte" (25.552). The other five instances are all harshly negative— the devil, for example, is "ful queynte" (23.482). But all the instances share a distrust of elaboration, of anything "queyntliche entayled" (14.200), reinforcing the Wycliffite value placed on ethical simplicity and doctrinal openness.

Characteristic of a general distrust of *queynte* stratagems, whether produced by human or diabolical ingenuity, is the Sloane *Secretum Secretorum* description of the body type of the strategist: "Who that has a right schort nek, he es ful queynte, sotel, gylous, and fraudus" (13.14). In *Cursor Mundi* we find: "The nedder [adder] that ys so quaynt of gyle... / That most con of croke and wyle" (739), and later, castigating women's adornments: "Yee leuedis...studis hu your hare to heir...hu to dub and hu to paynt, and hu to mak yow semle and quaint [here the result of craft: attractive]" (28015). In *Conquest of Ireland* Reymond is faintly praised for strategic "queyntyse," but denied the gentility of knighthood: "he [Reymond] was a man fre and meke, queynt and Purueynge; and thegh he wer Swyth hardy, and wel taght in wepyn, of queyntyse and of Sleght in fygh[t], and of Stelth in battayl, he Passid al othyr...he was bettyr ledder of hoste than knyght" (99.22). In the Chester Play, Satan uses the term to refer to his stratagem in Eden (21.198; 218.14).

Considering its association with the unusual and mysterious (as when Merlin's claim to walk with dry feet on water and make rivers appear is met with the narrator's "these be queynte craftes" [*Merlin* 309]), it is not surprising that *queyntise* turns up in connection with witchcraft. In *William of Palerne*: "ɜif thi wif of wicchecraft be witti, riɜt wel i hope sche can with hire connyng & hire queynt charmes, make him to me a-ɜen" (4136). Lydgate's *Troy Book* tells of a drink made "by quentyse eke of hir instrumentys" (1.135), and the *Siege of Troy* explains how Achilles' mother, a witch, had taught him "faire quayntyse" (1339). A bishop in Mannyng's *Handlyng Sin* commanded a witch to cast a spell: "do thy quentyse" (519). The link with witchcraft, though, is just the extreme expression of a more generalized sense of woman's exotic nature; the Middle Ages also asked Freud's famous question "What does woman want?" which posits both an unknowable and an historically constant "want." Woman's "to-be-looked-at-ness," in Laura Mulvey's coinage (14–26), marks the female as a domain of knowledge (hence, to "know" a woman), particularly her sexual equipment, which is called her *queynte*, but as a domain which is arcane, exotic, dangerous, and not usually recommended. As a male defensive move, all femininity is tainted seductive and unknowable, "she is the witch, he the bewitched," and at its outer limit of mysogyny and fascism the failure of pure militaristic nationalism is a morass figured as "the vagina of a giant whore" (Theweleit 304, 392).

One thing this chapter argues is that the double (and seemingly paradoxical) view of woman as both unfathomable enigma and eternal

~~essence~~ ~~belongs~~ ~~as~~ ~~well~~ ~~to~~ ~~pre-Freudian~~ ~~medieval~~ and early modern discourses about the feminine and that the bifurcated—and fused—meanings of *queynte* provide its trace. Sheila Delany argues that punning and other kinds of disorder in language are liberating, and while I agree that they are *linguistically* liberating, I do not find that their *social* effects necessarily are, although it is an empowering gesture for criticism to identify misogynistic language ("Anatomy" 30–32). In this case, paronomasia and bivalence mark as female a more generalized sense of adornment, over-elaborateness, cunning, and chicanery, sometimes reaching all the way to witchcraft.

Discourse queyntliche entayled

The possibilities for puns and other erotic wordplay created by this situation are amply seized upon by Middle English writers. Intricacy and its threatening underside are nicely captured in Chaucer's phrase describing a gown in his translation of *The Romance of the Rose*: "al toslytered [slit] for queyntise" (569). Such a gown is slashed just enough to show its beautiful lining—a nice trope for a style of medieval sartorial display and also for a cultural preference for indirection and sleight. This peek-a-boo strategy turns up frequently in passages where medieval writers put the term *queynte* to use. Lydgate's practice is a common one: the subject of discussion or narrative situation is sexy and someone is said to behave deviously, *queintly*. In the *Troy Book,* he writes: "Hercules...Hir to comfort dide his besynes, Al feynigly...As this louerys ful queynt can it make, / Til thei han had hooly her plesaunce" (1.3690), and "Medea the maiden made hym [Jason] all new, / By craft that she kouth of hir coint artys" (125). In *Pilgrimage*, "She [Chastity] wyl no queyntaunce han with me [Venus]" (13208), the pun is hard to miss. Stephen Scrope's *Othea to Hector* deploys the pun twice in connection with Criesyde: "Cresseide was a gentilwoman of grete beaute, and yit she was more queint & sotill to drawe peopill to hir" (102.14), and "Queynte him not...lete him beware that he aqueinte him not with such a lady as Cresseide was" (102.29). Thomas Hoccleve defends women in his "Letter of Cupid to Lovers" but admits that they are generally accounted "sly, queynt, and fals, in al vnthrift coupable." *Lessons of the Dirige* puns on both *queynt* and *corage*: "My spyryt shal be feble and feynt...When I am fallen in any age; My dayes, make I neuer so queynt, Shullen abrege and a somwhat swage, And I ful sone shal be atteynt Whan I haue lost myn hote corage" (447).

Piers Plowman offers a yet more obvious sexual pun in the C Text: "Mede mornede tho and made heuy cheere / For the comune called hure queynte comune hore" (5.161). The A Text has "I... was war of a womman wondirliche clothid... / In red scarlet robid & ribande with gold; / There nis no quen queyntere that quyk is o lyue" (214). But Langland has other uses for the term, sometimes (but rarely) merely "ingenuity": "the pileris weren y-peynt...And queynteli i-coruen" (161), and more often an argument for plainness not unlike Wycliffite senses: Surquidous and Spille-loue threaten to color the cart cristendom "so queyntely and couered vnder [oure] Sophistrie / That Conscience shal no3t knowe who is cristene or hethene...With swiche colours and queyntise cometh pride yarmed" (B, 19.347–51). The threat of successful deceit is the first note sounded in the A version: "Summe putten hem to pruide, apparaylden hem ther-after / In Cuntinaunce of clothinge queintliche de-Gyset" (1 prol. 24). Since some of Langland's instances of *queinte* acknowledge its female domain, the sense "craftiness" invites that suggestion by forcing a reader/listener to select from the two possibilities.

The *Pearl*-poet provides a number of positive instances of *quaint*. *Pearl* uses *Koyntyse* to mean "Wisdom" (690) and *Patience* calls God's unfathomable forgiveness "quoynt soffraunce" (417). In *Saint Erkenwald* it refers to wonderful sounds (889, 133) and an undecayed body (74). In Christ's parable of the raggedly dressed wedding guest in *Cleanness* the term refers to proper dress (160), spiritual savvy (54) and intricate carvings (1382, 1457); and in *Gawain* it refers to lovely cushions (877) and meals (999). These associations with exalted skills and effects make the instances in decidedly sexual contexts especially interesting. In *Cleanness*, Lot protects the angels who are his guests by offering his unruly neighbors the sexual use of his virgin daughters, claiming that they are "rype, and redy to manne" and "tayt [attractive] arn and quoynte" (869, 871). This "quoynte" can mean beautiful, but the sexual aura of the passage works against its meaning that alone. In *Gawain* the lady upbraids Gawain for not speaking to her of love, considering that he must be "so cortays and coynt of your hetes" (1525). Another such instance occurs in the much-discussed "anti-feminist tirade" in which Gawain accuses the ladies of the household: "wyth hor kest [contrivance] han koyntly bigyled" their knightly guest (2413). Once again, the nature of the beguilement was so clearly sexual that one can hardly see this line as meaning simply "clever." When Bertilak describes Morgan's role in the events Gawain has just survived, he attributes her powers to "koyntyse of clergye, bi craftes wel leried" from Merlin (2417), conflating the themes of female wiles (considering Morgan's history with Arthur) and clerical over-ingenuity to evoke witchcraft.

The most famous Middle English instance of *queynte* must be the identical rhyme of the couplet in Chaucer's *The Miller's Tale* in which Nicholas the Clerk of Oxenford comes to a sexual understanding with his landlord's young wife Alisoun:

> As clerkes ben ful subtile and queynte;
> And prively he caughte hire by the queynte.
>
> (I.3275–76)

Although this passage is sometimes referred to as punning, there is no pun in the second line—there *queynte* means "woman's sexual part" and nothing else. There may be an anticipatory doubleness in the first of the two lines, though, like that of many instances already discussed. What is really funny about this passage is the *lack* of scholarly subtlety Nicholas actually uses on Alisoun, especially in comparison with his over-elaborate plot to keep her old husband out of the way. The first *queynte*, then, is comical because it calls on what must have been a familiar association of clerics with arcane wisdom and craftiness, only to manifest another late fourteenth-century anti-clerical stereotype— the unabashed seducer of women—in the next line.

The two directions for the term in this couplet may be followed in several other Chaucerian instances. The most obvious appearance for the sexual direction is Alisoun of Bath's handbook on taming old husbands in *The Wife's Prologue*. Whether she is faithful or not, she taunts: "Ye shal have queynte right ynogh at eve" (III.332). What's the matter, she scolds them, "Is it for ye wolde have my queynte allone?" (III.444), only to reassure them that she does not, in fact, "selle," since if she did she would be "freshly" turned out.[2] In some manuscripts Alisoun's "I hadde the beste quonium [a euphemism from Latin] myghte be" (III.608) appears as the homelier *queynte* instead. These are not puns either but simply namings, although Alisoun does pun once, when she opines that women want what they cannot have and cease to value it if available—this is a "queynte fantasye" (517), an odd quirk in their makeup, but one which pointedly involves sex. The effect of these forthright namings for the discourse of *The Canterbury Tales*, though, is to place the sexual meaning of *queynte* clearly in play as one component of the reader's or hearer's expectations.

Chaucer's other implication for *queynte* concerns verbal (usually clerical) sophistication. This is the Canon's Yeoman's implication when he explains: "Oure termes ben so clergial and so queynte" (VIII.752). None but adepts can follow the cant that surrounds the "elvysshe craft" of alchemy. (The Yeoman says he learned from a clerk the pleasure of seeing others in painful bafflement because they could not follow fast talk, in a slight nod toward the Wycliffite position.) To be clear and reasonable, as the narrator in *The Book of the Duchess* expresses it, is to be "nouther towgh ne queynte" (531), an idiomatic phrase found quite frequently in Middle English. The third instance of *queynte* in *The Miller's Tale* unites sexual implication with that of verbal intricacy. Poor old John, puzzled, but impressed, by Nicholas's prediction of the flood, "to his wyf he tolde his pryvetee, / And she was ware, and knew it bet than he, / What all this queynte cast was for to seye" (I.3603–05). The "queynte cast" here is clerical sophistry, indeed a clerk's strategem, and, equally strongly, a cast to get queynte. This is a consummate pun; it functions both thematically and syntactically, and it depends on the establishing of both senses of the word in the Chaucerian lexicon.

   Before leaving *The Miller's Tale*, I want to comment on yet another of the many ways it replies to *The Knight's Tale*. Warm critical positions have been devoted to protecting the scene in which the parfit gentil narrator declines to describe Emelye bathing as a rite before the shrine of Diana (e.g., Benson 23–47). The Knight dares not tell, and "yet it were a game to heeren al" (2286). As Emelye awaits a sign from the goddess,

> Sodeynly she saugh a sight queynte,
> For right anon oon of the fyres queynte
> And quyked agayn, and after that anon
> That oother fyr was queynt and al agon;
> And as it queynte it made a whistelynge.
>
> (2333–37)

Here all but the first instance of *queynte* clearly means "quenched," "went out," and the first means something like "marvelous." These do not seem to me to be puns which meet all grammatical specifications, but a second variety of double meaning which colors and is colored by the narrative context. These dying and quickening fires are, after all, portents of Emelye's sexual career—they are about her sex, which the knightly narrator has valiantly tried *not to mention* directly (assuming the Knight's gentility; if Terry Jones is right that he is intended to be read as a mere lowborn mercenary, the case for an obscene pun would be even stronger). My point is that the plot itself and the narrator's cautiously averted glance cannot but bring the sexual meaning to mind. This narrative strategy is consistent with the frequent uses of *occupatio* in the Knight's telling; he is continually announcing that he will not describe something. His lifelong habit of eschewing vileynye in speech cannot protect him from the unpredictable sliding together of signifiers nor his discourse community's (and perhaps his own) pleasurable *frisson* at the result.[3] The first "queynte" in this passage is registered from Emelye's point of view. Its immediate implication ("strange, mysterious") is, of course, also linked with a pagan "clerical" subtlety, perhaps even stratagem, since the deities in all three temples deceive their worshippers. But, again, this particular mystery concerns Emelye's sealed or available sexuality. The Knight had referred to Arcite earlier in the tale as subject to the changing moods of "thise loveres in hir queynte geres" (1531), and the mystery is erotic there too. What Chaucer has done through the Miller's forthright namings and punnings with *queynte* is to make the timidity of the Knight's discourse about sex the butt of his joke, even in using *yqueynt* to mean "quenched" in an explicitly sexual context when Absolon's "hoote love was coold and al yqueynt" (3754) by his unfortunate kiss.

Country matters

Although John Florio's Italian–English dictionary uses *quaint* to mean "woman's priuities" as late as 1598 (*Becchina*: "a womans quaint or priuities"), in the practice of most early modern writers, the Middle English *queynte* has split into artful, curious, or proud, spelled *quaint*, and veiled suggestion of the sexual organ spelled *cunt* or *coun*try. The Middle English past tense and participle *queynte* or *y-queynte* for "quenched," dropped out with many other Early Modern English morphological standardizations, eliminating the possibility of word-play like Chaucer's in *The Knight's Tale* and *Troilus*. What seems to have happened Hock calls "tabooistic distortion"; a signified regarded as unmentionable is called up in a disguised form "without actually uttering the awesome word" (305).

The rebukes offered by courtesy books in the late Middle Ages stand as testimony to its low standards of hygiene and "social propriety" concerning bodily functions, but those books may have gradually modified people's behavior, first at court and later more broadly. The sixteenth century saw attempts to raise standards of taste in ordinary households, and the direction was to control or disguise the workings of the body "lower stratum," in Bakhtin's phrase. Another contributing factor is the standardization of the various dialects spoken and written in Britain, a result, of course, of the rapid growth of an English printing industry and its relatively centralized establishment in London. The localized languages of the mystery plays (which were banned anyway in 1576), Rolle's *Psalter*, and *The Book of Margery Kempe* were overwhelmed by the output from the presses of London and the continent, largely in a London dialect, and increasingly subject to surveillance and censorship from court and city. Whether one lived in the city or not, a copy of the Bible in English, *The Book of Common Prayer*, and Foxe's *Acts and Monuments* was likely to be present in a nearby church. Benedict Anderson's argument that the nation is an imagined community with a solidarity which depends in part on its revered truths being available in the vernacular (46) is deeply relevant here. A specifically English form of moral and civil behavior was reinforced by the uniformity Elizabeth legislated for religious observance and, from another, less obvious, quarter, by the popularity of the London theater.

When a nation begins to image itself a community, it must imagine itself as a particular *kind* of community. In terms of our present subject, one feature of that Englishness was the projection of a certain propriety, law-abidingness, and open dealing, in contradistinction to the sexual license (pox as the French disease) and malign ingenuity (Italian poisons) of Catholic Europe. Partly as a consequence of the national image of propriety, the Middle English *queynte* as the name of a female body part occurs in writing less and less often. The more obvious puns, even in popular pamphlets, are hard to find; wordplay itself is driven to deeper subtleties. But art is energized by libido and the need for subterfuge, and its play with the word *queynte* by no means disappears. What this new world requires of its language is, simultaneously, the *frisson* of sexual nuance and the fastidiousness befitting English restraint.

Edmund Spenser is a master of innuendo. His instances of *quaint* (nine of them) in *The Faerie Queene* may all be read as "intricate," "unusual," or "exhibiting exotic tastes," as in Florimell's willingness to sit down on a cottage floor because she was "nothing quaint / Nor s'deignfull of so homely fashion" (3.7.10.5) or the "queint elect" colors of the hyena-like beast called in by the witch later in the canto (22.5). Yet even in these seemingly inoffensive cases, *queint* comes up in erotically saturated scenes, and the verbal company it keeps include words like "rude," "lewd," "kindling," "corage," "uncouth," and "blood," all of which can suggest sexual licentiousness. The hyena is explained as a beast "that feeds on womens flesh as others feede on gras." Scudamour describes the "second paradise" in Book IV thus: "Nor could hart wish for any queint device, / But there it was, and did frail sense entice" (10.22.8–9). In Book V, the text endorses Britomart's virginity and her "queint disguise" of knighthood to protect her in her dynastic quest, and yet the word occurs in an interpretation of her dream that she was mated by a crocodile and gave birth to a lion (cantos 16–20). This does not work like paronomasia, even in its subtle versions, but as a feature of the general coloring of the scene—if her dynastic fate is to unfold, Britomart will have to come to terms with the physical body she is currently suppressing by disguising as male.

Philip Sidney plays archly with the possibilities inhering in both *quaint* and *country* in Book II of *New Arcadia*. Musidorus, disguised as the shepherd Dorus, is courting a rustic named Mopsa as a screen lady for Pamela, his true love. "Mopsa, though in my conscience she were even then far spent towards me, yet she answered her that for all my quaint speeches she would keep her honesty close enough" (139.24–26). "Honesty" here is clearly sexual purity, so the *quaint* must mean sexually seductive, although Dorus's elaborate court manner must also seem exotic to this simple woman. A sly Zelmane (Pyrocles in female disguise) comments to Dorus's mentor in the rural arts, "I shall grow skilful in country matters if I often have conference with your servant" (141.10–11). This is a layered joke, which is intended to further the deception of Musidorus's disguise, while it allows Zelmane/Pyrocles to talk with his cousin about love and pastoral terrains (country-ness); it is as if the courtly fiction, itself disguised as rural, condescends to revisit a crude past era. All the while, the poem maintains its standard of linguistic propriety and elegance.

Shakespeare's Touchstone does some consummate punning in his phrase "country copulatives" (*As You Like It*, V.iv.55). He means those intending the sex act, but his "country" could refer either to where the couples live or to what they want. The "country footing" Iris calls for in the wedding masque in *The Tempest* (IV.i.38) is surely to be read as an old-fashioned fertility celebration, now imitated (and of course distanced from Ferdinand and Miranda) by refined and courtly magic, suggesting both condescension to rural habits and a highly sanitized version of what might earlier have been unabashedly obscene. Puck's "country proverb known" (III.ii.458) in *A Midsummer Night's Dream* is that "man shall have his mare again." Puck is direct and earthy where

Paris, answering Diomede's charge that Helen is a whore, seems to cooperate with the charge: "You are too bitter to your country-woman." Diomede returns "She's bitter to her country," which is not a complete pun syntactically (as Paris's is) but which keeps the innuendo going (*Troilus and Cressida*, IV.i.68–69). The Frenchman in *Cymbeline* who reports the drinking bout in which the men were praising "our country mistresses" has the same steamy underlayer (I.vi.57).[4]

Hamlet's "country matters" (III.ii.116) pun is important to the unfolding tensions of the play. Sitting down at Ophelia's feet, he asks her,

> Lady, shall I lie in your lap?
>
> OPHELIA: No, my lord.
> HAMLET: I mean, my head upon your lap?
> OPHELIA: Aye, my lord.
> HAMLET: Do you think I meant country matters?
> OPHELIA: I think nothing, my lord
> HAMLET: That's a fair thought to lie between maids' legs.
> OPHELIA: What is, my lord?
> HAMLET: Nothing.

Hamlet is always one step ahead of Ophelia in this scene, making her think he is propositioning her and then embarrassing and chiding her for thinking so. (In his over-heated excitement about the quaint device of the mousetrap he has designed, he carelessly undermines her trust in him and perhaps in her emotional stamina.) He is also playing to Gertrude's supposition that he is merely a madcap lover, and to Claudius's desperate hope that his unpredictability ends there. But Hamlet may also be regarded as not able to keep his disguises and his inner life controllably separate—he is inadvertently revealing his desire to make both Ophelia and Gertrude think about their bodies, and to win this small measure of sexual control of both of them from Claudius and Polonius (Freud).

Shakespeare also plays a subtler game with *quaint*, as do other early modern playwrights.[5] Katherina's and Hero's *quaint* gowns are probably merely curiously designed, fashionable—although both of them are elaborately described as "toslytered." The rhetorical skills of various courtiers in the *Henry VI* plays are merely ingenious, although the possibility of over-elaborateness which deceives is lightly suggested. But in several instances, the context is so sexualized that an echo of sense may be clearly heard: Ann Page appears dressed "quaint in green" to identify her to a lover in *Merry Wives*, and the "quaint mazes in the wanton green" have been disrupted by the marital dispute between Titania and Oberon in *A Midsummer Night's Dream*. Portia's proposal that she and Nerissa imitate "fine bragging youths" who can "tell quaint lies" suggests bravado in general, but also sexual boasting. "Fine apparition! My quaint Ariel" seems to combine implications of the artful and exotic appropriate to Ariel's special nature, but it links him/her as well with sexual unfathomability.

In John Webster's *Duchess of Malfi*, Bosola describes himself as court intelligencer as "a very quaint invisible devil in flesh" (I.ii.181). While *quaint* here can be glossed as simply "cunning," the conjunction with hiddenness, flesh, and witchcraft would seem to feminize it. Bosola certainly regards his role as a spy as unmanly, stripping him as it does, of his moral agency. The coincidental falling together of Old French *coint* with Germanic *cunt* into Middle English *queynte* allows the formation of this very chain of associations. That chain connects intelligence—as both discernment and spying—witchcraft, and a piece of female flesh, and is anchored ultimately to women, to some secret knowledge or efficacy gendered female. The worldly-wise, like Chaucer's Robyn the Miller, regard this mystery with an awe they also extend to "Goddes pryvetee," and do so quite frankly. Norbert Elias's thesis in *The Civilizing Process* that "a stronger restraint" of emotion, language, and manners is related to the formation of the early modern nation-states describes early modern England fairly well, at least in terms of its printed texts. That stronger restraint which defined English proprieties suppressed several of the terms referring directly to the body and its "lower stratum" functions, including one of the medieval senses of *queynte*. Yet the resiliency of the double-entendre *queynte/quaint* through more than two centuries of social change suggests the durability of the links between its early meanings, even as its sexually inflected suggestions must become ever subtler.

10
Sely/Silly

The silly buckets on the deck
That had so long remained
I dreamt that they were filled with dew;
And when I awoke, it rained.

Samuel Taylor Coleridge, *The Rime of*
the Ancient Mariner

I have worried from time to time about those silly buckets ever since I read Coleridge's poem for the first time in the ninth grade. Mention of the buckets immediately follows the Mariner's prayer of thanks to Mary for the blessing of sleep and participates in his salvation. Since a twentieth-century reading of *silly* would not do, I put down the striking diction of the passage to a general romantic attempt to evoke the Middle Ages. Only recently has the philological precision of the passage struck me. These buckets were *silly* as merely "useless," "of no account," when there was no rain for them to catch, but as "blessed and bringers of blessing" when the Mariner opened himself to the beauty of the sea snakes and thereby induced the rain.

Sely comes into Middle English from Old English *saeliȝ*, "fortunate," as "blessed, spiritually favored, carrying blessing." It is found as early as the Bodleian Homilies (1175) in that sense. The noun forms *selth* ("well being") and *unselth* or *onselth* ("misery") turn up in the thirteenth century, but after that records of them are slim.[1] *Sely* is available to Chaucer to translate "nuptiis felix" from Boethius's Latin to "wel and zelily ymaried," suggesting happily and perhaps even wisely married. Although in a few instances its sense of innocent as harmless shades into helpless, Middle English *sely* most often conveys a positive sense of guilelessness. A frequent implication of *sely*, therefore, contains a built-in irony about power, for calling a person *sely* in Middle English conveys both apparent victimization and ultimate moral enfranchise- ment. The affect associated with the term is pathos. The efficient capture of this implication for his retrospective form and fable in "silly buckets" accounts in some measure for the haunting ethos of *The Ancient Mariner* for the Romantic project.

The story this chapter tells is about the gradual abandonment of a structure of feeling valorizing innocent piety (the valley that shall eventually be exalted) for a more entrepreneurial sense of human control of knowledge and social welfare. Under pressure from Protestant insistence on personal moral vigor, the subject position of passive innocence marked by *sely* loses privilege steadily, and the word itself slides toward its surviving sense. The *OED* includes no instances under "happy" after 1483, none under "blessed" after 1400, and only one under "innocent, harmless" after 1604—and that one (a reference to "what seely shepherds may have gathered from an angel's song") uses archaic diction for rhetorical effect. In the Paston letters, "sely labour, which is no labour" is called sloth (II.22); that is, in 1461 *sely* could appear bereft of its hallowed associations. By the middle of the sixteenth century, a few instances connect defenselessness with low estate—the "silly lass" loved by a king and the "silly heardman" stand- ing astonished, and by 1600 Camden could refer to a "seely soule" as merely simple-minded. *Richard II*'s "silly beggars" sitting in the stocks in Shakespeare's play are both hapless and unwise (V.v.25). But between its many medieval instances as "blessed" and its early modern instances as "foolish," *sely/silly* passes through an oddly nuanced asso- ciation with women and sheep.

Sely saints

Sely is common in Saints' Legends (which pre-date our period) and in miracle plays, and its implications are deeply respectful in these genres. *Sely* is given as the response in a Primer from around 1425: "Cely art thou, hooli virgyne marie, and worthiest al maner preisyng" (*MED*). "The Jewish Boy" from Vernon 124b–125 describes its miracle, the unharmed child, and all the people "Wondred on that selly siht, / And heried God with good entent" (*MED*). Julian of Norwich uses the word for people in general, not just women and children: "our good lord shewed that it is full great plesannce to him that a sely sowle come to him naked, pleaynly" (*Showings*, Long Text 5.34–35). In this formu- lation, every soul properly disposed (and spiritually exposed) pleases

God by its unpretentiousness and vulnerability.[2] These instances link the *sely* with the godly, and Chaucer's *Legend of Good Women* echoes its predecessors in the Legend genre by treating (however ironically in the end) its female protagonists as holy innocents betrayed. A disproportionate eight instances of his 43 occur in the *Legend*, four in the story of Dido alone, where *sely* is linked with her name as a leitmotif. Philomene, Progne, Phyllis, and Hypermnestra are also celebrated as hapless innocents. *Sely* is nicely situated by its association with holy women to carry off the pathos these tales insist on while at the same time it playfully undermines (conveying just a whiff of the emergent sense "foolish") their sober assertion of piety.

Lollard writers use *sely* to signal innocence and blessedness just as the orthodox do, although for them a somewhat different range of actions will merit it.[3] For example, *Piers the Plowman's Creed* tells the story of the narrator's search for someone who will teach him the Apostle's creed in plain language. Refused by the various fraternal orders, he sees Piers, "a sely man me by, upon the plow hongen" (Dean's edition 21.421). The first implications of *sely* here are connected with pity, as the man and his poor laboring family are described, and again *sely* is used (442). But as it becomes clear that this is the true Christian who will teach the narrator his creed, *sely* begins to take on its full early sense of "blessed." Piers instructs the narrator, and each calls the other *sely*, uniting them in the quest for holiness. Piers then warns him about the persecution of accused heretics (clearly Lollards) by prelates who disobey Christ's command and "sythen [then] the sely soule slen" (28.668). By this time the link is established between the Wycliffite "heretics," Piers, and the narrator. After *sely* has been so thoroughly implicated in the anti-fraternal case the tract is building, it is nonetheless used for friars. The narrator inquires about Piers's antipathy to "thise sely pore freres" and "thise sely men" (28.672, 675), giving Piers the occasion to reply with a thorough-going tirade against the friars. *Piers the Plowman's Creed* both rewrites the trope of the suffering female saint as a male Lollard evangelist, and also makes good use of the current implications of *sely* as "carrying blessing."

In all the poems of the *Pearl* manuscript, *sely* identifies remarkable or marvelous events. In *Pearl* the hour of salvation is a "sely stounde" (659), surely "blessed," and the "sely bestez" on Noah's ark are the recipients of God's pledge of salvation in *Cleanness* (490). The storm in *Patience*, "gret selly to here," might be read as "awesome." *Gawain and the Green Knight* is, of course, full of wonders: Arthur's hall (28), the "sellyly blered" eyes of the old woman in Bertilak's castle (963), the old boar in the forest, "the sellokest swyn" (1439), the fact that no chapel can be seen "and selly hym thost" (2170). The "vncely swyn" (1562) Bertilak hunted down was itself unlucky, but also provided rough sport compared with Gawain's seemingly protected leisure at the castle. Gawain calls his pursuit of the Green Knight "a selly I may not forsake" (475), surely a marvel and even, in the end, a blessing Gawain tries to carry back to the court.

In such a semantic economy—a dominant sense which combines innocence with pity and an emergent *naïveté* hinting at foolishness— Chaucer uses *sely/silly* for a full range of effects in *Troilus and Criseyde*. Troilus is depicted as a hapless innocent at several key points: when he is asked about his love by Pandarus (I.871), when Pandarus presents his case to Criseyde (II.683), and when he visits her deserted house (V.529). Criseyde is figured as the "sely lark" caught by a powerful sparrowhawk (III.1191), in a passage that hints at a nice irony by glancing back at Troilus in the grasp of an inexperienced lover's shame: "sely Troilus [gan] for to quake / As though men sholde han led hym into helle" (I.871). Troilus himself speaks in the older idiom ("blessed" or "fortunate") when he resolves to die: "For sely is that death…That…cometh and endeth pain" (IV.503–04), but in a newer ("of little account") when he worries that in the Greek camp Criseyde will devalue the "sely Trojans" (V.525). Finally, though, Chaucer's narrator leaves us with an enigma when he refuses to chide "this sely womman" Criseyde "Further than the storye wol devyse" (V.1093–94). Is she now to be regarded as the innocent betrayed by a cosmic arrangement of circumstances and mores or, in an emergent sense of *sely*, as a foolish woman who betrayed a faithful martyr of love?

The Canterbury Tales demonstrates Chaucer's virtuosity in doing things with words even more vividly. Although Custance was not an official saint, *The Man of Law's Tale* tells her story in the Saints' Legend style:

> Greet was the drede and eek the repentaunce
> Of hem that hadden wrong suspecioun
> Upon this sely innocent, Custance;
> And for this miracle, in conclusioun,
> And by Custances mediacioun,
> The kyng—and many another in that place—
> Converted was, thanked be Cristes grace!
>
> (II.680–86)

All the accustomed features are included—the heroic-but-wronged woman seemingly helpless in her tormentors' hands, her divine deliverance, the conversion of onlookers, and the narrator's grateful prayer. The Clerk's "sely povre Griselda" (IV.948) and the "sely child" whose resolute singing for the Virgin Mary in *The Prioress's Tale* turned so dangerous (VII.512) are clearly being situated in this tradition, the boy from his first appearance in the story. It is also the way Harry Bailly feels the force of the Physician's tale of Virginia, "this sely mayde is slayn, allas!" (VI.292), stressing the destruction of an innocent. The Nun's Priest's description of the "sely widow" who lives a life of uncomplaining poverty (VII.4565) represents both a social and a spiritual ideal, a counter-figure to Chantecleer's flamboyance and pride. Saint Cecile's story, told in *The Second Nun's Tale,* is prefaced by a series of strained etymologies for "Cecile," designed (in the conventional style of Saints' Legends) to encapsulate the moral significance of a life in the name of the saint, although Cecile is nowhere in the tale directly called *sely*. Pathos is the stock response to be elicited by these instances of *sely*, although when seen as constituents of the larger frame of *The Canterbury Tales* that response is subject to various ironies. Griselda, for example, is blameless and pitiable (*sely*) when Walter sends for her to honor his new wife, but she quickly asserts a kind of willful obedience which gains her victory over her imperious marquis.

Chaucer also produces comic effects with *sely*. "Sely innocent" is the Cannon's Yeoman's lament for the duped priest who is the alchemist's victim, but it expresses contempt for his graceless and blind "conceit," taxing him with both intellectual and moral weaknesses. The hapless husband in *The Shipman's Tale* is *sely* as the bill-payer for his wayward wife even before the story gets under way (VII.1201), mock pity for a man simply foolish. The friar in *The Summoner's Tale* tries to claim the despised-by-the-world-innocent role as he solicits a donation from Thomas, but his "we sely friars" is a joke the Summoner presents as part of his picture of a duplicitous cleric. He uses the same word for Thomas's wife, the "sely innocent" who invites him into the house and whose simple piety deserves the term (III.1906, 1983). The turpitude of mendicants was often indicted on the grounds that they "penetrated houses" (both households and the house of conscience) as Paul had predicted of false teachers in 2 Timothy 3.6 (Szittya 287–313). (By an historical coincidence, the Authorized Version of that verse reads "Of this sort are they which creep into houses and leade captiue silly women," where Geneva reads "simple women."[4]) The two instances of *sely* in *The Summoner's Tale*, then, constitute a tiny, but elaborate, topical jibe.

Both of the two instances of *sely* in *The Merchant's Tale* feminize men and evoke an emergent sense of *sely*. Long suffering "sely Damyan" is mockingly figured as a helpless innocent, and Harry Bailly interprets the whole story as one which castigates women for their plots against "us sely men" (IV.1869, 2423). The Wife of Bath has fun with *sely* too. She upbraids her old husbands for dispraising *sely* (presumably long-suffering) wives, and calls Socrates a "sely man" for suffering Xantippe's abuse (III.370, 730), but her *tour-de-force* is her reference to her husband's "sely instrument" (III.132). This last brings together all that the Wife wants to stress: that the genitals are God's gift and there-fore blessed, that men (evoked by their distinctive part) are a little helpless, and that, put this way, the whole controversy over proper sex within marriage is a bit foolish.

The sustained irony of the quitting contest between the Miller and the Reeve, though, is on a yet bigger scale. Ten of the 24 instances of *sely* in the *Tales* are found in these two tales. *Sely* is a leitmotif for John the Carpenter, just as "hendy" is for Nicholas. The effects are complex: locally, there is some pathos for the simple, loyal husband—"this sely carpenter"—wronged by the clever student, while at the same time the generic shape of the story as fabliau makes John the old jealous husband fair game and inflects *sely* as foolish. By the end of the tale, though, a still-larger picture emerges in which the sly outfox each other, and John's position is to some extent redeemed (while also feminized) as the innocent undergoing harm. This is a reading based on the shape of the whole Canterbury sequence, which posits and then reconfigures even simple generic forms like the fabliau, not a claim about Robyn's intended message—for him "sely carpenter" may be intended simply as belittling the pilgrim carpenter Osewold (as Osewold believes). The "sely tongue" that Osewold the Reeve invokes in his prologue is a foolish tongue (I.3896). The clerks John and Aleyn are called *sely* three times, clustered around their embarrassing attempt to catch their horse. Perhaps the joke involved in the Reeve's personal requital is that it takes a real master plotter like Nicholas to hoodwink a carpenter, but a miller can be duped by mere naïfs. The wind blowing from the future varies and freshens Chaucer's usage.

Sely sheep

The strenuous, individualistic Christianity of the Reformation in England stressed internalized spiritual struggle and vigorous ethical and civic campaigns (even for women), challenging a dominant structure of medieval religious feeling. Where God alone is to be accorded obedience, and human innocence is theologically impossible, the lamb-like ideal marked by *sely* is destined to fade, and indeed only a generation or two after the return to England of the Marian exiles it seems to have become residual. In sermons and devotional tracts, the centrality of saints' lives as models of patience in suffering gave way to direct commentary on vernacular scriptural texts. John Foxe's *Acts and Monuments* was intended to supplant the *Golden Legend* with the stories of martyrs who lived vigorous and controversial lives and suffered for the vision of Apostolic Christianity during the dark centuries of papist superstition. *Sely* appears in this book in its emergent sense "foolish," though with a strong sense of victimization (II.793.17). But *sely* did not altogether disappear into *silly* in the sixteenth century. Its positive valences were particularly suited for the genres which made use of the pastoral's emphases on simplicity, nature, and female chastity. A good many of these instances feature sheep and women. For example, over one third of Spenser's uses of *sely* concern sheep (12 of 31 instances). For Shakespeare, too, many instances concern sheep directly (5 of 23), and most are self-conscious about their posited rusticity, as in Proteus's quibble with a servant in *Two Gentlemen*: "a silly answer, and fitting well a sheep" (I.i.81).

Why sheep? One explanation is that they are required by the pastoral form admired by the English in recent Italian writing, especially that of Ariosto and Tasso, as well as in works from antiquity. The pastoral reanimated an agrarian and politically uncentralized England as the setting for its restaging of medieval romance. Then again, sheep were accorded a high and unchallenged place in Christian imagery; Christ is both shepherd and Pascal Lamb. Sheep and, more particularly, lambs held their uncontested place in European Christianity, being continually contrasted with pigs (which have a "time out of mind" association with the disgusting, and into which unclean spirits were cast in Mark 5) or goats (which are condemned to God's left hand at the final judgment). In everyday life, sheep are not kept in or near the household, like dogs, and therefore do not become "creatures of the threshold," those "most likely to take on ambiguous meanings" (Edmund Leach, quoted by Stallybrass and White 47). They were far enough from the house to retain their links with the apostolic, the rural, and the sacred, but not understood as wily or aggressive.

For such reasons, sheep were not culturally coded to induce fear or loathing. But perhaps they should have been. Sheep were the basis of England's most important exports—raw wool and woolen cloth. Their

heightened role in the economy was praised by some, but seen as the
root of England's social ills by many others, including the character
More in *Utopia*:

> Your shepe that were wont to be so meke and tame, and so smal
> eaters, now, as I heare saye, be become so great devowerers and so
> wylde, that they eate up, and swallow downe the very men them
> selfes. They consume, destroye, and devoure whole fieldes, howses,
> and cities.
>
> (Robinson's translation 23)

More's analysis here is, of course, a critique of the enclosures, which
forced much of the hereditary peasantry from their homes to seek
urban or wandering employment in England's early steps toward
"modernization" and "free labor." Although More's uses of *sely* do not
focus on sheep, I want to use his ambivalence over the word to intro-
duce those versions of the pastoral utopia which do.

In Ralph Robinson's translation of *Utopia*, *sely* never occurs unequivocally as foolish. In two of its seven instances, Hythloday explains why
the Utopians abhor blood sport, since the pleasure taken in watching
"a selye innocente hare murdered of a dogge" (76) or in slaughtering
"seelye and wofull beastes [Latin: 'timidum']" (77) in hunting expedi-
tions is vicious. In Book I, the "poore selye, wretched soules" in
contemporary England are presented in similar roles of innocence and
victimization. Late in Book II, the similarity is made explicit.
Hythloday's argument is that laboring men are no happier or wealth-
ier than beasts, worse off, in fact, because the beasts are free of worry,
unlike the "seilye poore wretches [who] be presently tormented with
barreyne and unfrutefull labour" (112). Hythloday's sympathies are
clearly signaled in his medieval inflection for *sely*, and he uses it for
himself in Book I: what if "I selie man [Latin: 'rursus'] should rise up
and will them to tourne over the leafe" when the King's other coun-
selors are all urging national expansion through foreign war (36), and
for the "silie poore Utopians" in Book II, when wealth-loving foreign
ambassadors are trying to dazzle with rich clothing and jewels. In both
cases the early medieval sense of ethical purity set apart from worldli-
ness is being invoked. But *Utopia* as a whole offers a choice between his
full-scale endorsement of Utopian life and the skepticism of the character More, apparently willing to allow the Renaissance philosopher
the garb of holiness, but arguing for more practical political interven-
tions to produce a result, not perhaps altogether good, but less bad

("not verye badde"). I agree with Stephen Greenblatt that "More" and Hythloday represent Thomas More in dialogue with himself, still at this point in his personal history unable to subdue entirely his Luther-like desire for radical reform, but well aware of the havoc such reform would work in the world (*Self-Fashioning* Chapter 1). Whether one thinks *sely* here denotes sainted or foolish behavior depends on the assessment of the whole argument of *Utopia* which seems to me evenly and precariously balanced.[5]

Edmund Spenser generally links *silly* with the central trope of the pastoral genre, the care of sheep. This reference points toward both the eclogues of antiquity and the teaching (rather than sacrament-dispens-ing) function of the Reformation pastor. In the Dedicatory Epistle of *The Shepheardes Calender* "E.K." acknowledges the author's debt to Chaucer, and the poem's retrospective vocabulary is evident in its implications for *sely*. The "seely sheep" despoiled by irresponsible (read: "Popish") pastors (September) are innocent victims. A good many of Spenser's instances involve self references, in which the speaker claims innocence and bids for pity. Colin Clout explains his absence from court life in these terms: "I silly man ... Durst not adven-ture such unknowen wayes" (668–70). In *Amoretti* 20, the poet figures himself as, not only silly, but a lamb, who opines that lions usually disdain to eat "silly lambs" who acknowledge their power—the power, of course, of the cruel mistress. Sonnet 63 figures the poet as a "silly barke" imagining safe harbor ahead. As he popularizes the phrase "sely sheep," Spenser's practice is strongly appropriative—he drains his medieval/fairy world of its grounding in Catholicism, making his links with Christian innocence to a non-institutionalized (rural), apostolic simplicity.[6]

The Faerie Queene both evokes the Christian and chivalric past, and re-configures that past as amenable to Protestant structures of feeling, especially in Book I. Una first appears leading a white lamb on a leash, and she herself is "So pure an innocent, as that same lambe" (1.1.5.1), and at the same time the heir of powerful monarchs. The association of lamb, lady, moral worth and potential victimization (like Christ on Palm Sunday, she rides an ass and "inly" grieves) provides a traditional medieval pattern. But the link with *silly* is consistently complicated. The self-described "Silly old man that lives in hidden cell" (1.1.30.6) would seem to call up an unproblematized medieval image, but events prove this simple hermit to be the conjuring magician Archimago bent on separating Redcross and Una. His apparent austerity of life seems at first apostolic, but his discourse, strewn with saints, popes, and ave-Marys, came from a langue filed "smooth as glas" (see "Glose" above; 1.1.35.7). The "silly man in simple weedes forworne" (1.4.35.1) who falsely reports the death of Redcross is again Archimago in disguise. The fact that in this case he is mistaken, rather than lying, may signal the emergent sense of *silly* as "foolish." (Duessa, too, calls herself "silly Dame, subject to hard mischance" [1.2.21.3] and "silly maid" [1.4.47.7].) The only straightforward instance of innocent help-lessness in Book I is the "seely Lamb" (1.6.10.4) in an elaborate simile for Una's state among the woodgods; Una never calls herself *sely*.

Book II continues to discredit characters who claim themselves to be *silly*: Trompart, who is actually "Wylie witted and growne old / In cunning sleights and practick knavery" (2.3.9.5–6), and Occasion, who is far from being the "silly weake old woman" she claims to be (2.4.45.5). The little bird saving its silly life from a hawk (2.3.36.3) is the only innocent in sight. But the flexibility of Spenser's pattern of linguistic implication becomes clear in Book III, where Britomart and Florimel are referred to as "silly maid" and "silly Virgin" by the narra-tor. The non-ironized medieval usage is disrupted by the lament of the undiscerning and feminized Squire of Dames (3.5.51.1) and two refer-ences to Malbecco (the old goat), the first by himself to elicit pity and the second by the narrator, who is simply accusing him of folly. A particularly rich instance is the Captain's calling Pastorell "one silly lasse" (6.11.12.6) in order to make her seem a less valuable commod-ity to the merchants who want to buy her. *He* means that she is a rather inconsequential prize for him to be allowed to keep for himself, but the traditional associations of *sely* with helpless innocence are bound to register as well.

Philip Sidney relies heavily on the subtleties of *sely* in *The New Arcadia*. Many of its instances occur with pastoral emphases and tend to mean both "rustic, non-courtly" and "ineffective" (5.21; 446.20). In at least one case the connotations of "rustic" are reversed in favor of derivative, and consequently weakened, classicism: "Poor painters oft with silly poets join / To fill the world with strange but vain conceits" (212.6), suggesting the modern range of *silly*. Some play off old against new inflections of the word; for example, making her complaint against the woman-deceiver Pamphilus, his accuser alleges that "he flies so into the favour of poor silly women" (238.8). There is clearly an accusation of foolishness being lodged against women here, but the charge would be pointless if the claim of innocence were not also being pressed. A much stronger equivocation is produced by Zelmane in her masterful manipulation of the peasants' revolt. At a climactic

point, she stands alone against the mob: "if, in fine, it be so that so
many valiant men's courages can be inflamed to the mischief of one
silly woman, I refuse not to make my life a sacrifice to your wrath"
(285.31–33). This is a brilliant appropriation of the residual aura of the
saint's life as blessed, a sacrifice of one on behalf of many, an imitation
of Christ. At the same time, the choice of *silly* as a female-inflected
term works in a chivalric discourse in which "courages" is the male
term. The peasants are accused, on the one hand, of playing the role
of the mob asking Pilate for Jesus' death, and, on the other, of taking
unmanly advantage of a woman's lack of military prowess—a lack
disproved in the combat just carried out, and in fact unfounded, since
"Zelmane" is merely a disguise for Pyrocles.

Philoclea's defiance of her tormentor Cecropia is just as brilliant, but
in a different cause. "Thou mayst well rack this silly body, but me thou
canst never overthrow" (422.6–7). This is exactly the claim of the
Saints' Legends; Chaucer's Cecile defies Almachius's power by saying
that he can "oonly lyf bireve, / Thou hast noon oother power ne no
leve" (VIII.482–83). But the *silly* performs other work in this passage as
well. Philoclea is also devaluing her body, claiming it is weak, foolish,
or associated with the animal kingdom (as *silly* so often is in the
pastoral). *She* would not mind its loss altogether, as long as Cecropia
could be prevented from defiling it by forcing Philoclea into a
marriage with her son. Both sets of implication here connect Philoclea
with medieval sainthood, but there is no transcendant reference:
Philoclea's loyalty is offered to an earthly lover, one to whom her
parents have not given her in marriage. The appropriation of *sely* here
is a step toward the fusing of romantically inflected sexual desire and
Christian marriage.

Silly men

Perhaps the most striking feature of Castiglione's *Courtier* in Hoby's
translation is the gender inflection of *sely*. The several occurrences
which describe men suggest "foolish" as the predominant sense; the
sely men in Hoby's translation are, in fact, victims of jests (cf. 164, 171,
173, 232), and none of the aura of protectedness or blessedness seems
to apply to them. Even the passage which discusses the social grace of
euphemism ("alwaies covering a vice with the name of the next vertue
to it") is given a masculine example: "calling him that is sawcie,
bold...him that is seelie, good" as an unflattering trait (31). But for
women, Hoby uses *sillie* in praising those who were saintly but never

widely recognized. "Imagin then how many there have been of whom there is no mention at all: because the sillie poore soules are kept close without the pompous pride to seeke a name of holinesse" (203). The "seely soule" who died protecting her chastity (225) is a clear instance of innocence passing over into blessedness, and "seelie vertues" should not be put to vile uses (193). Some instances, still signaling innocence, suggest suffering or victimization as well, as with the "seely poore creatures taken with so many entisements" (233). Sometimes the sense of victimization is very strong, as in the warning against the witty "nipping" of women because on this point they "are in the number of sillie soules [Opdycke's translation: "are to be numbered among the weak"]...and therefore deserve not to be nipped in it, for they have not weapon to defend themselves" (169).

Arthur Golding's rendering of *The Metamorphoses* exhibits the same pattern: *sillie* for innocent threatened types like sheep, doves, lambs, fish, women and babies, with stress on their helplessness, and in one instance a soul "lately dead" wandering among the fogs of the Styx is called a "siely Ghost new parted" (92.541). In his touching rendition of the rape of Proserpine, Golding gives us a victim so young that when she lost her collected flowers in attempting to escape Pluto's grasp, "such a sillie simplenesse hir childish age yet bears, / That even the very losse of them did move hir more to teares" (111.501–02). In this case, *sillie* directs attention to the girl's uncomprehending sexual innocence and unfocused fear, without damage to her dignity. Other sixteenth-century instances share these implications of *naïveté* and the resulting pathetic tone. Samuel Harsnett's *Declaration of Egregious Popish Impostures* sees Catholic exorcism as "A Stygian comedy to make silly people afraid" (quoted by Greenblatt, *Shakesperian Negotiations* 170–71). Puttenham alleges that "God raised a reuenger for the silly innocent women" who were reviled by "some old malicious Monke" (14.15). Florio's Montaigne exhibits no instances of *sely* as innocent, but a good many as "simple" or "harmless," including ants (102.29), lice (107.33), kids (125.12), women (134.10), and a laboring man (131.33). But mankind as a whole is *silly*: "this silly and wretched creature man" (161), "silly wretch" (95), and the "silly weapons of [his] reason" (94), and when men are called silly, they are rarely being praised.

The street-wise English of the coney-catching pamphlets and city theater tend to use *silly* in its surviving sense for describing both men and women. To Gilbert Walker in *A Manifest Detection of Diceplay*, *silly* and even *silly souls* refers to the foolish, incautious victims of card-sharps. They are not divinely protected, female, or even innocent of greed themselves. Thomas Harmon's "seely man or woman" (*Caveat for Common Cursitors* [1566] in Kinney's *Rogues, Vagabonds* 118.9) is simply a victim of highwaymen. Thomas Dekker's *The Wonderful Yeare* (1603) has "he that can so cosen himselfe, as to pocket vp praise in that silly sort, makes his braines fat with his owne folly" (*Plague Pamphlets* 5.13), and the same unequivocal tone is evident in the *Gul's Horn-booke* (8.29, 11.29, 50.9).

The drama of the period is a little less single-minded about *silly* as "foolish," but that is nearly always its first implication, Christopher Marlowe's plays excepted.[7] Webster's Castruchio excuses himself for not laughing at a joke: he "scorn'd to seem to have so silly a wit, as to understand" (*Duchess of Malfi*, I.ii.49–50) and Mendoza in John Marston's *The Malcontent* schemes to supplant his "seely lord" (II.v.97–98) and calls Ferneze a "seely novice" (I.vii.73–74). "Vulnerable because foolish" is the implication of the Swordsmen in Beaumont and Fletcher's *A King and No King* and of Tim's reference to his duped father in Middleton's *Chaste Maid* as "my poor silly father" (II.ii.8). The modern sense is clear in most of Shakespeare's uses, as in *Othello* when Iago calls Roderigo a "silly gentleman" for offering to drown himself because of his rejection by Desdemona. Roderigo's reply, "It is silliness to live when to live is torment" (I.iii.307, 308) contrasts in tone with the desire of Chaucer's Troilus for a blessed, "sely," death. "Worthless" is what Autolycus means by calling his occupational skills a "silly cheat," a crafty use of the modesty topos to enlist sympathy (*Winter's Tale* IV.iii.28). The Widow's refusal to be brought to the "silly pass" of the wife-testing in *Taming of the Shrew* (V.ii.124) also suggests triviality. Orsino probably intends to recommend the "silly sooth" of the sentimental love song he orders to be played—"simple truth" the note in Harrison's edition calls it—but the audience may well see that sentimentality as flaccid and self-indulgent, silly in the emergent sense. The most memorable instance of this—dismissive—kind is Hippolita's reaction to the "rude mechanicals" play: "This is the silliest stuff that ever I heard" (*Midsummer Night's Dream*, V.i.212), but her dismissiveness is tempered in that Bottom has stumbled into quoting—or rather anticipating—Paul to the Corinthians on blessedness.

By the early seventeenth century, then, "foolish" seems to have become the established first meaning for *silly*. Two plays—*Bussy D'Ambois* and *Volpone*—though, make the paronomasia *sely/silly* important contributors to their overall interpretation. George

Chapman implicates the term *silly* in his treatment of sexual passion. Tamyra's temporizing speech about women's debt to nature in *Bussy D'Ambois* claims that Nature must "sweep away the silly cobweb / Of our still-undone labors" (III.i.49–50), suggesting both the cobweb's fragility and unwisdom. That cobweb is, in terms of the plot, the moral scruple that will keep Tamyra faithful to her unworthy husband in spite of her passionate attraction to Bussy. The play as a whole stands neatly balanced as to how the love affair is to be read (and indeed how all of Bussy's epic—or is it merely heedless—rashness is to be read). If the love is sin, Tamyra's "silly cobweb" is evidence of her willful misreading of the moral world, and the word should be read as *sely*, fragile, but saintly. If the love is being represented as heroic defiance of misguided (*silly*) tradition, an historically distant sexual revolution is being hinted at. *Bussy D'Ambois* resembles *Dr. Faustus* in that both are plotted like admonitory moralities, but rhetorically tuned to Renaissance aspirations for new worlds of profit and delight, each of these potential effects undercut by the other.

This brings us to Ben Jonson and *Volpone*. It has been suggested from time to time that Celia bears the name she does to further the play's depiction of the weakness of residual values in the face of the rapacious proto-capitalist schemes of characters like Volpone and Mosca: that she is foolishly outdated—silly. Celia certainly acts out the role of the female saint in the legends, preferring to "take down poison, / Eat burning coals, do anything" rather than visit Volpone privately (III.vii.94–95). But her eloquent insistence on the value of her sexual purity moves neither her niggardly, calculating husband nor her warmer, more ruthless assailant. It doesn't acquit her in court either, and all that keeps the play from a thorough-going nihilism is the comic overreaching which allows one knave to unmask another. Bonario's name signals his role in this allegory, and insofar as he is paired with Celia, his identification draws hers toward its Latin derivation "heavenly" (which Volpone acknowledges by courting her in the guise of Roman deities), and its Germanic roots call attention to protection by God because of innocence. Jonson's audiences are not being called to the side of the rapist, and yet this fiercely unsentimental play is not sanguine about Celia's safety. In exhibiting the irrelevance of Bonario and Celia's structures of feeling to the flow of events, Jonson is coming close to calling his heroine *silly* rather than *sely*.

"Cely art thou, hooli virgyne marie" was a response uttered by the faithful in the fifteenth century, but by the early seventeenth English

Christians were paying little homage to Mary in public worship and *sely/silly* had come to connote incapacity rather than awe—the silly answer befitting a sheep in Shakespeare's *Two Gentlemen*. Early modern discourse finds other terms, less associated with Catholicism's often female saints, for sympathetic reference to distressed innocence and valorizes instead intellectual grasp and personal force—the style of both Protestant and capitalist modes. Like the once neutral *lewed* and the once authoritative *gloss*, *sely* suffered a fall in prestige during the period of this study, but for *providence* the opposite is true, as the word for workaday provisioning was transformed under the influence of Calvinist Protestant modes of thought to theological and national importance and dignity. The fact that words may either lose or take on prestige in the process of historical change—rather than undergo an inevitable linguistic decline—points up the social and cultural nature of the process.

11
Thrift

Think of it as thrift.

> Mrs. Lovet in Stephen Sondheim's *Sweeny Todd*,
> persuading Sweeny to let her use the
> corpses of his victims for her meat pies

Thrift is derived from the verb "thrive." As early as *Hali Meidenhede* (1230) and as late as the late nineteenth century, it is found meaning "thriving," either physical or spiritual. Both Langland and Chaucer use it in this sense, and New England farm communities still refer to especially abundant crop growth as "thrift." Trevisa, in translating Bartholomaeus Anglicus, rendered *virorem* as "thrift" and *non proficiunt* as "faileth of perfect thrifte" (226.17). Spenser's plan in his *View of Ireland* is for English soldiers in Ireland leaving the military to "fall to thrift," by which he means husbandry (122); as he explains later, husbandry is "the nurse of thrift and the daughter of industry" (157) and the basis of his proposed reform of the Irish economy. Occasionally *thrift* takes on the sense "enterprise," as in Ripley's *Compend of Alchemy*, "also I wrorзte jn sulphour & in vitriall...and thus I blewe my thryfte at ye cole....My clothys were bawdy my stomake was never holle" (1883), or Lodge's "Reply to Gosson," "your giddy brain makes you leaue your thrift" (I.3). Sometimes this thriving is imagined rather directly as monetary or military profit ("pore mennys thrift"), sometimes as a more general, or even a distinctly spiritual, increase. The "ill thrift" that two of the shepherds in Towneley's *Secunda Pastorum* wish on the third when he asks for food seems a general curse (150), until the birth of Christ appears in the play to complicate the meaning of food itself.

What constitutes thriving or offers the means to thrive is clearly dependent on social, religious, and economic conditions. Its history is an instance of the successful appropriation into the early modern period of the cultural privilege a term had accrued in Middle English. From the late Middle Ages to the early seventeenth century, shifting social conditions and values stretch the word between two quite distinct meanings: nobility in status or manner and economy with resources—propriety and frugality. How the two potentialities within the term are deployed allows us to glimpse the medieval definition of wealth—lands, titles, and inheritance—giving way to monetary earnings in the early modern period, but even when its major emphasis began to fall on prudent saving, *thrift* retained its very positive moral aura. In his *Meditations*, Bishop Joseph Hall comments that "So devotion is counterfaited by superstition, good thrift by niggardliness" (99). A later example—and a very striking one—of thriving non-materially is Coverdale's "The entrie vnto immortall thrifte is throughe losse of transitorie thynges," but it does seem to depend for its striking effect on an understanding that thrift usually involved keeping a tight hold on "transitorie thynges." The ideological force of *thrift* works to naturalize first the proprieties attendant on feudal relationships and later the individual restraint required by urban nuclear families. Such restraint was raised to the level of a moral imperative by Protestant emphasis on the God-ordained nature of secular callings and the stewardship of economic resources. The value the Middle Ages placed on *fredom* and *kyndenes* as uncalculating generosity is replaced in Puritan communities by strict account-keeping. Mrs. Lovet's proposal that nothing be wasted is an extreme (and, of course, perverse) example of that parsimony with resources.

Thriving in the Middle Ages

"Propriety" is clearly the preferred meaning of *thrift* in medieval writing, occurring in five times as many passages among those dated before 1500 than "frugality" (not counting Chaucerian instances, which are likely to be undecidable). Armies consist of "thrytty thousand" knights "thryfty in armes" in the alliterative *Morte Arthure* and many other narratives, ladies bear *thrifty* children, Adam's descendants behaved "vnthryftyly vchon other" (*Cleanness* 267), readers are warned against *unthrifty* language, and many events take place "in thrifty wise." The Paston letters deplore a riotous neighborhood with "so many vnthriftys that it was gret parell to thrifty men to duelle there" (2.581). In *Knight of Tour Landry*, "unthrifty women" are defined as unchaste, and Thomas Hoccleve indicts some women as "sly, queynt, and fals, in al vnthrift coupable" ("Letter of Cupid to Lovers" 152). "By my thrift" as a mild oath is found frequently in Middle English and as late as David Lindsay's *Ane Satyre of the Thrie Estaitis*. The Hunterian medical treatise from 1425 suggests getting a "thriftye phisicien" to superintend a patient's purge (104), and to "thriftilye" sew up an incision (107), bind up a wound (126), and cauterize the root of a canker (150). Because of their immediate practicality, these medical uses seem especially persuasive cases of *thrift* as "appropriate," "suitable."

In Middle English even the charge of economic thriftlessness is usually accompanied by a hint of more general impropriety, as in Lydgate's *The Hors, the Shep, and the Ghoos*: "In thyn expences make no waste / Grete excesse causeth unthrift in haste" (28). His more common usage is directly moral: "These ben the children of tristesse, that slepyn in slouthe and lachesse / veyne and ful of ydelnes and al maner unthrift" (*Pilgrim Soule*, Caxton's printing, III.viii). In the *Troy Book*, Lydgate's narrator describes the elaborate banquet King Cellius prepares for Hercules and Jason, modestly denying that he commands the descriptive power to present the diversity of courses served up "ther-with-alle the noble officeris / Ful thriftely serued... / With alle deintes that may rekned be" (1.1538–41). Here the sense of propriety as abundance and display decisively denies the emergent potentialities of *thrift*, suggesting that propriety in a royal setting is extravagance. Yet in his *Fall of Princes*, Lydgate fuses the two senses in his rebuke to aging lovers:

> Thou vsist many riche restoratiff
> In suiche vnthrifft tencrece thi corage,
> Of ribaudi thou fill in such dotage,—
> How maist thou thanne rebuke me? For shame!
> Which in such caas art blottid with diffame.
>
> (VII.474–80)

These old men are the more blameworthy because sexual appetite must be supplemented through the use of "restoratiffs"—that these are "riche" suggests that "vnthrifft" is wasteful of resources, that they increase "corage" (here, clearly, sexual) suggests turpitude. The balance falls on lack of thrift as a moral failing, but interestingly implicates economic imprudence as well.

A similar fusion of implications is evident in the phrasing of the Ashmolean *Secretum*:

Yf any kyng have eyther of these 2 vices, that is to sey, avarice or prodigalite, he oweth thurgh thryfty counseill and full grete diligence, to purveye to gete vnder hym a discrete, trewe, chosen man, vnto whom he shall commytte the disposicion of the comone wele.

(33.12–16)

The "thryfty counseill" is certainly appropriate, proper advice, but because of the particular vices the king is worried about, it must also be counsel to parsimony, and not wastefully sought. In Fortesque's *Governance of England*, the term seems to indicate an echelon of the citizenry without rank, but with some property, unlikely to join an uprising "ffor dred off lesynge off their gode" (148). The Proceedings of the Privy Council (1443) refers to *thriftimen* as a kind of estate, along with prelates, knights, squires, and "other cominaltees within the countree of Lincoln aforesaide" (5.414). This usage of *thrifty* strongly implies both "frugal "and "proper," "decent."[1]

A different balance is struck by the preacher's metaphor in one of the Worcester Sermons where an *vnthrifti* man "hath noyther fruit nor leues vp-on hym, is nat able to come to non estat, no degre of wrchepe her-afterward" (36). The figure of the barren tree is biblical, and traditional in its indictments of a generally unproductive life, both spiritually and temporally. But the monetary implications of *thrift*, hinted at by *estat*, gives the metaphor itself a thrifty doubleness in which both meanings function, either together or separately, for differently situated hearers or readers. Such complex effects, made possible by certain fluidities in the social formation, are the stock in trade of poets like Chaucer. As instances of the "playfully creative ambiguity" Dominick LaCapra defended from the flatness of the ideal speech situation, Chaucer's range of effects in managing the implications of *thrift* is impressive. The non-ironic feudal sense "propriety" is sometimes unchallenged, sometimes undercut by faint traces of playfulness, and sometimes marked by strong suggestions of the emergent sense of the mercantile, the calculating.

Trojan court and Canterbury highway

In the courtly *Troilus and Criseyde*, *thrift* usually either simply means "thriving," "fortunate," or it clearly refers to aristocratic proprieties. Both hero and heroine are referred to as the "thriftiest"—for Troilus the attribution is linked with friendliness, gentility, and freedom (the natural *sprezzatura* conferred by royal birth), for Criseyde with ultroctivonons. At a crucial moment in Book I, when the arrow of love enters Troilus's heart as he glimpses Criseyde in the temple, he "gan her bet beiholde in thrifty wise" (I.275). Here Troilus's looking is *thrifty*, proper, because it almost immediately becomes prudent and secretive as he keeps his sigh unheard and composes his face into its "pleyinge chere" to hide his loss of composure. These are the actions of a prince who cannot put his emotional state on public display, a leader among youths whose male camaraderie depends on uncommitted gazing on women, and a lover who (it would seem instinctively) observes the secrecy proper to "courtly love."

In disclosing Troilus's love to Criseyde, Pandarus is skillfully calculating, resorting to a torturously deferred chain of confidences, but he uses the word *thrift* to characterize Criseyde's success in winning a prince's affection: "And right good thrift, I prey to God, have ye, / That han swich oon ykaught withouten net!" (II.582–83). He is congratulating her on being "thriving," or "lucky," but the word is also implicated in Pandarus's repeated attempts to make Criseyde the one with snares and nets—if we both die, he says, "Than have ye fisshed fayre!" (II.328). So far Criseyde has not been a plotter; her beauty is a power of nature like that of the "faire gemme" (II.344). To consider her options, she sets herself a "caas" to debate, in the course of which she reflects that Troilus might have "the thriftieste" woman in the town for his love (II.737). While the trend of the stanza suggests that this means "most desirable" or "worthiest," the details of her fabricated "caas" concern the risks involved in loving. Her reflection that Troilus's dependence on her ("And yet his lif al lith now in my cure. / But swich is love, and ek myn aventure" [II.741–42]) constitutes an entrepreneurial advantage is nicely captured by the ambiguities of "aventure" as either "chance" or "exploit." With these reflections she does begin to consider shaping events through calculated actions.

"Good thrift have ye!" is frequently a casual greeting in the poem, but Pandarus's "by my thrift" (III.871) may indicate his busy agency in promoting the affair. Still more pointedly, "by my thrift" is Criseyde's oath promising her return to Troy (IV.1630). At stake is her claim to the self-possession and cunning to outwit her father's "queynte pley" and her willingness to undertake risk to fulfill her plighted trouthe. The two senses of this claim appeal to different implications for *thrift*: the emergent "calculating" and the courtly "noble." In *Troilus and Criseyde*, the social proprieties are not just referred to but defined, and that definition contains a hint of the calculation which is presented as necessary to this kind of propriety. Calculation, in turn, retains the taint of its connection with Criseyde's treacherous father, who left his city when "this Calkas knew by calkulynge...that Troie moste ben fordo" (I.71 and IV.1398). And throughout the poem, Pandarus is shown to be manufacturing proprieties, disguising the lovers' motives and actions from each other and perhaps even from themselves. In this overtly feudal, courtly fiction, it would seem that the modulations of the word *thrift* constitute a small gesture which strikes at the naturalness of the aristocratic code, a hint that it is a construction for protection rather than an inherent sign of nobility, a contradiction Castiglione's *Courtier* will also explore.

On the road to Canterbury, some distance from the courtly scene of *Troilus*, other proprieties are called for, most of them suited to more pragmatic, sometimes market-oriented, sensibilities.[2] The "thrifty tale" the Man of Law at first says he cannot conjure up (II.46) is a memorable one suitable for his heterogeneous audience. Within his tale the merchants of Syria are sought after for their "thrifty" merchandise, in a fully economic instance of *thrift*, which may then be read back into the lawyer's earlier desire for a thrifty story and forward into her father's mercenary motives for marrying Custance to the Sultan, eliciting the bourgeois Harry Bailey's admiration for a "thrifty" morally improving tale (II.1165). In *The Merchant's Tale*, January's description of Damyan as a "thrifty man right able" (IV.1912) provides a delightful irony at January's expense, since Damyan's expeditiousness serves *him* efficiently but his feudal master improperly. The clerk in *The Franklin's Tale* greets Aurelius and his brother *thriftily* in Latin, a proper address for an educated elite (V.1174), but his *thrift*, as craft, is quickly linked to his uncanny knowledge of why they have come and recalls the denunciation of magical practices the Franklin-narrator has just delivered. Still further down the social scale, the husband in *The Shipman's Tale* admonishes his wife to conduct a "thrifty household" in his absence, a clear double entendre involving sexual and fiscal proprieties and frugalities which in this tale are poles apart. *The Canon's Yeoman's Prologue and Tale* contain five instances of *thrift* and *thrive*, more than any other tale. The tale begins and ends with warnings that anyone who comes into the alchemical trade will lose his thrift; what will be lost is both moral and social thriving.

Harry Bailey warns the raucous Miller not to insist on speaking immediately after the seemly Knight by begging him to "werken thriftily" (I.3131). I like this instance especially, since it makes use of a term from courtly proprieties to chide one of the lower-class pilgrims, holding him, as it were, to a standard set by his "betters." Yet by the end of the Miller's hilarious, ingenious, bawdy tale almost everyone, Onewold the Reeve excepted, was laughing together. The Miller's insistence on his improper intrusion into the order and decorum of the tales has produced a re-ordering, a parsimonious (because brief) and proper (because conducive to festive harmony) contribution to the pilgrimage. This moment fuses the sense of *thrift* as propriety with that of frugality without losing the edge of either and yet with the social import of humorously turning the usual order of protocol on its head. As a "playfully creative ambiguity," which discloses social contradictions rather than papering over them with mystifying equivocation, this passage can hardly be rivaled.

Early modern thriftiness

Frugality with resources is not scorned in the Middle Ages, but neither is it the overarching metaphor for value it will become. The greater prominence of urban and mercantile modes of production and exchange for many English people turned it into such a metaphor, aided by Reformation emphases on personal responsibility for one's calling and earnings. Lutheran and Calvinist arguments that all callings are equally holy opened a field for moral speculation at a time when new modes of trade and investment, greater social mobility, and wider circles of literacy required such speculation. The Book of Common Prayer does not use the word *thrift* itself, but it values parsimony in asserting that only it and the Bible will be needed for the conduct of the church, "by the means whereof the people shall not be at so great a charge as in past time they have been" (165). The saving is realized in clarity and (presumably) lack of dispute, but also in requiring fewer "authorities" to be bought and consulted. As these newer social and ethical discourses succeeded in including the still very positive term *thrift* within their domain, the word lost its aura of aristocratic propriety and became increasingly associated with a range of virtues we now call "middle class." Sixteenth-century discourse presents, I think, a clear case of appropriating the high positive valence of a term—in which a romance hero and heroine can be described as "thriftiest"—for use "within the logic of another political discourse," one inclined toward deciding, managing, and saving.

The range of meanings for *thrift* in the sixteenth century is indicated on the side of mixed implications by writing such as George Whetstone's, whose title of one section of *Rock of Regard* (1576), "The Garden of Unthriftiness," indicates its inclusion of "a number of vain, wanton, and worthless sonnets" which make the rest of the book more profitable by exposing "hot desires" (313). Thomas Tusser, less whimsically, named one of the poems in his *Five Hundred Points of Good Husbandry* "The Ladder to Thrift," which advises both economic parsimony ("climb to thrift by husbandry") and moral propriety. Robert Greene tells the fable of the ant and grasshopper in *A Groatsworth of Wit* in which, of course, the thrifty ant wins, and the grasshopper repents, admonishes the young, and dies comfortless. In Skelton's "The Bowge of Court," "unthriftiness" clearly appears as "impropriety," but in "The Tunning of Elinour Rumming" "Her thrift is full thin" suggests an economic meaning as the principal one. One of Sir Thomas Wyatt's Epistolary Satires explains laughter as "not at thee, but at thy thrifty jest," a proper joke that takes us back to Robyn the Miller (CLI.80). Defining *thrift* as monetary saving, the old servant Adam in *As You Like It* declares that he has "five hundred crowns, / The thriftie hire I saved under your Father" when he offers to help Orlando (II.iii.39).

Thrift occurs frequently in Thomas More's English work. It appears in both light and weighty English works over the whole range of its available meanings, sometimes with notable effectiveness. In "A Merry Jest," *thrift* means thriving, the means to thrive, saving, and, less directly, propriety; the theme of the poem is about staying within one's proper craft, a reminder that moral arguments for craft are not limited to Protestant circles.[3] In the course of the debate over sanctuary in his *History of King Richard III*, More's Buckingham argues that "unthriftiness" has brought the thieves and manquellers who hide in churches to nought, implying both the neglect of a craft by which they might have thrived and the impropriety of the seeking of sanctuary. *The Supplication of Souls*—More's reply to Simon Fish's attack on the doctrine of purgatory—contests Fish's claim that the poor should be given the alms currently used to support a self-indulgent clergy. More's ingenious answer (which risks making a devastating concession) is that worse social ills would result from the sudden turning loose of so many "vnthryfty / lewde / and nought . . . as he wolde haue them all seme" (156). If an over-numerous clergy impede egalitarian social progress, and if they are really as wicked as they are made out, defrocked they would merely add to the population of outlaws. The word "vnthryfty" makes More's point in both the system of production and consumption and that of moral "works." Speculating on the effects of replacing Catholic preaching with Luther's or Tyndale's, he alleges: "Then shall folk waxe ydle and fall to vnthryftynesse. . . . Then shall vnthryftys flok togyder and swarme abowte and eche bere hym bolde of other" (168).[4] The role "vnthryftynesse" plays here is crucial: thrift is respect for the "natural order," which bolsters its claims through both the coercive power of masters and rulers and the ideological power of God's anointed. Such passages seem comments on both impropriety and economic waste. In debating the social role of the clergy and the consequences of Protestant readings of the Bible, More meets Protestant reformers on their own pragmatic ground, rather than moving to more traditional theological arguments.

The senses of *thrift* in More's discourse are echoed in Philip Sidney's *New Arcadia*, where we read about a moated castle, "the work of a noble gentleman, of whose unthrifty son" (Dido's father) had bought it (244.34). The present miserly owner maintained it so badly that Pyrocles opines: "if that were thrift, I wished none of my friends or subjects ever to thrive" (246.26–27). The whole episode delivers a neat little defense of a *via media* in the use of wealth at the expense of both the wastrel son (the phrase "unthrifty son" will turn up in *I Henry IV* as well) and the miserly Chremes, who lamented the loss of his goods more than the threat to his daughter or his own disgrace. In *The Faerie Queene*, Wrath causes "unthrifty scath," both harm and loss, and life and goods are wasted in "thriftlesse howres" (1.4.35.3; 1.5.51.8). The "thriftless wast" is waste of life energies as well as goods and is paired with "lustful luxury" (2.12.9.3). And personified "Unthriftihead" appears in Cupid's train in the maske in Book III, canto xii. Thomas Wilson's *The Arte of Rhetorique* presents a rhetorician's learned resources as if they were negotiable goods, which demonstrates the inroads frugality had made as an ideal: "A good thriftie man will gather his goodes together in time of plentie, and lay them out againe in time of need: and shal not an Oratour have in store good matter, in the chest of his memorie, to use and bestowe in time of necessitie?" (209). Stephen Gosson's argument in *The School of Abuse* against novel inventiveness in stylistic matters carries on More's sense of *thrift* as right order: "vnthrifty scholers, that despise the good rules of their ancient masters & run to the shop of their owne devices, defacing olde stampes, forging newe Printes, and coining strange precepts" (85, cf. 124, 135). Gosson also seems to employ the word in its oldest sense, as "means to thrive," as in "Let them not look to liue by playes, the litle thrift that followeth theire great gain" is a sign that God has cursed the whole enterprise (196). But Gamaliel Ratsey commends acting in London as *thrift,* a way to get ahead financially, according to *Ratsey's Ghost,* a pamplet about him published after his death in 1605 (quoted in Gurr 81).

The cony-catching pamphlets make the same assumption, with mock solemnity about the ways one might thrive (or is it, finally, mocking?). They are all about thriving, and thriving improperly. *Thrift* appears in them often in phrases like "a ready way to thrift" (Gilbert Walker, *Manifest Detection of Diceplay* [1552] in *Rogues, Vagabonds* 82) or John Audeley's "Rinse Pitcher is he who will drink out his thrift" (*Fraternity of Vagabonds* [1561] in *Rogues, Vagabonds* 99). Thomas Dekker's *The Wonderful Yeare* gives a mocking account of England springing back into life at James's accession in 1603. Among the revivals is that of "the thrifty Citizen [who] casts beyond the Moone, and seeing the golden age returned into the world againe, resolues to worship no Saint but money" (*Plague Pamphlets* 23). The plague takes its toll of the worthy as well as the "vnthriftie servant" (33), and warns the parent of "one onely sonne" that he might be taken by plague, although he might be "thriftily ... the young Landlord of all thy care-full labours" (30). Each of these instances seems to play with the equivocation between respectability and frugality with the point that plague respects neither. *The Gul's Horn-booke* advises sleeping late as a means to thrift, "both in sparing victuals (for breakefasts therby are saved from the hell-mouth of the belly) and in preserving apparell" (22). Here the equivocation is obvious because the gaping hell-mouth is a still-recognized medieval image of the reward of sins like sloth. Gallants are advised not to frequent crowded ordinaries where the likes of "Thrift Atturney's" might be customers (45), and to encourage the "unthriftinesse of such yong tame pigions" in order to laugh condescendingly at their discomfort (59).

In plays about "citizens" the epithet "unthrift" carries a real sting in the discourse of the characters, but that very fact may be part of the subtle humor these plays invite, both by showing how concerned with monetary thrift these worthies are and by contrasting their purely economic judgments of value with the older sense of thrift as propriety.[5] The class-marked quality of the term is also seen from the other side, when, for example, Webster's Duchess of Malfi tactfully divests herself of princely hauteur by speaking of economic *thrift* in her wooing scene with Antonio, and puns on *husband* at the same time: "It's fit, like thrifty husbands, we inquire / What's laid up for tomor-row" (I.ii.285–86). The tone the Duchess conveys is one of tender concern, but the same phrase, "thrifty husband," is offered by Maffe to Bussy D'Ambois as an insult, implying that he is unfit for court (I.ii.212). Bussy here stands for earning his way, having earlier claimed that "unsweating thrift is policy" (I.i.124), gain gotten by trickery rather than effort. *Thrift*, as good order in households and kingdoms, marking the increasingly important division of the producer from the freeloader, yet suggests the artisanal rather than the gentle, and this fact illuminates Shakespeare's social map of England.

Hal, Shylock, and Hamlet

Shakespeare uses *thrift* in the Henriad to pose some of the major themes of the plays. In *Richard II*, the metaphor of "thriftless sons" who waste their "scraping fathers' gold," clearly uses monetary frugality as its vehicle, although York's aristocratic "honor" being senselessly wasted by Aumerle is its tenor (V.iii.69). This scene begins with Henry's plaintive query, "Can no man tell me of my unthrifty son?" (1), which is itself, in all the meanings of thrift, the over-arching theme of the plays to follow. Having "rudely lost" his place in council, Hal has, as Henry sees it, abandoned chivalric military prowess and political acumen (the royal crafts): he has literally and figuratively spent the royal family's credit by behaving without aristocratic propriety.[6] In Hal's failure to protect the family's interests, Henry sees a recurrence of the very reason he had returned to England from banishment: "my rights and royalties / Plucked from my arms perforce—and given away / To upstart unthrifts" (II.iii.122).

In the 1590s, when Puritan insistence on thriftiness was used to attack the "unthrifty waste" of the theater, *The Merchant of Venice* plays out the entire range of socially available meanings. In the first scene of the play, Bassanio attempts to present his "quest" for Portia's hand as a courtly romance in which *he himself* risks all to win the lady—that is the point of his elaborate reference to Jason and the golden fleece as he asks Antonio to lend him the money. His use of *thrift*, then, is an attempt to call up associations with medieval quest romance. But since the passage is an unrelenting plea for a monetary loan, it is difficult to read his "I have a mind presages me such thrift" as anything less than a prediction of not just success in general, but of monetary success. Using Nerlich's schema for historical shifts in "the ideology of adventure," we can see Bassanio's rhetoric invoking the "courtly-knightly" associations of his proposed quest, while the plot reveals how embroiled it is in the cash nexus.

Later in Act I, Shylock means money by "well-won thrift, / Which he [Antonio] calls interest" (iii.51), and he is evoking the newer range of meanings of *thrift* most closely associated with Puritan thinking. Like Bassanio, he intends to call up positive associations for *thrift* but from a different, self-consciously shrewder, vantage point: Jacob's sheep are "a way to thrive...And thrift is a blessing" (89–90). Later he tells Jessica that "fast bind, fast find" is a "proverb never stale in thrifty mind" (II.v.54–55), in a phrasing which will haunt him during the trial scene, when in his thrift he binds himself to what he believes to be an intelligible legal code. *Merchant* is a direct, although complex, analysis of Elizabethan anxieties over the power of the cash nexus and the growing legal establishment which regulated, but also legitimized, it (Cohen 765–89; Engle 20–37), including the thrill of horror the courtroom crisis evokes when Portia subtly re-interprets a contract previously thought unambiguous. Lorenzo's list of lover's trysts on beautiful evenings ends with "In such a night / Did Jessica steal from the wealthy Jew / And with an unthrift love did run from Venice" (V.i.14–16). Lorenzo means a love which, in the free-hearted medieval manner, did not count the cost. But it was also an improper love in more than just its lack of parental authorization; it took a sentimental and over-optimistic view of the power of the stolen money to buy into the mode of life valued by "Christian" Venice. This glancingly-registered doubt contributes to the larger obstacles to full romantic comedy closure in the final act of the play.

Hamlet's "where thrift may follow fawning" surely trades on the single meaning of gain, and so does the Player Queen's avowal that second marriages are made with "base respects of thrift, but none of love" (III.ii.62 and 183). In both of these cases monetary thrift seems the enemy of aristocratic propriety. But the really interesting instance of thrift is Hamlet's explanation of Gertrude's o'erhasty marriage: "Thrift, thrift, Horatio! The funeral baked meats / Did coldly furnish forth the marriage tables" (I.ii.180). The wit involved bears Hamlet's distinctive stamp—it suggests the displacement of deep and bitter emotion and the pesky wakefulness of penetrating intellect. It discloses Hamlet's grievance within his only frank friendship and yet pretends to blunt that disclosure with equivocation. It imputes impropriety of a serious sort by using a word which in 1600 still can mean "propriety," but which, in this passage, displaces the direct sarcasm toward the second meaning of "middle-class parsimony." In its immediate context, it seems to refer to Claudius's claim (earlier in the scene) that discretion fought with nature to explain the quickness of the marriage. Like Hamlet's "a little more than kin and less than kind," it comes close to accusation, but commits him to no treason—just the tactic he will tax himself with continually during the rest of the play— he not only unpacks his heart with words, but with ambiguous, teaᴄing wordꜱ. In hiꜱ tauntꜱ, hᴇ iꜱ accusing Claudius and Gertrude of inaugurating a new, diminished order, in which base respects of thrift replace the epic virtues of Hamlet's father's reign.

The inclusion of retrospective uses of *thrift* contribute to what many of Shakespeare's commentators regard as his nostalgia for the feudal past, yet that past is invoked in a way which nibbles away at its status as an ideal. Hamlet's deep malaise might be described as a desire for return to a "prelapsarian" state in which his Oedipal energies were kept in check by the authority of an unassailable father. Henry's political ambitions rest on his ability to reestablish the authority of a regime in which no one can kill a king with impunity, even though it was he himself who had discredited it by his successful usurpation. Both instances signal a robust skepticism about a past in which to thrive is to be proper, and that signal is writ large in *Merchant of Venice*, where, as in *Timon*, the connection between economic realities and social proprieties is directly scrutinized. Bassanio's attempt to suggest that his premonition of *thrift* results from his uncalculating aristocratic propriety is ultimately unconvincing, and Shylock's appeals to *thrift* as a virtue count it the virtue of a very different social formation. His kind of thrift neither placates Antonio nor appeals to the young Venetians, but the play as a whole even-handedly discredits extravagance as much as this species of calculating self-discipline, including the emotional extravagance to which Lorenzo refers.[7] The ambiguities of *thrift* in the Shakespeare plays are not easy to decode, but that very difficulty suggests a "playfully creative ambiguity" which reveal social contest, rather than a glib whitewash for the current regime.

Early in the history of the word *thrift*, its implications of propriety naturalize a social scheme built on carefully delineated feudal hierarchies. Even when tinged with "frugality," these Middle English examples include that economic prudence within an ampler claim of appropriateness—until Chaucer's unsettling playfulness injects into even an aristocratic tale such as *Troilus and Criseyde* a touch of worldly expense-minding, and a free-for-all like the *Miller's Tale* opens the question of narrative thriftiness (polite propriety, but also efficacy) for the whole Canterbury anthology. Later, under pressure from mercantile and Reformation cultural influences, the strong positive valences of *thrift* were captured for new social ideals. Vincentio in *Measure for Measure* alleges that

> Nature never lends
> The smallest scruple of her excellence
> But, like a thrifty goddess, she determines
> Herself the glory of a creditor,
> Both thanks and use.
>
> (I.i.37–41)

The familiar biblical injunction not to hide one's talents is presented as usury—every loan, even nature's loan of virtue to the upright, demands "use," both employment and interest. In *Merry Wives of Windsor*, Falstaff falls to middle-class vices in announcing "I am about thrift," as he plots to seduce and swindle Mistress Page and Mistress Ford. In doing so, and euphemistically appropriating the Protestant's word to name his project, Falstaff admits that the prerogatives of his birth will no longer sustain him. He must, like the financially success-ful aristocrats in Lawrence Stone's analysis who join business ventures and lend money at interest, employ his resources (in his case bravado and charm) in an urban, bourgeois arena. He is "about thrift," and so is seventeenth-century London.

12
Virtù/Virtue

they continuously praise virtue; but they never speak as if power would be theirs tomorrow and they would use it for virtuous action. In fact, they want to receive the Eucharist, be beaten by the Turks, and then go to heaven.

Rebecca West, *Black Lamb and Grey Falcon*

I thought once of making a little fortune by my person. I now intend to make a great one by my vartue.

Henry Fielding, *Shamela*, Letter 10

Rebecca West is reflecting on a medieval Serbian poem about a Tsar who chooses a heavenly kingdom over a time-bound earthly kingdom, allowing himself and his troops to die in a state of grace. This belief system, she says, accounts for the continuance of poverty and oppression in the face of the knowledge that they are wrong. The history of the word *virtù/virtue* participates in the irony West invokes in her meditation on Yugoslavia in *Black Lamb and Grey Falcon*. The point of this passage is made by contrasting *virtue* to *power*, but the primary Middle English meaning for *virtue* was "power." The *Middle English Dictionary* has between 1050 and 1100 citation slips for *vertu* in its various spellings, very few of which can be construed as unambiguously meaning "goodness."

Virtue comes into English through Anglo-French and Old French from Latin *vir*, "man," hence "manliness," "manly prowess." Thomas Elyot's *Book Named the Governor* acknowledges that derivation: "A man is called in Latin *vir*, whereof, saith Tully, virtue is named. And the most proper virtue belonging to a man is fortitude" (186.29–31). In classical thought, the word "fortune," often envisioned as Lady Fortune, was used for the "circumstantial insecurity of political life," and its counter-term *virtus* for the fortitude and talent to suffer or reshape it heroically, in a political venue that largely excluded women. J.G.A. Pocock describes a frequent figure for this tenet in *The Machiavellian Moment*: "a masculine active intelligence was seeking to dominate a feminine passive unpredictability which would submissively reward him for his strength or vindictively betray him for his weakness" (38, 37). In the Middle Ages, the meaning of *virtue* broadens into "distinctive power," as in *Dives and Pauper*, "God bad erthe and ӡaf it vertue and nature to bring forth gres, trees and fruth of many sondry kende.... God ӡaf gres, trees and herbis diuerse vertuys" (1.145); excellence in general, as in Trevisa's translation of Higden's *Polychronicon* which alleges that people used to live longer, so they were able to obtain "glorious vertues, as astrology and geometry" (2.231); and finally, but less commonly in Middle English, moral excellence.

Vertues are an order of angels, mentioned in Romans 8.38, Ephesians 1.21, and Colosians 1.16—an order which in Scot's *Discoverie of Witchcraft* is said to contain some devils. How far from automatically meaning "goodness" early medieval usage fell is indicated by the assertion in the *Southern Legendary* that the planets exert such influence that "euere ase heore vertue is: Some lechours, some glotones, and some of othur manere" (312.428). Wimbledon's sermon at Paul's Cross contains this paraphrase of Revelations 18.3, concerning the whore, "the kyngis and the marchaundis of the erthe haueth do lecherie with, and of here vertu they haueth be maad riche" (551–52). Biblical translations before 1611 use "power" as the usual meaning of *vertu*, specifying moral strength if that is intended. The Wycliffite Early Version renders II Corinthians 1.18: "we ben greuyd aboue vertu, or myӡte, so that it anoyӡede vs, ӡhe, for to lyue." *The Benedictine Rule* enjoins love of God "wid al yure herte and wid al yure saul and wid al yure uertu" (8.14), and Coverdale's rendering of Wisdom 19.19 suggests the sense "specific efficacy": "The fyre had power in the water (contrary to his awne vertue)." The Geneva Bible gives Philemon 3.20 thus: "That I may knowe him, and the vertue of his resurrection," where the Authorized Version of 1611 has "power of his resurrection."

By 1611, the wording of the *Rule* and the Geneva Version may have seemed somewhat out of keeping with the more modern usage of *virtue* as moral rectitude, particularly female sexual continence. It is this sense—the female's preservation of a technical sort of virginity—that Fielding satirizes in *Shamela*. Moreover, many early modern examples are fully conscious of the equivocation between power and goodness, as when the King in *Love's Labors Lost* taxes the Princess with having forced him to break his oath of celibacy by "The virtue of [her] eye," and she replies: "You nickname virtue; vice you should have spoke; / For virtue's office never breaks men's troth" (V.ii.348–50). The semantic history of *virtù/virtue*, then, traces a shift from its dominant medieval associations with a strongly active and masculinized "power" to a passive and feminized "chastity."[1]

The specific virtues of things

Within medieval horizons, the things of the world have severally their special powers: armies and men have theirs, but also minerals, plants and planets. A late Middle English book of medicinal recipes by Gilbertus Anglicus ends on this summary note: "To thre thinges God зeveth vertu: to worde, to herbes, and to stonis. Deo gracias." The major writers (except Hoccleve)—Chaucer, Gower, Langland, the *Pearl*-poet, Malory, Rolle, Trevisa, Wyclif—mention the *vertues* of planets, stones, herb, venoms, and other natural objects. The translators use *virtue* to render Latin "efficacia," "virtutem" (e.g. Trevisa, *Bartholomeus* 219a/b and 220a/b). And the *Stanzaic Life of Christ* describes Christ's appearance to all creation, even that without life, which is to say, without *vertue*:

> Sum creatur has beyng
> wyth-out vertu any more,
> As ston & erth & sich thing,
> that neuer hade lyuyng her bifore.
>
> (881–84)

Vertue often means a specifically military power. As early as *Arthour and Merlin* (1300) we find: "Seigremor & his hadde swiche vertu, that on of his, зif the other was feld, ther oзaines twenti he queld" (7074), and as late as 1588 Queen Elizabeth, in her speech to the troops at Tilbury, promises to be the rewarder of their "virtues in the field" (Rice's edition 96). In Wyclif's translation, Luke 10.19 is rendered, "I hau зouun to зou power of... tredinge, on serpents and scorpiouns, and on al the vertu of the enemy," and I Maccabeus 1.4, "And he gadride vertu, and ful strong oost." In Lydgate's *Troy Book* Achilles says to Hector, "For I ful ofte, in werre & eek in fiзt, / Haue felt the vertu & the grete myзt / Of thi force, thoruз many woundis kene" (3.3796), and in

Melusine we find: "he...came & smote Zelodius vpon his helmet, by suche strengthe & vertue that he made hym to enclyne vpon his hors neck al astonyed" (226.24).

Medieval lapidaries explain and dispute over the specific virtues of the minerals, as when the *Newberry Lapidary* asserts that "Mochel were they [stones] more open in vertues and miracles... & in many place shulde haue myghte where Mirre ne herbe ne rotes ne myghte noȝt auaylen ne helpen" (3.21). Romances are full of virtuous gems, as in the *Pearl*-poet's "vertuous stones" in both *Cleanness* (1280) and *Gawain* (2027), Malory's "coronal of gold besette with stones of vertue dere" (12.27.254), and (a late example) Stephen Hawes's *The Pasttime of Pleasure*: "With perles and rubies rubicond. Mixte with emerauds so full of vertue" (127). Some stones have malign powers: *Mandeville's Travels* asserts that there is an island of cruel women who, it is said, have "precious stonys in here eyne growende, that yif they lokyn vpon a man with an egre wil and a wrothful that thour wertu of that ston they slen that man with a lokyng" (Bodley Version 111) and that a diamond should be carried on the left side, "for it is of grettere vertue thanne than on the right side" (105). The lapidaries often hint at an enigmatic connection with language: Lapidary Dc 219 (1450) reads: "And Salamon & Moyses the prophete & and seint Iohn the euangelist, that knewe the vertues of stones & wordes" (17).

The medicinal powers of various herbs include "byndyng" (Trevisa), purging phlegm (Trevisa), cleansing and drying "noyous humors" (Hunterien 95), causing women to abort or to expel a child dead in the womb (*Diseases of Women* 2.69), curing horses of illness or preventing them from falling, and causing piss to flow (Gilbertus Angelicus). *Agnus Castus* claims: "The vertu of this herbe is that he wylle gladly kepe men and women chast" (119). The features of the body have their *kyndeli vertues* to digest food and make fingernails grow. An *Anatomy* from the *Welcome 564* manuscript describes the circulatory system thus: "Sangueyn or blood is the norischinge of the body and frend to kynde and the mooste vertu aboute the herte and rote of bodili lijf " (51b/a). It also offers classifications of, for example, imaginative (a mental and anatomical virtue, found in the first ventricle), assimilative, expulsive, and retentive bodily vertues (21a/b). *Lanfranc* lists among the causes for things burning up, "for sum vertu in hem schulde wexe" (343.33), some power exceed its normal limit.

In all these cases, the *virtue* of a thing—an army or military hero, a mineral or gem, an herb or bodily fluid—is its efficacy, its power to produce results. Each virtue represents, as Pocock puts it, "masculine,

active intelligence ... seeking to dominate feminine passive unpre
dictability," either an intelligence wielded by persons (as in military
affairs) or an intelligibility embedded in created nature itself.

Christian virtues

In medieval discourse, the great repository of power is, of course, God
himself, and his power is often referred to in Middle English as his
vertue. Wyclif's Early Version customarily uses the term this way, for
example, Jeremiah 16.21: "I shal shewen to hem myn hond & my
vertue & thei shul wite for name to me is lord" (see also Judith 16.16;
Luke 4.14; Romans 1.16; and I Corinthians 4.21). Christ's healing
powers are referred to in the same way, as in Matthew 13.58: "He dide
not there manye vertues for the vnbyleue [unbelief] of hem," and
Mark 6.5: "He myȝte not make there ony vertu, no but heelide a fewe
sike men."[2] Divine *virtue* is also said to reside in sacred artifacts. In
Stripping the Altars, Eamon Duffy quotes many witnesses to their
effects: Robert Reynes copied the names of God and magical words
into his commonplace book, claiming to avert various disasters by "the
grace of God *and the vertue of these names*," and an unnamed farmer
used "the grete vartu and grace" of certain prayers to revive his injured
ox (276, 296). Fortescue denies that female monarchs can be anointed,
the holy oil being the agent of the king's special healing powers: "The
Kynges of England have ben enoynted in theyre hands and by vertue
and meane therof God commonlie healeth sickness" (quoted in
Chrimes 7). The mass and shrift have specified powers called *virtues*
(*Handlyng Sin* 2303, 12075); so do the passion (Rolle 34, *Castle of
Perseverance* 3140), baptism (*Gesta Romanorum* 767.13), and the
eucharist (*Speculum Christiani* 182.13; Nicholas Love's *Mirrour* 204).
Pecock's *Repressor*, defending the use of holy images, argues that some
users find in them "sum godli vertu ... If thou clepist a godli vertu such
a vertu which is causid of God into a creature aboue the worching of
kinde" (I.153).

Between the divine and the human, there are many unseen beings.
Trevisa's *Bartholomeus* explains that *vertues* (L. *virtutes*) are the seventh
order of angels, "here seruise is to do vertues & miracles. In hem prin-
cipaliche the vertu of god schineth and therfore they beth I-clepid
vertues" (16a/b). The nine orders given in the *Speculum Sacerdotale* are:
angels, archangels, principalities, potentates, dominions, virtues,
thrones, cherubim, and seraphim (189). In *Adam and Eve* we find:
"thanne there camen twelve aungels and two vertues, that is to seye,

two othere ordris of aungels" (86). And in Lydgate's *Life of Oure Lady*: "The high Angels and virtutes all, / Presith hym as thay ben wonte to done" (3.841).

The usefulness of symmetry for dramatizing abstract ideas and rendering them easier to remember resulted in many schemes to match seven specific virtues with the already firm categories of the seven deadly sins. The best known of these fused three theological (or divine) virtues (faith, hope, and charity) with the four cardinal virtues—specified as early as *Ayenbite of Inwit* (1340) as righteousness, prudence, strength (L.: *fortitudo*), and temperance—to fill out the number seven and counter the seven deadlies. The opposition of the seven virtues to the corresponding vices must have been fairly well understood quite early, in that the *Lay Folk's Catechism* seems to take a general knowledge of it for granted: "In the seuen vertues... that ilk man sal use, / And in the seuen dedley sinnes that man sal refuse" (20.57).[3] *Apocalypse* connects the cardinal virtues with the four evangelists: "the lioun strenthe, the calf temperaunce, the man riȝwijsnesse, the egal prudence" (24.14). The *virtues* are presented as efficacious against the sins with which they are matched, which preserves the sense that they are powers while linking them with various aspects of goodness.

Julian of Norwich uses *vertu* lavishly in describing her *Showings*, and always with a primary emphasis on "power." But the peculiar tilt of Julian's theology toward the palpable presence of God nearly erases any distinction between power and goodness. "Charyte gevyn is vertu" (Long Text, 84.13) urges both the power and the goodness God bestows and people receive. She prays for her evencristen to be "in the same vertue and grace that we awe to desyre to oureselfe" (67.29). When it is used to discuss chastity in the early Middle Ages, *virtue* means "efficacy," as in *Hali Meidenhad* (1200): "Engel & meden beoth euening i uertu i meidhades mihte" [virgins are the equal of angels because of the power of maidenhood] (12.154). Many later writers continue to stress the power of chastity: *Aelred of Rievaulx's de Institutione Inclusarum*: "Strecche out therfor al thy wille in kepynge this maydenhode and atteyne, if thou maist come to that vertu that thou may holde honger, delices; pouerte, rychesse" (386; see also 352 and 420). Note that in these instances chastity is *a* virtue (i.e., a power), and *virtue* and chastity are not yet synonyms, although they sometimes keep company.

With this array of nuance available for *virtue*, Chaucer can expect to be understood to mean efficacy in referring the *vertu* of the spring rain to "engender" the flower (I.4) and the "vertu expulsive" that would allow the poison in Arcite's system to be purged (I.2749). Introducing Friar Huberd in *The General Prologue*, as "vertuous" (I.251) may be taken as "good" in the hands of the pilgrim Chaucer and "powerful" in those of the ironic author Chaucer. Custance's *vertu* is a guide to all her works in *The Man of Law's Tale* (II.164). In the Physician's stress on Virginia's "owene vertue unconstreyned" (VI.61) Chaucer comes closest to making *vertu* and *chastity* synonyms, in the style of emergent usage. His other tales about chaste women use *vertue* as a more general descriptor of their moral lives, including their fairness and compassion. The Prioress praises the Virgin Mary's *vertu* but seems to mean by it "power to help," and the Second Nun does not call the aggressively chaste Cecile *virtuous* at all, although Cecile uses the term to defend the Christian community's rectitude (VIII.457).

The virtù of *The Prince* and the virtue of the lady

The linguistic legacy *virtue* inherited from the Middle Ages was highly positive and broad in range, indicating the efficacy of natural and religious objects, and, increasingly, personal moral strengths which granted powers over self and others. For Thomas More, as for Dame Julian, both the senses "power" and "goodness" are invoked and often fused, and we may read the fact that the term so often occurs *with* "good" (as in "good vertuouse people" or "goodnes and vertue") as either intensive or additive pairs. But More's implications for *virtue* fell into disuse later in the sixteenth century. The male-inflected sense "power" split off from a more particularized sense of goodness associated with female chastity. An important influence prying apart earlier meanings was Machiavelli's *The Prince*. Machiavelli's influence was felt early and pervasively in England, and it took a variety of shapes, of which the most obvious was the stage villain "Machiavel." Although there was no openly printed English translation of *The Prince* until that of Edward Dacres in 1640, English manuscripts of it were in circulation, including one said to have been the work of Thomas Kyd, read, at Cambridge by Christopher Marlowe. Gabriel Harvey mentions his desire to borrow it, using the Machiavellian keywords *politic* and *policy* five times as he makes the request (*Letter-book* 135.1, 141.14, 174–75, 79). Translations into French (1553) and Latin (1560) were also available. Cardinal Reginald Pole claimed that as early as 1529 Thomas Cromwell had read *Il Principe* in Italian at Henry VIII's court. But most early seventeenth-century readers found Machiavelli chiefly through the "Contre-Machiavel," Innocent Gentillet's French *Discours...contre Nicolas Machiavell* (1576), which Simon Patericke translated into English in 1602.

Although his influence was central to the shifts in the meaning of *virtù* in the sixteenth century, it was not because Machiavelli used the word in novel ways—his usage looks directly to the Latin *vir*, and even to Boethius's view of the relation of fortune to virtue specifically, as Pocock has argued (Chapter 6). *The Prince* contains 70 instances of *virtù* and various translators have tried to find accurate equivalents for it; Robert Adams renders it as "strength," "energy," "merit," "talent," "capability," "skill," "powers," "ability," "strength of character," "character," "vigor," "shrewdness," "acuteness," "effort," "courage," "virtue," "craft," "bravery," "good customs," "value," "qualities," "valor," and "manhood." What Machiavelli does *not* mean is "goodness," except in three instances in the famous fifteenth and sixteenth chapters, and as "goodness" he does not praise it as a quality of the prince. Patericke's translation of the *Contre-Machiavel*, on the other hand, steadily implies that *virtue* does mean "goodness" in his equally frequent usage of phrases like "goodness and vertue" (six instances in Maxime 27 alone). What shocked in Machiavelli's treatise was not his insistence on *virtù* as power—that was common in both ancient and medieval discourse—but his ruthlessness in separating "power" from the late medieval connection it was forming with *virtue* as "goodness." In J.H. Hexter's view, it was the "magnetic force of *stato*" (Machiavelli's conception of the state) which "altered the orbit of the most ordinary of all words used for discriminating between right and wrong" (192). Hexter's metaphor of an orbit rather than a fixed meaning is useful (although for my purposes "trajectory" would be even better), but I disagree that *virtue* was already settled in the "right and wrong" orbit when Machiavelli wrote. The influence of his *Prince* impeded the bond between power and goodness from becoming an automatic or ordinary usage in early Modern English, by treating principled, manly action— what Robinson took More to mean by calling Henry VIII "in all royal virtues a prince most peerless" in *Utopia* —as working best in the polit- ical realm when it is a pious charade or holy pretence. In a famous passage Machiavelli writes: "In actual fact, the prince may not have all the admirable qualities we listed, but it is very necessary that he should seem to have them....To preserve the state...he should be ready to enter on evil if he has to" (Chapter 18 of Adams's translation).

The English assimilation of the Machiavellian insight rests on the phrase, "to preserve the state." A private person who dissembles *virtue* but embraces evil when necessary is merely a hypocrite, and the Middle Ages had plenty to say about hypocrisy. The new element is the protection of a unified national totality governed by the real strength ("where there are good arms there are bound to be good laws"—*Prince* 35) and feigned goodness of the prince, supported by the deluded opinion of the masses. Although Machiavelli's name and stance were associated in the English popular imagination with wicked Italy—the Medici in particular—and easily assimilated into a general anti-Catholic program, radical Protestants were also intensely interested in maintaining a strong, unified English nation, which they regarded as providential to the eventual salvation of Europe (Chapter 8 above). The fascination of Machiavelli's political theory lay in the possibility that the practice of it might succeed in preserving the state they needed—they were not content to be beaten by the Turks and then go to heaven as in Rebecca West's example—yet any direct appeal to it was damaging to their cause. They had to differentiate English *virtue* from Italian *virtù* as strongly as possible.

Two reactions were made to *The Prince* and the controversies it spawned. The more obvious was the widespread use of Machiavelli's name as a synonym for political skullduggery; the less obvious was the reluctant and cautious admission of the "reason of state" into much seventeenth-century English political thinking, acknowledged by all religious factions (see Mosse, *Holy Pretense*). The trickle-down effect from these high-level discussions which allowed some relaxation of private moral strictures in governing the nation was a popular accept-ance of nationalist goals, and one way of furthering that nationalism was to locate a special brand of wickedness in an Italy associated with Machiavelli. A character with his name introduces Marlowe's *Jew of Malta*; he is mentioned by Jonson in *Volpone*, and alluded to only slightly more obliquely by Shakespeare in his characterizations of Richard III, Claudius in *Hamlet*, and Edmund in *Lear*. Robert Greene in *Groatsworth of Wit* and Thomas Lodge in his reply to Stephen Gosson, refer to the "Machiavel" as the master of dissembling. The sign "Machiavelli" did double duty, then, directly by teaching certain lessons of real-politik and the "reason of state," and indirectly by providing a catchword for an unprincipled Italy and its superstitious religion. If *virtù* means what Machiavelli advocates in *The Prince* (or was accused in the contra-*Machiavel* of advocating), then the English *virtue* must be distanced from it, and the link with unprincipled force (either measured violence or the intellectual force of deceit) erased; increas-ingly the word would signal its secondary medieval sense of "goodness."

The practice of English writers later in the sixteenth century largely bears this out. In his translation of *The Courtier*, Hoby usually implies "goodness" by *vertue* (except in phrases like "by virtue of") and he uses the word a great deal. The *vertue* called "recklesnesse" (*sprezzatura*) is precisely a liminal case, since it is most certainly a strength the courtier must develop, and may be regarded as either a genuine goodness—a grace in both senses—or a clever social mask. In Golding's translation of *The Metamorphoses*, *virtue* means goodness when it is used for persons, but power when used of herbs (three of 22 instances).[4] Puttenham's *The Arte of English Poesie* uses *vertue* to mean "goodness" about three times more frequently than to mean "power," and the power involved is that of language: "enargia" (161). For Hooker in the *Laws*, both meanings of *virtue* are available, although "goodness" is considerably more frequent. When virtue is treated as "power," that power is justice, an attribute of both scripture (or God himself) and certain kinds of law (42, 98). Gosson uses *virtue* to mean "moral rectitude" in his anti-theatrical tracts, and uses it often. So does Florio in his translation of Montaigne, although some scattered instances of *virtù* do appear, as when the remora, brought into a ship, no longer retained "that powerful virtue which it had being in the sea" (113). Dekker's *Gul's Horn-booke* uses *vertue* ironically to summarize all the ridiculous peculiarities of the gallant, as either mock strengths or mock claims to goodness (32.10), and advises "let it be your special vertue" not to offer deference to anyone, no matter what claims to it he might have (40). None of these references to power is likely to trigger thoughts of Machiavelli's *virtù*.[5]

If Machiavelli's leitmotif throughout *The Prince* is *virtù*, Sidney's in *New Arcadia* is *virtue*. The term occurs in at least 200 instances, and these belong to two distinct senses. When it refers to strength or power, the setting is commonly a chivalric trial at arms, which rarely implies naked force devoid of some positive moral trait. When it refers to goodness, it often describes a female and alludes to her chastity and fidelity in love.[6] Both the male- and female-inflected instances are deployed so as not to suggest Machiavellian *virtù*, but at certain points *New Arcadia* seems to allude to *The Prince* in raising questions about the nature of virtue. In a good example of the male inflection, Pyrocles on the brink of suicide finds that "virtue and her valiant servant anger, stopped him from present destroying himself" (432.7–8). *Virtue* here is connected with a voice calling "Revenge!" either heard or hallucinated, and is related to "noble anger" and epic rashness—male inflected and conducive to violence. A more complicated instance is the lady's willingness to "read a lecture to your [Pyrocles's] virtue" (237.30). She is pausing in a quasi-military attack, so physical force cannot be the sole meaning of *virtue* here. She is teaching revenge against a deceiver of women, which implies that she wants Pyrocles to link just dealing with his prowess. What she does not mean, though, is anything that implies chastity, the more usual female-associated direction.

Sidney seems to allude to *The Prince* in describing Philoclea falling in love: "while she might prevent it she did not feel it, now she felt it when it was past preventing—like a river, no rampires being built against it til already it have overflowed." Machiavelli's similar image is of fortune flooding the land and changing its configurations: "Yet this does not mean that men cannot take countermeasures while the weather is still fine, shoring up dikes and dams, so that when the waters rise again, they are either carried off in a channel or confined where they do no harm" (Chapter 25). Both these passages invoke rational efficacy—the sphere of free human agency against fortune, Machiavelli's antidote for the natural and political contingencies that might limit the prince's powers of action, Sidney's against the unpredictable power of love. *Virtue* in this text is also presented by Musidorus as the power of reason to protect freedom. He reprimands his cousin for his loss of "virtue" resulting in thraldom on account of love: "To what pass are our minds brought, that from the right line of virtue are wired to these crooked shifts! But O love, it is thou that doost it" (109.28–30). (Musidorus's formulation sounds like Pocock's description of the classical "masculine active intellect" overcoming "feminine passive unpredictability" [38].) Yet the *virtue* of Pamela, Philoclea, and Zelmane is most vigorously demonstrated when they are in love and imprisoned, and it is pointedly contrasted with their imprisonment. Philoclea is described as ending a speech "with so fair a majesty of unconquered virtue that captivity might seem to have authority over tyranny, so foully was the filthiness of impiety discovered by the shining of her unstained goodness" (363.12–15). Here the term suggests efficacy in a military sense (unconquered), and at the same time goodness, even saintliness (unstained), and of course both are embodied in a woman and enacted in a love relationship, allowing the two senses to contribute to the same effect.

There is also an intertextual reference to Machiavelli's virile sense of *virtù* in Pyrocles's spirited defense of women's *virtue* against the argument for reason Musidorus is pressing upon him.

And certainly (for this point of your speech doth nearest touch me) it is strange to see the unmanlike cruelty of mankind, who not content with their tyrannous ambition to have brought the others' virtuous patience under them, like childish masters think their masterhood nothing without doing injury to them, who (if we will argue by reason) are framed with the same parts of the mind for the exercise of virtue as we are.

(72.30–73.2)

The narrative will consistently prove Pyrocles to have been right in this insistence; Pamela and Philoclea will demonstrate the reason and resolution requisite for *virtue* as readily as Pyrocles and Musidorus themselves. In fact, Philoclea comes to Pyrocles in prison during the final sequence to comfort and upbraid him much as Lady Philosophy appeared to imprisoned Boethius. But Pyrocles's argument moves on to consider the sense of military prowess. It is the "sweetness of their dispositions" which makes women see "the vainness of these things which we account glorious" (73.4–5); in refraining from trials by arms, then, women would seem to have more virtue than men. The fable of *The New Arcadia* will play out this half-serious assertion in the *seeming* military superiority of the Amazon Zelmane, who is actually Pyrocles disguised. At the same time, the valorized "real" women display their courage through their willingness to suffer in defense of their chastity and fidelity without taking arms, even against lions. Perhaps they see the vainness of these things. The appropriated ideological force of *virtue*, the text's most obvious marker of value, therefore oscillates between the manly exercise of chivalric prowess and the specifically female exercise of resolute chastity. Thus Sidney has attempted to wrest the implications of *virtue* from the "taint" of the Machiavellian male struggle for power through force and deceit by consistently linking the term with just action and by prominently giving the quality to women.

The *virtues* of the central female characters in *The New Arcadia* are rendered in heroic colors, but their powers are deployed in protection of their chastity. The next step is to treat their chastity *as* their virtue. Consider the rape fantasy in this description of the country of Guiana by Walter Ralegh. Guiana "hath yet her maydenhead, never sackt, turned, nor wrought, the face of the earth hath not been torn, nor the vertue and salt of the soyle spent by manurance.... It hath never been entred by any armie of strength, and never conquered or possessed by any christian Prince" (Hakluyt 408, discussed by Montrose 12).

Guiana's claim to "vertue" is seen here as lying in its secluded female virginity.

Virtue staged

The Roman sense of virtue as manly force against the vagaries of fortune is present in the English stage tradition through the influence of Seneca's plays and essays. Christopher Marlowe calls up a vivid, though not unpunished, image of this male-inflected resolution, and makes a strong and consistent reference to Senecan *virtù*, especially in the two parts of *Tamburlaine*, which contain most of the instances in Marlowe's drama (the only exception being a eulogy for Zenocrate in Part II [III.ii.24]). Later in that play, Tamburlaine's military prowess and resolution are called "sacred vertues" when he is on his deathbed (V.ii.11), in keeping with almost all the other 17 instances.[7] Marlowe seems to make no effort to avoid the Machiavellian associations with his Senecan inflection for *virtue*, and his soberness in using it contrasts nicely with, for example, the mercurial wit of Thomas Middleton's practice a decade or two later. Middleton's *A Trick to Catch the Old One* plays off male- and female-inflected senses of *virtue*: Witgood fears his debts might cost him "a virgin's love, her portion, and her virtues" (I.i.22), "her virtues" being a euphemism for social powers of some kind as well as an acknowledgment of her chastity and dismisses his courtesan, whom he accuses of trying to unravel his wits, his "wilt leave no virtue in me?" (I.i.30) clearly meaning "efficacy." Moneylove praises the "virtues" of his intended, meaning her financial powers. The despicable Lethe in *Michaelmas Term* thinks Susan's mother obeys "some small inferior virtue" which keeps her from consenting to their marriage (I.i.218). Shortyard, one of Quomodo's operatives in the same play, "held it [his] best virtue" to plot against his crafty master (V.iii.84)—this is a neat equivocation, since he could mean his strongest power or his finest good deed.

Both of John Webster's plays acknowledge the gendered bifurcation of the term. *The Duchess of Malfi* presents a debate about the contending claims of virtue and birth, plotted as Antonio's "right" to the Duchess's hand. As the play presents the issue, birth grants power both through succession to princedoms—the bloodline—and a willingness to shed blood (manly prowess). *Virtue* is left with those implications of "goodness" to which "power" is the counter term. The Duchess's love for Antonio is his wages for so long serving *virtue* ("rectitude") and power relations force her to woo him obliquely, away from the path of simple *virtue* ("candor") (I.ii.355, 363). The Duchess tells Bosola that those born without high station are best able to establish their virtue through action—Bosola calls it "A barren, beggarly virtue" (III.v.120–21). If *The Duchess of Malfi* is interested in *virtue* which has been denied its powers of action, *The White Devil* examines that *virtù* which vaunts its power at the expense of a sense of *virtue* as "goodness."[8] Vittoria claims she must address the court at her trial as if she were a man:

> my modesty
> And womanhood I tender; but withal
> So entangled in a cursed accusation
> That my defence of force like Perseus,
> Must personate masculine virtue to the point.
>
> (III.ii.131–35)

"Masculine virtue" is power of action (as Monticelso has made clear in arguing for princes to become soldiers to give them a "stock of virtue" [II.i.102, 106]) and of free-spoken discourse. Flamineo uses the phrase late in the play, and even more obviously forces the two senses of *virtue* apart: "Know many glorious women that are fam'd / For masculine virtue have been vicious" (V.vi.241–42) and called the 49 daughters of Danus who killed their husbands "a shoal of virtuous horse-leeches" (V.vi.162–63).

A patriarchal ambiance in Shakespeare's plays is strongly evidenced in their insistence on the virginity of the marriageable women and sexual faithfulness of married ones, in both cases called *virtue*.[9] Hero's *virtue* is at issue in *Much Ado*, Isabella's and Marianna's in *Measure for Measure*, Perdita's in *Winter's Tale*, Marina's in *Pericles*, Hermione's in *Winter's Tale*, Gertrude's in *Hamlet*, Desdemona's in *Othello*, and Imogene's in *Cymbeline*. Although these women are all "innocent," the drift of the plays supports the importance of patriarchal control (self-exercised, of course, by the women) of female sexual desire, but the case of *Measure for Measure* warrants further comment.

Measure for Measure is about both justice and chastity, and both are referred to as *virtue* in the play, the former associated with Duke Vincentio and Angelo, the latter with Isabella. In a speech which twice insists on Angelo's "virtues" (I.i.31 and 33) as probity and discernment which must be exercised in public life to justify his having them, the Duke appoints Angelo as a justicer, who may "enforce or qualify the laws" (65). What the Duke sees in Angelo (or is he merely laying a trap to precipitate his fall?) is a man capable of justice, the most obviously missing ingredient in Machiavelli's account of the attributes of the prince (Hexter 209). Escalus calls Angelo "most strait in virtue" (II.i.9) too, but he reflects on Claudio's peril with "some rise by sin and some by virtue fall" (38), an apt description of what is about to happen to Angelo as Angelo himself sees it. In the next scene, Angelo will blame Isabella's chastity, *her virtue* for his sexual warmth (II.ii.162, 183). He sees an infernal plot to tempt his saintliness with a saint. Angelo's reasoning could be put down to simple sophistry, but I would argue for a more interesting moral terrain, one which interrogates the play's general acquiescence in the overvaluation of female chastity. Angelo and Isabella are legalists and eager to win whatever competition they are in. Isabella's chastity is so complete, so well defined, that Angelo fears he cannot win except by destroying it, even though that will disqualify him as a justicer. He is genuinely attracted to her insofar as sexual attraction involves admiration, but his rigid self-image renders him loath to recognize *a virtue* higher than his own. The situation is exacerbated when Isabella fails to take him seriously, thinking that "his virtue hath a license in it" (II.iv.145) merely to test her, that it is a judicial ploy—in effect, that he is the just man the world accounts him. But when Claudio wants her to change *her* definition of virtue by sacrificing her chastity to save his life, she vehemently refuses—she cannot relinquish the female virtue-as-chastity to consider Claudio's argument about justice.

The contest for *virtue* between Angelo and Isabella results in Angelo's failure to remain just, and Isabella's success in remaining chaste, at the price, she thinks, of causing her brother's unjust execution. Without the machinations of the Duke, this plot would scarcely belong among the comedies, problem or otherwise, but it would stand as testimony to the bifurcation the word *virtue* has undergone. A great deal, therefore, depends on the credibility of the Duke. Though we have no reason to think him sexually incontinent, he is a Duke of dark corners in his secretive management of the lives of his subjects. He thinks of himself as just, figuring himself in terms of "the whitest virtue" when he complains of Lucio's calumny (III.ii.187), and claiming of Marianna, "I have confess'd her and I know her virtue" (V.i.527). To take him at his own valuation compromises what early in the play seemed to be a rigorous demand for just dealing; to find him merely selfishly devious makes Isabella the victim of yet another flawed, self-described saint. Marianna asks in the judgment scene for "sense in truth, and truth in virtue" (V.i.226), but it is hard to see how the logical lines in this play are connected, how public justice and personal purity are being valued by the plot. Rather than a clear *exemplum* of *measura*, the play manifests a cultural impasse, brilliantly registered, but not overcome.

In George Chapman's *Bussy D'Ambois*, the intellectual problem of the play appears at once, with Bussy's declaration that he will "bring up a new fashion / And rise in court for virtue" (I.i.129–30)—and the play goes on to exhibit 24 more instances of *virtue*. The earliest suggestions are that the term means "goodness" ("I am for honest actions, not for great"), but Bussy's first exploits—his exasperating the Guise by courting his wife and his triumph in a rather pointless duel—place that definition in question. Bussy's praise of Tamyra's "renown'd" virtues (II.i.218) refers to her reputation for sexual fidelity, and Tamyra's rebuff of Monsieur's suit ("Mine honor's in mine own hands, spite of kings" II.ii.9) echoes Bussy's self-possessed tone. The virtue her husband Montsurry expects of Tamyra—sexual fidelity—contrasts sharply with the *virtue* he ascribes to Monsieur—ruthless power (II.ii.74). The Friar teaches Bussy to lie to Tamyra: "for the direct is crooked" (II.ii.174). The play is thus constructed like *Measure for Measure* in its assignment of valor to men and chastity to women under the sign *virtue*, while blurring the moral tone of its major actions.

If *Measure for Measure* is a problem comedy, perhaps *Bussy D'Ambois* is a problem tragedy. It certainly creates unresolved doubts about its many invocations of *virtue*. Bussy's *virtue* may be a matter of his bold powers of action in a decadent and servile court; that is his construal of his story. He soliloquizes about *virtue* as he ponders his poverty "in a green retreat": as great seamen in tall ships, who have put a girdle round the world, come near their haven they must call upon a poor staid fisherman to guide them in, so

> We must to virtue for her guide resort,
> Or we shall shipwreck in our safest port.
>
> (I.i.25–32)

Such a full-blown epic simile could either be seen as marking the seriousness of Bussy's moral vision or as presenting a flattering self-image, like Claudio's notion in *Hamlet* that his kingly "divinity" will hedge him off from harm. Similarly Tamyra, in transgressing *virtue* as it has been defined on her side of the gender divide, either exhibits what Webster calls "masculine virtue" in managing the aftermath with such courage and loyalty or becomes merely a hardened adulteress once she consents to the liaison with Bussy. In sum, the rhetoric of this play may be seen to work either for or against its plot concerning the *virtue* of both genders. This uncertainty creates interpretive problems every-where: the insistence of King Henry (the seemingly normative character) that Bussy is the "complete man," the complicity of the Friar, and the status of conjuring. Extravagant playfulness character-izes the language, as when Bussy speaks of "the vicious virtue of [Monsieur's] busy sense" (IV.ii.5) or the villain Monsieur, describing Nature says:

> Nature lays
> A deal of stuff together....
> Of strength or virtue, error or clear truth,
> Not knowing what she does.

(V.ii.11)

A similarly extravagant tone describes the Escher-like ethical turnings of *Bussy D'Ambois*, and allows Chapman some vivid (even when not entirely coherent) dramatic effects.

The early modern stage signals both the active masculine intelligence which meets fortune with brave defiance and the female refusal of unauthorized sex with the powerful signifier *virtue*. Three centuries later a male character in Hannah Folger's American novel *The Coquette* writes to another man, "I would not be understood to impeach Miss Wharton's virtue; I mean her chastity. Virtue in the common accepta-tion of the term, as applied to the [female] sex, is confined to that particular, you know" (quoted in Smith-Rosenberg). Although the letter-writer (not to mention Fielding in *Shamela*) objects to this usage—chastity is "of little importance, where all other virtues are wanting!" he writes—it has a long life in the English language on both sides of the Atlantic and is a surviving sense. The masculine inflection, however, seems to be sliding from residual to archaic. *Virtue* as "manly resolution and fortitude" may still be understood, but it is relegated to life-worlds of the past; "the common acceptation of the term" does not describe current heroes without a hint of irony. *Virtue* as the signifier for the simultaneous and linked power and goodness Hytholday claims for the Utopian system, largely abandoned in early modern usage, was never vigorously reclaimed.

After Words

[Chinese] ideographs are like bloodstained battle-flags to an
old campaigner.

Ernest Fenollosa, *The Chinese Written Character as a
Medium for Poetry*

Ernest Fenollosa's brief essay, never corroborated by academic
Sinologists but introduced into discussions of poetics by its editor Ezra
Pound, insists on the superiority of Asian language systems over their
European (Aryan) counterparts. In Eastern languages:

> etymology is constantly visible. It retains the creative impulse and
> process, visible and at work. After thousands of years the lines of
> metaphoric advance are still shown, and in many cases actually
> retained in the meaning. Thus a word, instead of growing gradually
> poorer and poorer as with us, becomes richer and still more rich
> from age to age, almost consciously luminous.
>
> (p. 25)

In the precincts of such a language, no one would have to "feel
painfully back along the thread of our etymologies and piece together
our diction, as best they may, from forgotten fragments" (p. 24), which
is rather like what I seem to have been doing in this book. In such
linguistic precincts, the luminosity of words themselves would render
unnecessary Gadamer's claim that the later readers' new horizons
require new interpretive efforts, since the whole history of meaning
would be always already present. There would have been no need for
Habermas to argue that all language is deformed by particular ideological pressures controlled by relations of power and labor, since

189

those relations would also be readable in the sign itself. In fact, if new social developments could not make language users forget their old allegiances, the semantic shifts chronicled here might not have occurred at all. But in fact there is no such language, nor could there be—the weight of each word would quickly become too cumbersome for ordinary communication.

The eleven words treated in this book were detached from the social logic of the late Middle Ages and supplanted within that of the early modern, sometimes by deliberate social planning, sometimes by a diffuse drift, usually by some combination of intended and contingent forces. We are left, then, within the Gadamer–Habermas problem space, from which a strictly logical exit seems impossible. The details of these eleven word-histories were written as eleven attempts to test Gadamer's thesis that language can give evidence of its own complicity with ideology: its own bending to dominant social ideals and practices, its own record of resistance and emergent meaning, and its own recovery of the residual. By and large, language did supply that evidence, supporting the skeleton of Gadamer's argument in ways he himself might not have envisioned. On the other hand, it is clear that much has been lost. Habermas's pessimistic conclusions about access to the past are confirmed by gaps in surviving evidence. It seems to me that neither Gadamer nor Habermas wins their debate conclusively, though the evidence for these particular words weighs more heavily on Gadamer's side. Explications of the ways people in past generations interpreted and responded to their social circumstances—completely evident structures of their feelings—can never attain full presence for us late-comers, but their words can bear enlightening testimony. As J.G.A. Pocock puts it, "men cannot do what they have no means of saying they have done and what they do must in part be what they can say and conceive that it is." When something new is required to be done, new words or old words with new valences must be summoned to inspire the doing.

And this brings us to the power of fictions, since it is not usually single words that give men (people) the power to do new things, but the weight those words convey for some community, present or imagined. It is because verbal fictions *play*—that is "move freely," "pretend," and "present as theater"—that they are so essential to social *work*. All three senses of *play* operate, for example, in Shakespeare's consummate amateur theatrical in Act II, scene iv of *I Henry IV*. Hal has been summoned to court to answer to his father for his profligate life. Before he actually goes, he enacts his going. A talented rhetorician himself, he moves himself from his own position in the imagined woodshed to his father's and back again, allowing his friend Falstaff, an even bolder rhetorician, to change roles as well. In the course of this play—as theater, as pretending, and as moving away from direct realities—Hal phrases the stance he will take when he appears before his father and commits himself to the course the rest of his life will take. When he is able to "say and conceive" what it is he must do: "Banish plump Jack and banish all the world," he replies in the words of a binding ceremony: "I do, I will." The "imagined communities" between which he chooses are present to him as fictions before he can act. The poetic, narrative, and dramatic fictions discussed in these pages—*The Canterbury Tales, Utopia, The New Arcadia, Hamlet,* and the rest—presented imagined identities and situations to their first audiences and inform our historical imaginations as well.

One emphasis of these word histories has been on the way the major issues of a particular text can be focused by attending to recurrent or weighted instances of a single word, *estate* running through *Timon of Athens,* for example, or *providence* in *The Atheist's Tragedy.* I find this focus not only a good way of understanding the effects these texts produce, but a good way of teaching students to begin to enter medieval and early modern life-worlds. Sometimes the interaction of more than one word is useful. The anonymous fourteenth-century poem "Who says Sooth, He shall be Shent," for example, may be explicated in terms of its implications for *queynte* and *gloss*:

> Thus is the sothe I-kept in close,
> And vche mon maketh touh and queynte;
> To leue the tixt and take the glose,
> Eueri word thei coloure and peynte.

(12–15)

Religious and political truth is hidden because it is ingeniously, *queyntly,* glossed. The man who says truth plainly is *shent,* "disgraced," "punished," or "ruined," for his unmasking of powerful (probably clerical) controls over discourse. *Queynte* here carries the clear sense of "overelaborate," but connotes as well something sinister, some political self-interest. *Glose* cooperates with that sinister element by being, not merely the explication of the text, but something *painted* over it to decorate and obscure it. The contention over medieval glosses is, therefore, evident in the poet's choice of the two contested words *queynte* and *glose.* The dominant discourse privilege given to Patristic glossing is undermined by the logic of the poem, and also by the strategic link it forms with clerical "quaintness" in general. The poem itself, then, must be read as anti-clerical, although it may have been written by a cleric (a dissatisfied friar, as Carleton Brown suggests). Social configurations can also be read *from* the poem. For example, the poet expects his reader to register the ingenuity called *queynte* as suspect, at least unedifying in producing secrecy where openness is needed, and perhaps dangerous to the spiritual health of simple people. Distrust in both the authoritative glossing system and the institutions which underwrite it is made available in this poem.

Anti-clericism on a more raucous note is heard throughout Chaucer's *The Miller's Tale*. John the carpenter makes a heartfelt appeal for the *lewed* estate when he sees his learned boarder Nicholas in a coma from, as he thinks, too much study. "Men sholde nat knowe of Goddes pryvetee. / Ye, blessed be alwey a lewed man / That noght but only his bileve kan" (I.3454–56). This works, of course, against both John and Nicholas—John because his simple belief system does not allow him to see through Nicholas's over-elaborate scheme (and because it is the student who grabs Alisoun by the *queynte*, apparently knowing the bald truths of life better than the "simple" man), and Nicholas because his insight into "Goddes pryvetee" is only a ruse and his educated cleverness only benefits him temporarily. *Sely* contributes to this layered joke in accompanying John throughout the tale, suggesting both its old sense of innocence wronged and its emergent sense of gullibility. Like the play with *lewed*, this bifurcation of *sely* allows John more sympathy than is usually accorded to the customary "old husband" of farce, making response to the tale more complicated, but it also suggests the immediacy of certain lived social contentions outside the tale. The Miller's contribution is framed by the word *thrift*, since he is admonished by the Host to "werken thriftily" by relinquishing his place in the storytelling order, but prevailing against the Host's status-driven sense of propriety, *thrift*, through his narrative virtuosity. Again, English society is readable through the tale, as *lerned* and *lewed* stake their claims and the senses of *sely* and *thrift* jostle one another for linguistic dominance.

It is my hope that these chapters have exhibited a previously unexplored approach to the Gadamer–Habermas debate, meshed social and semantic histories in the case studies of eleven words, and deepened the explication of some resonant passages in medieval and early modern fictions. Although these eleven words may not shine in the immediate way Fenollosa and Pound claim (quite wrongly) for

Chinese ideographs, I hope they will light up some future discussions of the social work and play of words. As with semi-precious stones, the glow of these particular words appeared with polishing.

Notes

Notes to Chapter 1: Introduction

1. Current conceptions of philology are enormously varied. For example, Jan Ziolkowski's edited book *On Philology* consists of eleven brief essays given as papers at a conference at Harvard in 1988. The definitions of philology operating in the volume range from philology as the groundwork for literary study to an identification of it with the whole of literary study. Barbara Johnson's contribution to the volume, "Philology: What is at Stake?," outlines the mutual distrust now obtaining between "philology" and "theory."
2. Hans Robert Jauss argues that in the Middle Ages, fictions were not valued for their power to enable new structures of feeling. They were permitted and privileged (in such measure as they were allowed), for two quite different reasons: as a "Platonic residue" in which the sense world imagined is the vehicle for presenting "the ideal reality belonging to eternal archetypes," and as a moral claim for presenting the sense world under the imperative of verisimilitude (9).
3. As Raymond Williams pointed out in *Keywords*, "The *OED*, indispensable as it is for our sense of the history of English, cannot alert us to those developments in ordinary speech that occur decades before they show up in manuscripts or printed books" (17).

Notes to Chapter 2: Corage/Courage

1. Often *corage* does not appear as valor where it might be expected. For example, in *Gawain and the Green Knight*, when Gawain's virtues are described in the scene of his first arming, his valor is mentioned twice, neither time using *corage*: his "forsnes" he took from the five joys of Mary, and when he saw her image on his shield, his "belde" never failed (645, 650).
2. Of the Chaucerian instances of *corage* and its variations (*corageous*, *courages*), 45 are in *Boece*; 8 in *Romaunt of the Rose*; 5 in *Troilus*; 3 in *Duchess* and *Legend*; and 37 in the *Canterbury Tales*.
3. The first two numbers refer to Caxton's book and chapter numbers, the next to the page and line numbers in Vinaver's edition of *Works*.
4. The argument from constitution is used in Ralph Robinson's 1551 translation of *Utopia* to mark both gender and class, as the lawyer in Book I claims that military retainers have "manlyer courages [Latin: "anima magis," more life-blood] then handycraftesmen and plowmen" [22]. Other passages in Robinson's *Utopia* also suggest that couage can be managed: men watched over by the dead are said to go about their business more *courragiouslie* (104) and eschew physical mortification to increase their courage (80).
5. *Courage* does not appear in *Dido*; in *Jew of Malta* it is a call to defensive

military valor, in *Edward II* the king addresses "couragious Lancaster" (I.iv.340); and in *Faustus* Mephostophilis bids Faust to "stab his arm couragiously" (II.i.50).

6. "Resolution" is also the implication of *courage* in John Florio's translation of Montaigne's essays in phrases like "stoutness of courage" and "harden my courage," as well as in Thomas Hoby's translation of Castiglione's *Il Cortegiano*. But in one playful passage of Bembo's rhapsody on love, one may construe the implications of *corage* as spilling over into "lust." The soul, figured as "she," is "contented to be lead by them [the senses], especially when they have so much courage, that (in a manner) they enforce her" (IV. 306.7). The vehicle of this metaphor is a rape scene, the soul the victim of the lust of the senses.

7. The cony-catching pamphlets, from Gilbert Walker in 1552 to Robert Greene in 1592, most often use *courage* to suggest valor, although one instance invites a layered reading . In Thomas Harmon's *Caveat for Common Cursitors* (1566), a young man following a prostitute in the hope of both restitution of property and sex from her, attacks her "upright man." He does this "being of good courage and thinking to himself that one true man was better than two false knaves" (Kinney's edition 136.23–25).

8. Where the Country Wench may intend the equivocation, Thomasine's "take courage," spoken to her daughter's suitor who is about to win Susan's hand, is probably registered as an inadvertent innuendo, but not one out of keeping with the context of the play. In Ben Jonson's *Epicoene*, Truewit puns when he urges the desperate Morose to welcome his female guests, with "Take courage, put on a martyr's resolution" and "Look upon her [his intended bride] with a good courage" (III.ii. 280 and 292).

9. The whole scene resonates closely with the mindset of fascinated fear of the armed or warlike woman, which Theweleit ascribes to his Freikorps authors. Early moderns indulged a less extreme form of this obsession in contemplating the Amazon, a representation both inspiring and frightening, and less likely to offend the English Queen. Sidney's *Apology for Poetry* defends poetry from the charge that it saps martial resolve in being an art "not of effeminateness, but of notable stirring of courage" (130.34), echoing Elyot's *Governor*.

10. Zelmane dazedly "her courage still rebelling against her wit" tries to hale "her wit to her courage" and come up with a plan which will save Philoclea from her nightmarish imprisonment. Bravery as well as sexual desire are involved in this passage without destructive contradiction (428.8–9, 14).

11. The first quotation is from a speech to Parliament on Marriage and Succession, 1566 (Rice's edition 812–14), the second from a speech on the execution of Mary Queen of Scots (89.23–24). Her address to the troops at Tilbury takes the same tone: "I have the heart and stomach of a king, and of a king of England too" (96.14–15).

Notes to Chapter 3: Estat/Estate

1. Alfred's gloss is mentioned by both Chrimes (95) and Mendle (25). The nature of estates theory as social imagination is stressed by Georges Duby in *The Three Orders*.

2. "The lady that is royalle [but married to a mere knight] shalle kepe the state that she afore in stode; the lady of lowe blode & degre [married to royal blood] kepe her lordis estate" (1091.2).
3. References to it do not entirely cease during the early modern period—the Authorized Version refers to a supper made by Herod "to his lords, high captaines, and chiefe estates of Galilee" (Mark 6.21)—but they become a good deal scarcer, although there are plenty of notations about the robes, cups, and seats "of estate." These ritual objects seem calculated to hark back to historical traditions no longer fully in force.
4. Middle English contains some such references, but since all are found in collections of wills and governmental documents, it would seem that the term in this sense was still specific to legal discourse, and no instance of it can be found before 1407. Chrimes asserts that *estate* was not used for "land," interest in land," "endowments," or "property" at all before the fifteenth century, and then only sparingly (89).
5. Later the preacher acts out an interrogation of a priest at the last judgment who is asked "Who stirid the to take vpon the so hise astaate?" (180–81). The sermon is quoted from the Duquesne Studies edition of 1967. An excerpt of it is printed in Owst *Literature and Pulpit* 550–51.
6. In immediate political terms, that meant that tribute paid by the English king to the Pope because of the submission of King John might justly be denied; Wyclif prepared that case to present to Parliament at John of Gaunt's urging, though it is not certain that the case was ever actually presented.
7. Pope Formosus was actually reduced to lay status by Pope John VIII before John was elected to the papacy in 891. Formosus was found unfit for the office and his acts rescinded by a court established by Stephen VII after his death in 896. Still later, that decision was reversed.
8. Early converts to English Protestantism were likelier to be urban artisans than either aristocrats and their servants and retainers or the rural peasantry, and Protestant leaders were ministers who had been "freed from feudal connections," many by the Marian exile (Walzer 14–15).
9. In 1592 one Thomas Wiggin was "translated" from his guild to that of the vintners in order to marry a vintner's widow, his fine waived because he was "a young man and his estate to be but small" (Rappaport 41).
10. For example, "Hence grew a very dissolution of all estates" (160.8) and "at the great parliament which was then to be held they should, in the name of all the estates, persuade the king" (220.14–15; cf. 326.8).
11. Ben Jonson's characters often use *estate* to assert their feudal importance, while they seek financial gain. In *Epicoene*, *estate* as position in the world is used early in the play, but by the end both Morose and Dauphine are speaking of the financial inheritance as Morose's *estate*. When Volpone torments Corvino about his wife's supposed adultery, his similar phrasing refers to an exalted public image as well as money: "You need not care, you have a good estate, / To bear it out" (V.vi.22–23).
12. There is a sleight of hand in the timing of this plot, akin to the much-discussed "double time-scheme" in Othello. Bassanio asks to try the casket test as soon as he has the opportunity, refusing Portia's invitation to wait in order to enjoy her company a bit longer (III.ii.1–25). Yet the loan from

Shylock is for three months. I think that this looseness in Bassanio's medieval/courtly sense of time is being contrasted with the legalistic time mode of capitalism in the Antonio vs. Shylock plot.

Notes to Chapter 4: Fre/Free

1. If Chaucer himself mistranslated either Latin *iugo* or French *ioug* ("yoke") as "judge," it makes little difference to my argument, since the passage plays on the tensions within *free* whether the priest considers himself above judgment or without the yoke (burden) of office (see Riverside's explanatory notes).
2. Christ is represented elsewhere in Margery's narrative as expressing the wish that other wives "myght be as frely fro her husbondys as thu art fro thyn" (212).
3. It was *The Courtier* rather than *Utopia* that James I evoked in his rhetorically grand defenses of "a free and absolute Monarche" (McIlwain's edition 54.21). These instances stress both the class privilege—nobility in the legal sense—and the unencumbered powers of action of the monarch himself. Unlike Hythloday's stress on the happiness of the citizens as the measure of the kingdom, James argues that the populace is aggrandized by the prestige of the prince, suggesting an unbroken link with medieval tradition.
4. The same scriptural passage, frequently cited in later Protestant discourse, is, for example, the key to most of John Bale's uses of *fre*, as when Ynglond accuses the Cardynall of transforming the nation from a "fre woman" to a "bonde mayd" (*King Johan*, 1684; cf. 2232 and 2596).
5. Even Bishop Cooper, answering one of the Marprelate tracts in *Admonition to the People*, admits that, "to make holy or vnholy those things that God hath left free . . . is one of the chief grounds of Papisticall corruption" (Pierce 167). In this matter he is, of course, agreeing with his radical Protestant opponents.
6. In the *Amoretti*, Spenser also engages in that bound/free paradox: "Fondnesse it were for any being free, / To covet fetters, though they golden be" (Sonnet 37, 13–14). That trope meshes closely (although indirectly) with the equally paradoxical sense of Christian freedom/commitment. The Envoy to the *Shepheardes Calender* imitates Chaucer's "go litle Boke," but continues "thou hast a free passeporte" (7). The *free* seems to imply both "noble," a franchise from the nobility, and "unconstrained" a chance for wide dissemination. A class-conscious note is struck in the next line, where the "lyttle Calender" is advised to walk "lowly . . . emongste the meaner sort," i.e., to avoid prideful comparison with Chaucer and Virgil (which the warning, of course, also invites). Passports had recently been issued to Elizabeth's disbanded troops to allow them to travel to their homes without being arrested for vagrancy.
7. Although estimates of London's population vary rather widely, all agree that the city sustained its spectacular growth during the sixteenth century through immigration, since its death rate was measureably higher than its rate of births.
8. Leeds Barroll has argued convincingly that the crown cannot have exerted so irresistible an influence as has been claimed for it, while in fact the

poorage, the City Fathers, the guilds, and Parliament all provided possible locations for resistance to the monarch's will (24).

9. *Family of Love* also alludes to freedom as sexual license, though without the mercantile reference: "Truly, husband, my love must be free still to God's creatures: yea, nevertheless, preserving you still as the head of my body, I will do as the spirit shall move me" (V.iii.425).

10. In other plays, Jonson produces different effects with *free*. In *Every Man in his Humor*, Knowell's epigramatic "Force works on servile natures, not the free" (I.i.208) contrasts with Kitely's assertion that before marriage he was "free master" of his own "free thoughts" (III.iii.19), the first making fuller use of the old meaning, the second the new. In *Catiline* the uses of free (14 of them) ring changes of perspective and register ironies within the political venue of "unfettered," ironies like Catiline's "I command you to be free" (I.i.581). An emergent usage,"not otherwise engaged," turns up in *The Alchemist*, when Face tells Kastril, "he, by that time, will be free" (III.iv.132)—the first instance of this usage I have found. In the same play Drugger is said to be "free of the city" in the legal sense (I.iii).

Notes to Chapter 5: Gloss

1. A similar attitude toward glossing is found in "Who says Sooth, He shall be Shent"(1390): "Thus is the sothe I-kept in close, / And vche mon maketh touh and queynte; / To leue the tixt and take the glose, / Eueri word thei coloure and peynte" (Brown 152–54). In Brown's view, internal evidence suggests a friar as author. It is possible that this poem was composed when Wyclif and the friars made common cause against certain ecclesiastical abuses, but it could simply indicate that Lollards were not the only witnesses to the misuse of glossing.

2. Britton Harwood argues that Imaginative tells the story of the woman taken in adultery, with its stress on Christ's writing on the ground, to establish "the Old Law *as something that must be interpreted*" and justify "the tradition of the gloss" (71, Harwood's italics).

3. Sometimes, but not often, he includes the word *glose* or *glosa*. He also relied on the glosses to Statius's *Thebaid* and Boccaccio's *Teseida* as he composed *The Knight's Tale*, suggesting that the scholarly practice was available to and respected by Chaucer. Even in these translations, *gloss* can appear as Fortune's seductive tool "glosynge wordes" (II.pr.3.64–65). A non-pejorative tone is evident in his remark that the whole story of Troy, "bothe text and glose" (333), was told in stained glass windows in the "Book of the Duchess" (*Riverside's* note suggests that the glose here may be an illustrative medallion sometimes used to clarify a written text).

4. Additional Chaucerian instances include the Manciple's refusal to flatter, "thou shalt nat been yglosed" and the Monk's reference to Lady Fortune's dangerous flattery, "Beth war, for whan that Fortune list to glose, / Thanne wayteth she her man to overthrowe" (VII.2140–41), a Boethian sentiment.

5. The three volumes of sermons edited by Thomas Arnold simply explain the text for each Sunday and holiday and draw out its ethical and social lessons. Although the "four senses" of Patristic exegesis are mentioned (I.30 and II.277–78), there are no attempts to explain all four.

6. This negative aura for *gloss* came to be widely deployed. John Knox argues in his *Appellation to the Nobility* that "the author of the gloss upon their canon" credits the pope with being able to "change the nature of things," making injustice into justice (138.26–37). John Jewel's *Apology for the English Church* warns against Catholic attention to council findings which distort the scripture: "Thus lurk they under the name of the church, and beguile silly creatures with their vain glozing" (89). Thomas Elyot's *Governor* calls the "innumerable glosses" which mince necessary ideas into fragments the "feces and dregs" of learning (53.21–23). The accusers of John Oldcastle in John Foxe's account are false spies "and glozing glaverers" (III.323.38). Richard Hooker warns in the *Laws* not to seek to "smother [truth] with glosing delusions" (49.36–50.1).
7. Wyatt's paraphrase of Psalm 6 ascribes "glosing bait" to David's enemies (175–76); in Psalm 51, David acknowledges God's preference for the sacrifice of a "sprite contrite" instead of "such gloze / Of outward deed as men dream and devise" (498–99).
8. Arthur Golding's translation of *The Metamorphoses* also treats glossing as sophistry, here poetic subtlety: "they shadowing with their gloses...too turne the truth too toyes and lyes" (11.530–31). Golding's other instance, "The glittering glosse of godlynesse beguyld her long" (192.547), points toward the modern "glossy advertisement."
9. In Yong's *Diana*, *glosse* refers to the amplification of a poem by an additional stanza ending with a line of the original: "He sung a glosse vpon this Dittie" (437). Gabriel Harvey's letters too provide positive, if playful, references *glossing*: "the charitable and fatherly glosse of Innocentius Tertius" (*Letterbook*, 76.1) and "The gloss / Is grosse: / The text / Is next" in his poem to his mistress (125.1–4), contributing to the poem's irreverent university tone by invoking the scholarly "text and gloss" formula.
10. He warns Leicester to avoid overinterpretation in the dedication to *Virgil's Gnat*: "Ne further seeke to gloze upon the text" (10) and assures Anne "I love not to gloze, where I love indeed" (5).

Notes to Chapter 6: Kynde/Kind

1. For example, Wyclif translates "contra naturam" as "aȝens kynde" (Romans 11.24) in his Early Version; Trevisa "innatas," "opera naturae" as "workes of kynde," in *Higden* (2.155, 3.293, 8.35) and in *Bartholomeus*, "virtutis naturalis" as "kinde vertu" (27). The medical treatise *Chauliac* uses *kinde* to translate Latin "naturale" (31).
2. Some translators use it to render the Latin *gratis*; Trevisa, for example, in *Bartholomeus* (198 and 233). I found two examples of *kind* as a verb: *Knight of the Tour Landry* extols the hind for caring for the young of other species, "and kindithe hem tille they may susteine hem selff" (112), and *The Faerie Queene* reminds the war-like Radigund that she "of men was kynded" not of bears and tigers (5.5.40.8).
3. Robinson's translation of *Utopia* also uses the very old sense of gender for *kynde*: priests may be women since "that kinde is not excluded from priesthode"; in church the "male kinde [Latin: "viri"]" sit before the goodman of the household, the "female kinde" before the goodwife

(108–09). David Lindsay's *Ane Satyre of the Thrie Estaitis* denounces celibate clerics who are a danger to women as long as "kynde of Nature In them growis" (2771), and Philip Stubbes uses *kind* as "sex" when he castigates actors for adulterating "the verite of his owne kinde" by impersonating women, the figures thus created being "*Hermaphrodita*, that is, Monsters of bothe kinds, half women, half men."

4. In *Castle of Perseverance* we read: "Thou hast ben to God vnkynde"; in *Ludus Coventry* there are apologies to God that his "vnkynde creatures" have grieved Him, and *Mankind* admonishes "Be not vnkynde to Gode" (280). *A Book to a Mother* has God accusing his "unkynde" children, and Margery Kempe accuses herself of being an "vnkynde" creature toward God (38.33; 207.25). The idea is frequently found in preaching and devotional writing: *Barlaam*, *Dives and Pauper*, *Chartier's Treatise on Hope*, *Mirk Festial*, *Wyclif's Lantern of Light* and sermons, *Prick of Conscience* and *Orchard of Syon*."

5. Medical works especially use *kynde* in this sense, as in *Anatomy Wellcome* (MS 64): "Sangueyn or blood is the norischinge of the body and frend to kynde and the mooste vertu aboute the herte" (51b/a), and *Lanfranc's Cirurgie* (1400): "Whanne tho [superfluities] ben y-dried, kynde engendrith fleisch" (14.11). So do books of recipes, like *Stockholm Recipes* (1450), which recommends letting a mixture "sethe there in his owyn kynde" (33.2) and keeping ground condiments away from everything except their own kynde (104.29). Ripley's *Compend of Alchemy* often uses the word to emphasize the systemic "knowledge" his work involves: "So doth our erth by kynde drawe done to hime his soule bore vp withe winde" (60a, cf. 45a).

6. All the medical treatises and many other texts refer to these "hetes": Lydgate, *Diseases of Women*, *Macer*, *Gilbertus Anglicus*, *Anatomy Wellcome* MS 64, as well as Wimbledon's sermon and Recipes from the Hunterian MSS 2378 (which gives an antidote for scalding).

7. In commenting on the shape of the whole, I am referring to the B text. The C text uses *kind* in addition as the grammatical category "gender": "As adiectif and substantyf vnite asken. / Acordaunce in kynde, in cas, and in numbre" (4.339); as "kin" or "offspring": "A book of the old lawe, that a-corsed alle couples that had no kynde forth brouhte" (19.224), and as "benevolent": "Beo unkynde to thyn emcrystene [fellow-Christian]" and risk condemnation (20.216).

8. Like so much in the Do-Best section of the poem, this vantage point on the gospel story has been hinted at, *Kynde's* being cousin to Christ, for example, and Abraham's assertion in Passus 16 that "creatour weex creature to knowe what was bothe" (215).

9. Among the very few instances of an older sense for *kind* is Hooker's mention of natural agents, who "keep the law of their kind unwittingly" (59.7–8).

10. This usage is rare in Middle English, although it does occur in the collection *English Poems of Charles of Orlean*: "Allas How euyr kouthe the god of kynde / A body shape so fayre and so goodly / And in it sett a hert so hard an hert vnkynde?" (185.5520–23).

11. Wyatt's translation of Psalm 38 makes use of the equivocation for a different end, invoking the medieval associations between *kind* and *kin*. "Reason and wit unjust, / As kin unkind, were farthest gone at need" (367–68). Here

it is the reason and wit of the natural man which were no more loyal than cruel/unnatural kinfolk's.

12. Spenser's *The Faerie Queene* contains the last example the *OED* has located for the meaning "gender," when Britomart is asked what made her "dissemble her disguised kind" (III.ii.4.7).

13. "Natural" and "benevolent" are both available to interpreting the blind King of Paphlagonia's (Shakespeare's Gloucester in *Lear*) confession of a "foolish kindness to my unkind bastard" (182.21–22). This can be read as a foolish naturalness, toward an unnatural "natural son" (as bastards were often called), a foolish benevolence toward an unbenevolent son, or a natural and tender-hearted love nonetheless foolish because of the unnaturalness of the boy. This repetition of a bifurcated term in which both instances call up both meanings is a neat rhetorical effect which Sidney's text makes use of often, but in this passage it is a strong indictment of the "natural order" which the old king sees as violated.

Notes to Chapter 7: Lewid/Lewd

1. Fourteenth-century English clerics were not all learned. Bishop Brunton charged that many parish priests could scarcely say their Pater Noster properly, and several campaigns to improve the level of clerical education were launched during the fourteenth century; see Owst, *Preaching* 15–20, and Pantin 238.

2. When Queen Elizabeth was told by Chancellor William Cecil that Cambridge University must be addressed only in Latin, she "marvelously astonied" her auditors by delivering a learned and graceful Latin paegyric (Rice's edition 71–73).

3. Among the many examples of this usage from the late fourteenth century are: Master Wimbledon's sermon, which depicts a soul appearing there "as a prest other [or] as a lewid man" (271); a 1390 translation of Robert Grosseteste's *Castle of Love*, which the translator begins: "Her byginnet a tretys / That is yclept Castel off Loue, / That bisschop Grosteyʒt made ywis, / ffor lewede mennes by-houe" (355.1–4); and an *Ars Moriendi* book aimed "not only at lewed men but also to religiouse men" (quoted in Duffy 316).

4. The first instance of "foolish" in the *MED* is from Trevisa's *Higden*, and the first instance of "worthless" is Langland's striking phrasing from the A-Text of *Piers Plowman*: "Chastity withouten Charite (wite thou forsothe), / Is as lewed as a laumpe that no liht is Inne" (1.163).

5. The *OED* gives only one instance of the sense "lay person" after 1553, and that is obviously antiquarian.

6. Here is the whole handful of sexually tinged instances given for this popular word in the *MED*: Trevisa's *Bartholomeus* warns against japing "with the genytal membres" "at a lewed likynge" (60b), Audelay's *Poems* (1426) upbraids those priests "lewyd in here leuyng...ʒe were choson to chastyte" (3.57), *Knyght of the Tour-Landry* blames a "leude look" for King David's fall into adultery (57.34), and in a tale from the *Gesta Romanorum*, an abbot defends his monk from the charge of making a knight a cuckold by saying "my monk is not so lewde, for to do such a dede" (Add., 421).

7. The power of the Latin prayers used to consecrate the host was, in Eamon

Duffy's view, regarded as "too sacred to be communicated to the 'lewẹd'";
it would save them whether or not they understood It (218). Duffy himself
defends the Latin mass as exhibiting "the decent obscurity of the learned
language" (110), and denies that ignorance of the language made the
service non-participitory for lay people.

8. In an examination before the star chamber in the Marprelate matter,
Attorney-General Popham accuses Penry of being a "seditious and leud
rebel" (Pierce 207). One Humphrey Newman is given a submission which
confesses the "lewdnes and greevousnes of my saide former practices," but
he refuses to sign it. In their turn, the Marprelate group inveighed against
the *lewd* ministers appointed by the bishops. Even the Bishop of
Winchester admitted that "some lewd and unlearned ministers had been
made," and Elizabeth had chided the bishops because she was receiving
complaints from the House of Commons about the "lewd life and corrupt
behavior" of their appointees (Pierce 109, 110).

Notes to Chapter 8: Providence

1. In *Conquest of Ireland purveynge* seems to bar one Reymond from a place
among elite knights on account of his practical bent: "he was a man fre and
meke, queynt and Purueynge; and thegh he in both were mych to preyse,
he was bettyr ledder of hoste than knyght" (99.22).
2. This contrast is reinforced by other textual signals: the Knight's handling
of time is leisurely, the Miller's hurried, even frantic; Emelye is described in
terms of brightness, philosophical value, Alisoun in terms of plants and
animals, sense-world values; causal links between events in *The Knight's
Tale* are narrated from the "heye heights of thinges," in *The Miller's Tale*
produced directly by the characters' actions (although John does look
down from the high rafters when he is equipping the tubs).
3. Blundeville's title is *The True Order and Methode of Wryting and Reading
Hystories*, sig. F3ʳ and F3ᵛ. I owe this reference to my colleague Beverly
Sauer.
4. In *The Holy Pretence*, George Mosse argues that Puritans need not be seen as
uncompromisingly otherworldly; many developed "a theology which was
well attuned to political action, and flexible enough to use all sorts of holy
pretences in carrying out its aim of building the godly society" (152).
5. The Queen herself also recognises the two senses of the word in public life,
acknowledging that Parliament's counsels in the matter of Mary Queen of
Scots have been "careful, provident, and profitable for the preservation of
my life" (95.13), but elsewhere insisting on "the providence of God"
(117.17–18). *Providence* is cited frequently in Greville's *Life of Sidney* (at least
26 instances), often as God's providence but also as the wise planning of
"providences of councells in treaties of peace, or aliance, summons of
warres" and the like (15) in real political life or fiction. *The Protestation of
Martin Marprelate* urges that in spite of their innocence the Puritans will
suffer under the bishops unless aided by "the providence of god and the
gracious clemency of her majesty" (4), but later praises the secrecy of those
who have hidden Martin's identity, calling *them* "provident" (15).
6. The fable of Prometheus figures "theternal woord of God, / His wisdom and

his providence" (453–54, 446). The usefulness of pagan texts was often defended as testimony to natural reason (Calvin's "secret guidance" as natures require it—1.16.4), but in this text Golding seems to be claiming Calvin's sense of "special providence" as well.

7. Spenser also uses *purveyance*, employing it in a typical early modern way for the more pedestrian matter of daily supplies: a siege will eventually succeed through "dispurvayance long" (III.x.10.3; cf. III.xi.53.9). His *Present State of Ireland* preserves the same distinction: *purveyance* for the provisioning of troops [139.4] and *providence* for God's plan for Ireland (44.32–33, 47.22).

8. *Provident* was not as likely to be treated so soberly. Thomas Middleton's *Michaelmas Term* uses it for the back door "convenient for a gentleman" who might be caught in fiscally or sexually compromising places (I.i.138) and for the "wise and provident father" Quomodo claims he has been just before his son reveals his contempt (IV.iv.28).

9. And by the end of the first scene he has conducted a slick piece of usury by investing money in his nephew's military commission to get him out of the way while he appropriates his nephew's whole inheritance.

Notes to Chapter 9: Queynte/Quaint

1. The Middle English signifier is spelled *queint(e)*, *quaint(e)*, *quoint(e)*, *quant(e)*, *quent(e)*, *quint(e)*, *coint(e)*, *koint(e)*, *koweinte*, *kint*, *wheinte*, *whaint(e)*, *waint*, and *wente*, in the list given in the *MED*. There are other spellings as well.

2. "Refresh" is Alisoun's euphemism for sex in her comment on King Solomon's polygamy: "wolde God it were leveful [lawful] to me / To be refresshed half so ofte as he" (37–38).

3. The timid narrator of *Troilus and Criseyde* "inadvertently" indulges in the same wordplay in V.543, when Troilus refers to Criseyde's empty house as "thow lanterne of which queynt is the light." This passage has the same overall structure as the three instances in *The Knight's Tale*, but may also make syntactic sense as a straightforward pun (Sheila Delany 18–19).

4. Some instances of *country* refer, of course, simply to the terrain or call attention to the rural scene. Duke Senior sees a stag bitter against the "country, city, court" attempting to usurp the rightful domain of the animals in *As You Like It* (II.i.59), arranging the three as if in ascending order of civilization.

5. Lodovico's description of Brachiano's death by strangling in *The White Devil*: "No woman-keeper i'th'world, / Though she had practis'd seven years at the pest-house, / Could have done it quaintlier" (V.iii.174–76) also links ingenuity with female sexuality. Instances in Tourneur's *Revenger's Tragedy* have the same coloring. Vendice explicitly credits female elusiveness—"a lady can / As such all his, beguile a wiser man" as he works his own disguise on the skull of his dead betrothed—"Have I not fitted the old surfeiter / With a quaint piece of beauty." Hippolito returns to the term by applauding the "quaintness" of his brother's malice, which he finds "above thought," i.e., no ordinary *cogitum* (III.iv.52–55, 109–10).

Notes to Chapter 10: Sely/Silly

1. Among the few recorded instances are Layamon's *Brut* (1300), which

describes the king's predatory son as "onsellishe lifuede...ᴣit ᴣeo [any young woman] were fuli and fore...he...makede hire hore" (3500); Walton's *Boethius* (1410): "Now am I set in sorowes and vnselthe" (13); and *The Conquest of Ireland* (1525): "euery gladnesse ys endet wyth sorowe, & euery selth hath unselth at the end" (50.8).

2. *Unsely* in devotional works suggests "cursed" or "depraved." *Speculum Christiani* refers to an *vnsely* soul forsaken by God (72.1); Judas is an "vnsely disciple" in Nicholas Love's *Mirror* (225); and a "wicche vnseely" was brought to the bishop in *Peter Idley's Instructions to His Son*. In the more secular genres, *unsely* might also mean to be unlucky: Hector is *onsely* on a certain day of battle (Yonge's *Secreta Secretorum 163.1*). Lydgate's *Troy Book* has "Eleyne...Hard & vnᴣely...Thou haste vs brouᴣt in meschef & in were" (2.4233) and "A! Priam Kyng! vncely is thi chance!" (2.3249).

3. Both the Early and Later Wycliffite Bible translations use *sely* to translate Latin "felix" and imply "blessed." The Early Version gives Wisdom 3.13 as "Sely is the bareyn & the vndefouled," and the Early Version of Wisdom 15.14 says "vnwise men & vnsely" where the Later Version substitutes "cursid." Wyclif's Later Version has "Y am an vncely man; who schal delyuer me." The Wycliffite *Lanterne of Light* stresses implications of innocent vulnerability in "& with this craft thei cacchen awey the goodis of thise celi widowis" (52).

4. The trope of a predatory institution invading the house of conscience was resilient, and turns up in John Jewel's Reformation treatise *Apology for the English Church* (English translation, 1567): "Thus lurk they [Catholic decrees] under the name of the church, and beguile silly creatures with their vain glozing" (89).

5. More's English tract *Supplication of Souls* answers Simon Fish's attack on clerical power and wealth, *A Supplication for the Beggars*. "Sely" appears in its first sentence to identify the bringers of the supplication, the reader's late relatives and friends, now "pore prysoners of god ye sely sowlys in purgatory" (111.6–7). Their helplessness (as the Yale edition glosses *sely*) is highlighted, since their continued suffering is the likely result of an acceptance of Fish's position. These souls are not guiltless, but they will presumably be saved eventually; thus they resemble More's readers more nearly than either spotless saints or hopeless reprobates and deserve prayers just as More's readers would wish to be prayed for, suggesting *sely* as "innocent." *Sely*, therefore, may be seen as a key term in positioning More's audience to receive the *Supplication*. In *A Dialogue of Comfort*, More embraces its emergent sense, like the "sely rude roryng asse" (111.3) and the "sely pore pismeres & Antes" (158.13). An instance which fuses strong elements of contemptible with fainter shadings of innocent and foolish is the description of the offspring of pusillanimity, "a sely whrechid girle & ever pulyng, that is callid scrupulosity or a scrupulouse conscience" (112.17–19).

6. Spenser's association of *silly* with rusticity may be seen in his objection to the arrogance of quartering English soldiers with an Irish tenant farmer: the "wretched poor man and the silly poor wife...glad to purchase their peace with anything" (*View of Ireland* 80.33–34).

7. In *Dido*, for example, Aeneas' men are welcomed to Carthage "as Jupiter to sillie Baucis house" (I.ii.41), "uncalculating," "rustic," unthreatening, but

ultimately victorious. In *Tamburlaine I*, Zenocrate calls herself a "silly maid" to save herself from the "lawlesse rapine" she initially fears from Tamburlaine (I.ii.10), and Tamburlaine asserts that his troops, who seem now "but silly country Swains" will eventually make the mountains quake with their conquests (I.ii.47).

Notes to Chapter 11: Thrift

1. Similarly, when the poem "Corruption of Manners" accuses the rich as "Ye prowd galonttes... With youre short gownys thriftlesse, / Have brought this londe in gret hevynesse" (*Political Poems* II.251), its disapproval is focused mainly on the immodesty of the dress, but secondarily on its financial extravagance.
2. Skill and practicality explain the arrangement of the Yeoman's peacock arrows "thriftily" under his belt (I.105), and the "thrifty clooth" the Wife of Bath denies having at home (III.238) may suggest her exalted sense of what is proper for her clothing, but she may be complaining that even simple cloth is denied by her husband's imputed niggardliness.
3. Thomas Cromwell's object is civil order in his endorsement of craft, "lest at any time afterwards they [the young] be driven for lack of some mystery or profession to live by, to fall to begging, stealing, or some other unthriftiness" (Royal Injunction, excerpted in Cressy 17).
4. William Harrison agreed; vagabonds are "a thriftless sort" who "lick the sweat from the true labourers' brows" ("The Description of Britaine," Holinshed I.10).
5. In Beaumont and Fletcher's *Knight of the Burning Pestle*, the citizen's wife mistakenly dismisses the intended hero of the play-within-the-play as an "unthrifty youth" (II.157), and later the heroine's father, too, calls him an "unthrift" (IV.132). The instances of *thrift* in Thomas Middleton's *Michaelmas Term* work the same way—Quomodo refers to his own "thrift and covetous hopes" for his son and the son's "rare thrift" in keeping through law what was gotten by craft (IV.i.39; IV.iv.22).
6. John Harington, translator of Ariosto's *Orlando Furioso*, describes the Prodigal Son of the scripture in the same terms, "given over to all unthriftiness, all looseness of life and conversation" (38–39). This description matches the Common Council's language restricting plays, "unthrifty waste of the money of the poor and fond persons" (Adams 109).
7. Another interesting instance of this kind is Viola/Cesario's sympathetic "what thriftless sighs shall poor Olivia breathe" in *Twelfth Night* (II.ii.40). "Unlikely to thrive," certainly, but perhaps "improper," or even, in view of the stress on monetary images in the wooing scene ("leave the world no copy," "schedules of my beauty" "will" as inheritance, and "recompensed"), archly prodigal.

Notes to Chapter 12: Virtù/Virtue

1. The expression common to both eras is "by [or through the] virtue of," in which "power" is the operant sense; the adjective *virtuous* usually means "morally good" in both.

2. Mannyng's *Handlyng Sin* alludes to Jephthah thus: "whan he had, thurgh goddys vertu, / Uf the batuylk peya and pru   he thanked god" (2853). The *Metrical Life of Christ* reads "Lazarus, he saide tho, / I comaunde thee so, / In the vertue of the Trinite...That thou rise in quycke astate" (1738–42). In Capgrave's *Lives*, St. Gilbert regarded the growth of his order as indicative of "Goddis vertu, and noot his."

3. The idea was kept before the people. *Speculum Christiani* bids "that euery curat expowne....The seuen principal vertuse" (6.9) and "The therde tabyl tretes of the werkys of mercy and of seuen principalle vertuse" (8.8). The *Castle of Perseverance* reads "Thus vycys ageyns vertues fytyn ful snelle [quickly]" (70) and "The seuene synnys I forsake / And to these seuene vertuis I me take" (1691).

4. The one notable exception occurs when one of the muses welcomes Pallas to their secluded spring but tells her "your vertue greater works than these are, calls you to" (108.342), implying that either her greater powers to act or her greater goodness require her in the larger world.

5. Instances of *virtue* as "power" did not disappear altogether: Samuel Daniel wrote of Edward III: "He builds up strength and greatness for his heirs / Out of the virtues that adorned his blood," suggesting efficacious inheritances, and Ralph Holinshed calls Henry V's "virtues notable" just after he has mentioned that he was a "terror to rebels and suppresser of sedition" (Daniel and Holinshed are quoted in Rollins and Baker). William Perkins delivered a sermon at Sturbridge Fair in 1593 which offered a commodity "from heaven, so it is a heavenly virtue and will work that which all the wealth in this fair is not able to do" (quoted in Agnew 140). In his political works, James I uses *vertue* to mean goodness; as in several usages discussed earlier, he is a retrospective thinker, perhaps one consciously attempting to reappropriate some medieval ideological forces to strengthen his office.

6. It is not unusual to allegorize *virtue* as female, and in the *Apology for Poetry* Sidney himself does so: "Poetry ever setteth virtue so out in her best colors, making fortune her well-waiting hand maid, that one must needs be enamored of her."

7. In *Dido*, Aeneas is welcomed to Carthage for his *vertues*, which may make glancing reference to his moral excellence, but certainly refers to his power to protect the city "from annoy" (I.i.78, 153). Edward is asked to cherish "vertue and nobility" (*Edward II*, III.i.167) in his barons—not goodness, but feudal battle prowess—and similarly Mortimer replies to the threat of prison that stone walls cannot "Immure [his] vertue that aspires to heaven" (III.i.257).

8. The play does include one instance of the feminized sense; in Act V, Zanche uses *virtue* to mean chastity. In addition, there is one instance in *The White Devil* which can be read as an inclusive use of *virtue*. In Atonelli's analogy to petals giving off perfume when crushed, "affliction / Expresseth virtue" (I.i.49–50), both the power and the goodness proper to it.

9. *Virtue* as "power" is not, of course, absent from Shakespeare's plays. An interesting instance of its particularly male inflection is Roderigo's despair over not being able to stop loving Desdemona: "it is not in my virtue to amend it" (I.iii.320).

References

Primary texts

A Fourteenth-Century English Biblical Version, ed. Anna C. Paues (Cambridge: Cambridge University Press, 1904).

Adam and Eve (from the Wheatley MS), ed. M. Day, EETS 155 (1921), 76–91.

Aelred of Rievaulx's de Institutione Inclusarum, ed. John Ayto and Alexandra Barratt, EETS 287 (London: Oxford University Press, 1984).

Agnus Castus: A Middle English Herbal, ed. G. Brödin, Essays and Studies on English Language and Literature, Uppsala University (1950), 119–96, 204–05.

Alexander and Dindimus (1450), *The Gests of King Alexander of Macedon*, ed. F.P. Magoun, Jr. (1929), 171–216.

Anatomy Welcome (1392), *MED* Library mss. 564.

Arderne, John, *Treatises of Fistula*, ed. D'Arcy Power, EETS 139 (1910).

Arthour and Merlin, ed. E. Köbling, *Altenglische Bibliothek*, 4 (1890), 3–272.

Assembly of Gods, ed. O.L. Triggs, EETSes 69 (1896).

Audelay, John, *Poems*, ed. E.K. Whiting, EETS 184 (1931).

Augustine,Saint, *The Confessions*, trans. E.B. Pusey (London: Dent; New York; Dutton, 1907).

Ayenbite of Inwit (Dan Michel's Ayenbite of Inwit), ed. R. Morris, EETS 23 (1866, rpt. 1895), 1–262.

Bacon, Francis, *Essays*, The World's Classics (London: Oxford University Press, n.d.).

Bale, John, *King Johan* (1538–40), Malone Society Reprints (London: Oxford University Press, 1931).

Barlaam and Josaphat, ed. W.C. Kayser (1877).

Beaumont and Fletcher, *A Chaste Maid in Cheapside*, ed. R.B. Parker (London: Methuen, 1973).

Beaumont and Fletcher, *A King and No King*, ed. Robert Turner (Lincoln: University of Nebraska Press, 1963).

Beaumont and Fletcher, *Knight of the Burning Pestle*, ed. John Doebler (Lincoln: University of Nebraska Press, 1967).

Benedictine Rule, Northern Prose Version, in *Three Middle English Versions of the Rule of St. Benet*, ed. E.A. Kock, EETS 120 (1902), 1–47.

Body Politic, the Middle English translation of Christine de Pisan's *Livre du Corps de policie*, ed. D. Bornstein (1977).

Book of Kervynd & Norture, Early English Meals and Manners, ed. F.J. Furnivall, EETS 32 (1868, rpt. 1931), 1–83.

Book of the Knight of La Tour Landry (1450), ed. T. Wright, EETS 33 (1868, rev. 1906).

Book to a Mother, ed. Adrian James McCarthy (Salzburg: University of Salzburg, 1981).

Brown, Carleton, *Religious Lyrics of the XIV Century*, 2nd edn (Oxford: Clarendon Press, 1970).

Brut, The or *The Chronicles of England* (1400), ed. F.W.D. Brie, EETS 131 (1906) and 136 (1908).

Calvin, John, *Institutes of the Christian Religion*, trans. Ford Lewis Battles, Library of Christian Classics (Philadelphia. Westminster Press, 1960), 2 vols.

Capgrave, John, *John Capgrave's Lives of St. Augustine and St. Gilbert of Sempringham*, ed. J.J. Munro, EETS 140 (London: Kegan Paul, Trench, Trübner, 1910).

Castle of Love, ed. C. Horstmann, EETS 98 (1892); F.J. Furnivall, EETS 117 (1901).

Castle of Perseverance: The Marco Plays, ed. F.J. Furnivall and A.W. Pollard, EETSes 91 (1904, rpt. 1924), 77–186.

Catholicon Anglicum, ed. S.J.H. Herrtage, EETS 75 (1881), 1–428.

Chapman, George, *Bussy D'Ambois (1604–05)*, ed. Maurice Evans (New Mermaid, New York: Hill and Wang, 1966).

Charles of Orleans, *The English Poems of Charles of Orleans*, ed. R. Steele, EETS 215 (1941).

Chaucer, Geoffrey, *The Riverside Chaucer*, ed. David Benson *et al.* (New York: Houghton Mifflin, 1987).

Chauliac, *The Cyrurgie of Guy de Chauliac*, ed. M.S. Ogden, EETS 265 (London: Oxford University Press, 1971).

Chester Plays, Part I (1607), Hrl 2124, ed. H. Deimling, EETSes 62 (1892, rpt 1926).

Chester Plays, Part II, ed. Matthews, EETSes 115 (1916), 241–400, 427–53.

Clanvowe, John, *The Works of John Clanvowe*, ed. John Scattergood (Cambridge, England: D.S. Brewer, 1975).

Clyomon and Clamydes (1599), ed. Betty J. Littleton (The Hague: Mouton, 1968).

Common Conditions, ed. Tucker Brooke (New Haven, Conn.: Yale University Press, 1915).

Conquest of Ireland, ed. F.J. Furnival, EETS 107 (1896).

"Constitutions of Masonry," *The Early History of Freemasonry*, ed. James Orchard Halliwell (London: T. Rodd, 1840).

Coverdale, Miles, *Paraphrase of Erasmus upon the New Testament*, Early English Books.

Croxton Play of the Sacrament, ed. O. Waterhouse, EETSes 104 (1909).

Cursor Mundi (1325), ed. R. Morris, EETS 57 (1874), 59 (1875), 62 (1876), 66 (1877), 68 (1878).

Dean, James (ed.), *Six Ecclesiastical Satires*, Medieval Institute Publications (Kalamazoo: Western Michigan University Press, 1991).

Dekker, Thomas, *The Gul's Horn-booke* (1608) (London: Dent & Sons, 1904).

Dekker, Thomas, *The Plague Pamphlets of Thomas Dekker*, ed. F.P. Wilson (Oxford: Clarendon Press, 1925).

Deloney, Thomas, *The Works of Thomas Deloney*, ed. Francis Oscar Mann (Oxford: Clarendon Press, 1967).

Destruction of Troy (1400), in *English Metrical Romances*, ed. W.W. French and C.B. Hale (1930), 809–19.

Destruction of Troy, ed. G.A. Pantin and D. Donaldson, EETS 39 (1869); EETS 56 (1874).

Diseases of Women (1540), MED Library MSS Dc 37.

Dives and Pauper (1410), ed. Priscilla Heath Barnum, EETSes 275 (1976).

Earliest English Wills in the Court of Probate, London, ed. F.J. Furnivall, EETS 78 (1868).

Early English Meals and Manners, ed. F.J. Furnivall, EETS 32 (1868, rpt. 1931), 215–18.

Elizabeth I, Queen, *The Public Speaking of Queen Elizabeth: Selections from Her Official Addresses*, ed. George R. Rice, Jr. (New York: AMS Press, 1956).

Elyot, Sir Thomas, *The Book Named the Governor* (London: Dent; New York: Dutton, 1963).

Elyot, Sir Thomas, *Castle of Health* (1541), Early English Books.

Elyot, Sir Thomas, *The Defence of Good Women*, ed. Edwin Johnston Howard (Oxford, Ohio: Anchor Press, 1940).

English Conquest of Ireland (1500), ed. F.J. Furnivall, EETS 107 (1896).

English Medieval Lapidaries, ed. J. Evans and Serjeantson, EETS 190 (1933), 17–37.

Fifteenth-Century Translations of Alain Chartier's Le Traité de l'Esperance and Le Quadrilogue Invectif, ed. Margaret S. Blayney, EETS 281 (London: Oxford University Press, 1980).

Firumbras and Otuel and Roland, ed. M.I. O'Sullivan, EETSes 198 (1935), 3–58.

Florio, John, *The Essays of Montaigne done into English* (1603) (New York: AMS Press, 1967).

Florio, John, *A World of Words, or Most Copious and Exact Dictionary in Italian and English* (1598) (London: T. Warren, 1659).

Foresque, John, *Governance of England* (1475), ed. C. Plummer (1885).

Foxe, John, *Acts and Monuments*, 8 vols (New York: AMS Press, 1965).

French, W.H. and C.B. Hale, *English Metrical Romances* (New York, 1930).

Genesis and Exodus, ed. R. Morris, EETS 7 (1865; rev. 1873; rpt. 1895).

Geneva Bible: A Facsimile of the 1560 Edition, ed. Lloyd E. Berry (Madison: University of Winconsin Press, 1969).

Gentillet, Innocent, *A Discourse upon the means of wel Governing...a kingdome...Against Nicolas Machiavell, the Florentine (Contre-Machiavel)*, trans. Simon Patericke (London, 1602; New York: Da Capo Press, Theatrvm Orbis Terrarvm, 1969).

Gesta Romanorum, ed. S.J.H. Herrtage, EETS 33 (1879).

Gests of King Alexander of Macedon, ed. Francis Peabody Magoun, Jr. (Cambridge: Harvard University Press, 1929).

Gilbertus Angelicus, *Healing and Society in Medieval England: A Middle English Translation of the Pharmaceutical Writings of Gilbertus Anglicus*, ed. Faye Marie Getz (Madison: University of Winconsin Press, 1991).

Golding, Arthur (trans.), *Countre Tyrannos*, Philippe du Plessis Mornay.

Golding, Arthur (trans.), *The XV Bookes of P. Ouidius Naso, entytuled Metamorphosis* (London: Willyam Seres, 1567).

Gosson, Stephen, *The School of Abuse* (1579) (London: The Shakespeare Society, 1841).

Gosson, Stephen, *Markets of Bawdie: The Dramatic Criticism of Stephen Gosson*, ed. Arthur F. Kinney, Salzburg Studies in English Literature (Salzburg, Austria, 1974).

Gosson, Stephen, *Playes confuted in five actions*, ed. Arthur Kinney (New York: Garland, 1972).

Gower, John, *The English Works of John Gower*, ed. G.C. Macaulay, EETSes 81 (1900), 1–456; 82 (1901), 1–478.

Greville, Sir Fulke, *The Life of Sir Philip Sidney*, intro. by Nowell Smith (Oxford: Clarendon Press, 1907).

Hakluyt, Richard, *Voyages and Discoveries: The Principle Navigations, Voyages, Traffiques and Discoveries of the English Nation*, ed. Jack Beeching (London: Penguin, 1972).

Hali Meidenhad (1200), ed. O. Cockayne (1866). rev. F.J. Furnivall, EETS 18 (1922), 2–66.

Hall, Joseph, *The Art of Divine Meditation* (Binghamton, NY: Early Ren. Texts, 1981).

Harvey, Gabriel (1573–80), *The Letter-book of Gabriel Harvey*, ed. Edward John Long Scott, The Camden Society (1884; rpt. Johnson Reprint, 1965).

Hawes, Stephen, *The Pasttime of Pleasure*, ed. W.E. Mead, EETS 173 (London: Oxford University Press, 1928).

Hilton, Walter, *An Epistle on Mixed Life* (1390), Yorkshire Writers, ed. C. Horstmann (1895), 270–92.

Hoby, Thomas, *The Book of the Courtier* (London: Dent, 1944).

Hoccleve, Thomas, *Letter of Cupid to Lovers* (1402), ed. I. Gollancz, EETSes 73 (1925), 20–34.

Hoccleve, Thomas, *Works*, ed. Fredrick J. Furnivall, EETSes 61 (1892), 72 (1897), and 73 (1825).

Holinshed, Raphael, "The Description of Britaine," in Holinshed's *Chronicles*, 6 vols (1566; rpt. England, 1807–08).

Hooker, Richard, *Of the Laws of Ecclesiastical Polity*, ed. Arthur Stephen McGrade (New York: Cambridge University Press, 1989).

James I, *The Political Works of James I*, ed. Charles Howard McIlwain (Cambridge, MA: Harvard University Press, 1918).

Jewel, John, *The Works of John Jewel*, ed. John Ayre, Parker Society (Cambridge: Cambridge University Press, 1848).

Jonson, Ben, *Works*, ed. C.H. Herford and Percy Simpson (Oxford: Clarendon Press, 1925).

Julian of Norwich, *A Book of Showings to the Anchoress Julian of Norwich*, ed. Edmund Colledge O.S.A. and James Walsh S.J. (Toronto: Pontifical Institute of Medieval Studies, 1978), 2 vols.

Kempe, Margery, *The Book of Margery Kemp*, ed. Stanford Meech and Hope Emily Allen, EETS 212 (New York and London: Oxford University Press, 1961).

Kinney, Arthur (ed.), *Rogues, Vagabonds and Sturdy Beggars: A New Gallery of Tudor and Stuart Rogue Literature* (Amherst, MA: University of Massachusetts Press, 1990).

Knyght of the Tour Landry, ed. T. Wright, EETSos 33 (1868, rev. 1906).

Knox, John, *The Political Writings of John Knox*, ed. Marvin A. Breslow (London: Folger Books, 1985).

Kyd, Thomas, *The Spanish Tragedy*, ed. Thomas W. Ross (Berkeley: University of California Press, 1968).

Laȝamon's Brut, or Chronicle of Britain (1225), ed. F. Madden (1847).

Lanfranc's Science of Cirurgie (1400), ed. Robert V. Fleischhacker, EETS 102 (London: Kegan Paul, Trench, Trübner, 1894).

Langland, William, *Piers Plowman: The B Version*, ed. George Kane and E. Talbot Donaldson (London: The Athlone Press, 1975).

Laud Troy Book, ed. J.E. Wülfing, EETS 121 (1902).

References 211

Lay Folk's Catechism (1357), ed. T.F. Simmonds and H.E. Nolloth, EETSos 118 (1901).

Le Freine: The Middle English Lai of Le Freine, ed. M. Wattie, Smith Studies in Modern Languages 10.3 (1929), 1–10.

Lessons of the Dirige: Twenty-Six Political and Other Poems (1450), ed. J. Kail, EETS 124 (1904), 107–20.

Letters of Alexander to Aristotle, ed. Thomas Hahn (New York: University of Rochester, 1978).

Libelle of Englysche polycye, ed. G. Warner (1926).

Lindsay, David, *Ane Satyre of the Thrie Estaitis*, intro. by Roderick Lyall (Edinburgh: Canongate Classics, 1989).

Lodge, Thomas, "Reply to Gosson," *The Works of Thomas Lodge* (New York: Russell & Russell, 1963), vol. I.

London Prodigal: Shakespeare's Apocrypha, ed. C.F. Tucker Brook (1918).

Love, Nicholas, *Mirrour of the Blessyd Lyf of Jesu Christ*, ed. Lawrence Powell (London: Henry Frowde, 1908).

Ludus Coventry or *The Plaie called Corpus Christi*, ed. K.S. Block, EETSes 120 (1922).

Lyarde: A Satire on Monks and Friars, Reliquiae antiquae, ed. T. Wright and J.O. Halliwell, 2nd edn. (1845), 280–82.

Lydgate, John, *Fall of Princes*, ed. H. Bergen, EETSes 121–23 (1924).

Lydgate, John, *Minor Poems*, ed. H.N. McCracken, EETS 107 (1911); 192 (1934).

Lydgate, John, *Pilgrimage of the Soule*, Caxton's printing (1483).

Lydgate, John, *Siege of Thebes* (1421), ed. A. Erdman, EETSes 108 (1911).

Lydgate, John, *The Hors, the Shep, and the Ghoos* in *Munchener Beitrage*, ed. M. Degenhart (1900).

Lydgate, John, *The Life of Oure Lady*, ed. C.E. Tame (London: Washbourne, 1879).

Lydgate, John, *The Pilgrimage of the Life of Man*, ed. F.J. Furnivall, EETSes 77 (1899); 83 (1901); 92 (1904).

Lydgate, John, *Troy Book* (1420), ed. H. Bergen, EETSes 97 (1906); 103 (1908); 106 (1910).

Macer: A Middle English Translation of Macer Floridus de Viribus Herbarum, ed. G. Frisk, Essays and Studies on English Language and Literature (Uppsala: University of Uppsala Press, 1949).

Machiavelli, Nicolo, *The Prince*, trans. Robert Adams (New York: W.W. Norton, 1977).

Malory, Thomas, *Works*, ed. Eugène Vinaver (London: Oxford University Press, 1971).

Man that luste, The (1st line) (1390), *Fourteenth-Century Lyrics*, ed. Carlton Brown, 152–154.

Mandeville, John, *Mandeville's Travels*, ed. P. Hamelius, EETS 153 (1919), 1–211; *The Bodley Version of Mandeville's Travels*, ed. M.C. Seymour, EETSes 253 (London: Oxford University Press, 1963).

Mankind: The Marco Plays (1475), ed. F.J. Furnivall and A.J. Pollard, EETSes 91 (1904, rpt. 1924), 35–74.

Mannyng, Robert, of Brunne, *Handlyng Synne* (1303), ed. F.J. Furnivall, EETS 119 (1901); 123 (1903).

Mannyng, Robert, of Brunne, *The Story of England by Robert Manning of Brunne*

(1338), ed. F.J. Furnivall, Rolls Series 87 (1887), 7–580 (Chron. Pt 1).

Marlowe, Christopher, *The Complete Plays*, ed. J.B. Steane (Harmondsworth: Penguin, 1969).

Marprelate Tracts, 1588–1589, Scolar Press Facsimile (Menston, England: Scolar Press, 1967).

Marston, John, *The Dutch Courtesan*, ed. Martin L. Wine (Lincoln: University of Nebraska Press, 1965).

Marston, John, *The Malcontent* (Menston: Scolar Press, 1970).

Medical Works of the Fourteenth Century, Harley (British Museum) 2378, ed. G. Henslow (1899).

Medieval English Anatomy from the Wellcome MS 564, ed. Robert Nels Mory (dissertation, University of Michigan, 1977).

Medieval Woman's Guide to Health, ed. Beryl Rowland (Kent, Ohio: Kent State University Press, 1981).

Medulla Grammatice (1425), *MED* Library.

Melusine, ed. A.K. Donald, EETSes 68 (1895).

Merlin, ed. H.B. Wheatley, EETS 10 (1865, 1875); 21 (1866); 36 (1869); 112 (1899).

Metrical Life of Christ, ed. from MS BM Add. 39996, ed. Walter Sauer (Heidelberg: Carl Winter, 1977).

Middle English Pilgrimage of the Soul (1413), ed. Merrel D. Clubb, Jr. (dissertation, University of Michigan: 1953).

Middle English Translation of Macer Floridus de Viribus Herbarum, ed. Gösta Frisk (Uppsala: Kraus Reprint, 1973).

Middleton, Thomas, *A Chaste Maid in Cheapside*, ed. R.B. Parker (London: Methuen, 1973).

Middleton, Thomas, *A Trick to Catch the Old One*, ed. Charles Barber, Fountainwell Drama Series (Berkeley and Los Angeles: University of California Press, 1968).

Middleton, Thomas, *Family of Love*, in *Works*, ed. A.H. Bullen (New York: AMS Press, 1964), vol. III.

Middleton, Thomas, *Michaelmas Term*, ed. Richard Levin, Regents Renaissance Drama Series (Lincoln: University of Nebraska Press, 1966).

Mirk, John, *Festial*, ed. T. Erbe, EETSes 96 (1905).

Mirror St. Edmunds: The Minor Poems of the Vernon MS 1 (1390), ed. C. Horstmann, EETS 98 (1892), 221–51; also, ed. F.J. Furnivall, EETS 117 (1901), 749.

Mirror of Salvation, ed. A.H. Huth, Rolls Series 118 (1888).

Mittelenglishes medizinbuch, ed. F. Heinrich Halle (1896), *MED* Library.

Montaigne, Michel de, *The Essays of Montaigne done into English by John Florio* (1603) (New York: AMS Press, 1967).

Morality of Wisdom: Who is Christ? The Marco Plays (1475), ed. F.J. Furnivall and A.J. Pollard, EETSes 91 (1904, rpt. 1924), 35–74.

More, Thomas, *Utopia*, written by Sir Thomas More and translated by Ralph Robinson (Hammersmith: Kelmscott Press, 1893).

More, Thomas, *Yale Edition of the Works of St Thomas More* (New Haven: Yale University Press, 1961).

Morte Arthure (1400), ed. J.D. Bruce, EETSes 88 (1903, rpt. 1930).

Myers, A.R. (ed.), *The Household of Edward IV: The Black Book and the Ordinance of 1478* (Manchester: Manchester University Press, 1959).

Nashe, Thomas, *The Unfortunate Traveller*. *Shorter Novels: Elizabethan*, intro. by George Saintsbury, Everyman (London: Dent; New York: Dutton, 1929; rpt. 1960).

Newberry Lapidary (1400), *MED* Library.

Northern Homilies, ed. C. Horstmann; *Archiv* 57 (1877).

Octavian, ed. G. Sarrazin, Altenglische Bibliothek 3 (1885).

Of Hawks and Horses: Four Late Middle English Prose Treatises, ed. W.L. Braekman, Research Centre of Medieval and Renaissance Studies (Brussels, 1986).

Orchard of Syon, ed. Phyllis Hodgson and Gabriel M. Liegey, EETS 258 (London: Oxford University Press, 1966).

Oxford Book of Sixteenth-Century Verse, ed. E.K. Chambers (Oxford: Clarendon Press, 1932).

Paston Letters (1422–1509), ed. J. Gairdner, 6 vols (1904).

Pearl-poet, The Poems of the Pearl Manuscript, ed. Malcolm Andrew and Ronald Waldron (Exeter: University of Exeter Press, 1987).

Pecock, Reginald, *The Repressor*, ed. C. Babington, Rolls Series 19 (1860–61).

Perkins, William, *Works*, ed. Ian Breward (Abingdon: Sutton Courtney Press, 1970).

Peter Idley's Instructions to His Son, ed. C. Evelyn, *MLA* Monographs 5, (1935), 80–200.

"Piers of Fulham," in *Remains of the Early Popular Poetry of England*, ed. W.C. Hazlitt, vol. 2 (1866), pp. 2–12.

Piers Plowman: The B Version, ed. George Kane and E. Talbot Donaldson (London: The Athlone Press, 1975).

Political Poems and Songs, ed. T. Wright, Rolls Series II, 174.

Proceedings and Ordinances of the Privy Council of England, ed. H. Nicolas (1834–37), 5.414.

Promptorium Parvulorum, ed. A.L. Mayhew, EETSes 102 (1908).

Prothero, G.W., *Select Statutes and Other Constitutional Documents Illustrative of the Reigns of Elizabeth I and James I*, 4th edn. (Westport, Conn.: Greenwood Press, 1983).

Proverbs of Hending, Altenglische Dictungen des MS Harl. 2253, ed. K. Boddeker (Berlin, 1878), 287–300.

Puttenham, George, *The Arte of English Poesie*, ed. Gladys Doidge Willcock and Alice Walker (Cambridge: Cambridge University Press, 1936, rpt. 1970).

Pylgremage of the Sowle, printed by Caxton (1483).

Ralegh, Sir Walter, *The Discovery of the Large, Rich, and Bewtifull Empyre of Guiana* (1596), ed. V.T. Harlow (London: Argonaut, 1928).

Records of the City of Norwich, vol. 1, ed. W. Hudson (1906); vol. 2, ed. J.C. Tingey (1910).

Ripley, *The Compend of Alchemy* (1471), MS Bode. Mus. 63, vols 41a–65a (*MED* Library).

Robert of Glocester's Chronicle, ed. T. Hearne (1724, rpt. 1810).

Robinson, Ralph (trans.), *Utopia* (1551) by Thomas More (Hammersmith: Kelmscott Press, 1893).

Rogues, Vagabonds, and Sturdy Beggars: A New Gallery of Tudor and Stuart Rogue Literature, ed. Arthur F. Kinney (Amherst: University of Massachusetts Press, 1990).

Rolle, Richard, *Psalter* and "Meditations on the Passion" (1394), ed. H.R. Bramley (1874).

Rollins, Hyder, E. and Hershel Baker (eds), *The Renaissance in England* (Boston, Mass.: Heath, 1954).

Romance of Sir Beviues of Hamtoun, ed. E. Kolbing, EETSes 46, 48 (1885–6; rpt. 1898).

Romance of William of Palerne, ed. W.W. Skeat, EETSes 1 (1867); rpt. 1898), 6–175.

Sandys, George, *Ovid's Metamorphosis Englished, Mythologized, and Represented in Figures* (1632), ed. Karl K. Holley and Stanley T. Vandersall (Lincoln: University of Nebraska Press, 1970).

Scot, Reginald, *Discoverie of Witchcraft* (1584; Totowa, NJ: Rowman and Littlefield, 1973).

Scrope, Stephen, *The Epistle of Othea to Hector*, translated from the French of Christine de Pisan, ed. G.F. Warner (Roxburghe Club, 1904).

Secretum Secretorum, Ashmole, ed. M.A. Manzalaoui, EETSos 276.

Seege or Batayle of Troye, ed. M.E. Barnicle, EETS 172 (1927), 3–163.

Shakespeare, William, *Shakespeare's Sonnets*, edited with analytic commentary by Stephen Booth (New Haven, Conn.: Yale University Press, 1977).

Shakespeare, William, *The Riverside Shakespeare*, ed. G. Blakemore Evans *et al.* (Boston, Mass.: Houghton Mifflin, 1974).

Sidney, Sir Philip, *An Apology for Poetry*, ed. Geoffrey Shepherd (London: T. Nelson, 1965).

Sidney, Sir Philip, *The Countess of Pembroke's Arcadia*, ed. and intro. by Victor Skretkowicz (Oxford: Clarendon Press, 1987).

Sidney, Sir Philip, *The Countess of Pembroke's Arcadia (The Old Arcadia)*, ed. Jean Robertson (Oxford: Clarendon Press, 1973).

Sir John Oldcastle, ed. Percy Simpson, Malone Society Reprints (Oxford: Oxford University Press, 1963).

Sir Orfeo (1330), in *Middle English Metrical Romances*, ed. W.H. French and C.B. Hale (1930), 323–344.

Sir Tristrem, ed. G.P. MacNeill, Scottish Text Society 8 (1886).

Six Ecclesiastical Satires, ed. James Dean, Medieval Institute Publications (Kalamazoo: Western Michigan University Press, 1991).

Smith, John, *Complete Works*, ed. Philip L. Barbour, 3 vols (Chapel Hill, N.C.: University of North Carolina Press, 1986).

Southern Legendary, ed. C. Horstmann, EETS 87 (1887).

Speculum Christiani (1400), ed. G. Holmstedt, EETS 182 (1933).

Speculum Sacerdotale, ed. E.H. Weatherly, EETS 200 (1936).

Spenser, Edmund, *The Poetical Works of Edmund Spenser*, ed. J.C. Smith and E. De Selincourt (London: Oxford University Press, 1961).

Spenser, Edmund, *A View of the Present State of Ireland*, ed. W.L. Renwick (Oxford: Clarendon Press, 1970).

Stanzaic Life of Christ, ed. F.A. Foster, EETS 166 (1926).

Stockholm Recipes, ed. G. Miller, Kölner Anglistische Arbeiten (Leipiz, 1929; MED Library).

Stonor Letters and Papers, 1290–1483, ed. C.L. Kingsford, Royal Historical Society, series 3: 29, 30 (1919).

Stow, John, *The Survey of London* (New York: Dutton, n.d.).

Stubbs, Philip, *The School of Abuse* (1579) (London: The Shakespeare Society, 1841).

Tale of Beryn, ed. F.J. Furnivall and W.G. Stone, EETSes 105 (1909).

Thoresby, John, *Lay Folks Catechism*, ed. T.F. Symmonds and H.E. Nolloth, EETS 71 (London: K. Paul, Trench, Trübner, 1901).

Thorne, Robert, "A Declaration of the Indies" (1527), in *Divers Voyages Touching the Discovery of America*, ed. John W. Jones, Hakluyt Society, 7 vols (London, 1850).

Three Kings of Cologne, ed. H.N. MacCracken, *Lydgatiana*, vol. 129 (1912), 3, Archiv, 51–68.

Three Middle English Sermons from the Worcester Chapter MS (1400), ed. D.M. Grisdale, Leeds School of English Language Texts and Monographs 5 (1929), 22–80.

Three Tudor Classical Interludes: Thersites, Jacke Jugeler, Horestes, ed. Marie Axton (Cambridge and Totowa, N.J.: D.S. Brewer, and Rowan and Littlefield, 1982).

Tourneur, Cyril, *The Atheist's Tragedy*, ed. Brian Morris and Roma Gill (New Mermaids, New York: W.W. Norton, 1989).

Tourneur, Cyril, *The Revenger's Tragedy* (1607), ed. Brian Gibbons (New York: Norton, 1991).

Towneley Plays (1500), ed. G. England and A.J. Pollard, EETSes 71 (1897; rpr. 1925).

Trevisa, John, *Polychronicon of Ranulphi Higden*, ed. C. Babington and J.R. Lumby, Rolls Series 41 (1865–86).

Trevisa, John, translation of Bartholomew de Glanville's *De Proprietatibus Rerum* (1398), MS Add. 27944, *MED* Library.

Tyndale, William, *The Obedience of a Christian Man* (Menston: Scolar Press, 1970).

Tyndale, William, *Wicked Mammon* (1528), ed. Henry Walter, Parker Society.

Usk, Thomas, *Testament of Love* (1385), in W.W. Skeat (ed.), *Chaucerian and Other Pieces* (1897).

Warner, William, *Albions England* (1592).

Wars of Alexander, ed. W.W. Skeat, EETSes 47 (1886).

Webster, John, *The Duchess of Malfi*, ed. Elizabeth Brennen (New Mermaids, New York: W.W. Norton, 1987).

Webster, John, *The White Devil*, ed. J.R. Mulryne (Lincoln: University of Nebraska Press, 1969).

William of Palerne (The Romance of), ed. W.W. Skeat, EETSes 1 (1887; rpt. 1898), 8–175.

Wilson, Thomas, *The Arte of Rhetorique* (Oxford: Clarendon Press, 1909).

Wimbledon's Sermon, ed. Ione Kemp Knight, Duquesne Studies, Philological Series 9 (Pittsburgh, Pa.: Duquesne University Press, 1967).

Wright, T. (ed.), *Political Poems and Songs*, Rolls Series (1859), 2 vols.

Wyatt, Thomas, *Sir Thomas Wyatt: The Complete Poems*, ed. R.A. Rebholz (New Haven, Conn. and London: Yale University Press, 1978).

Wyclif, John, *37 Conclusions*, ed. J. Forhsall (1851).

Wyclif, John, *A Lollard Chronicle of the Papacy*, ed. E.W. Talbert, in *JEGP*, 41 (1942), 175–93.

Wyclif, John, *Apology for Lollard Doctrines*, ed. J.H. Todd, Camden 20 (1842).

Wyclif, John, *de Officio Regis*, ed. A.W. Pollard and C. Sayle (1887).

Wyclif, John, *De Veritate Sacrae Scripturae*, ed. Rudolf Buddensieg (Leipzig: Dietrich, 1904).

Wyclif, John, *The Lanterne of List* (1400), ed. L.M. Swinburn, EETS 151 (1917).

Wyclif, John, *Works Hitherto Unprinted*, ed. F.D. Matthew, EETS 74 (1880).

Wyclif, John, *Select English Works*, ed. Thomas Arnold, 3 vols (Oxford: Clarendon Press, 1869).

Yong, Bartholomew, *Diana*, trans. from Jorge de Montemayor's *Diana* (Oxford: Clarendon Press, 1968).

Yonge, James, *Gouernance of Prynces* (1422), in *Secreta Secretorum*, ed. R. Steele, EETSes 66 (1894).

York Plays, ed. L.T. Smith (1885).

Secondary texts

Adams, Joseph Quincy, *A Life of William Shakespeare* (Boston, Mass.: Houghton Mifflin, 1923).

Aers, David, *Community, Gender and Individual Identity: English Writing, 1360–1403* (London and New York: Routledge, 1988).

Agnew, Jean-Christophe, *Worlds Apart* (Cambridge: Cambridge University Press, 1986).

Anderson, Benedict, *Imagined Communities: Reflections on the Origin and Spread of Nationalism* (London: Verso, 1983).

Bakhtin, M.M., *Rabelais and His World*, trans. Helene Iswolsky (Bloomington: University of Indiana Press, 1984).

Baldwin, Frances Elizabeth, *Sumptuary Legislation and Personal Regulation in England* (Baltimore, Md, 1926).

Barroll, Leeds, *Politics, Plague and Shakespeare's Theater: The Stuart Years* (Ithaca and London: Cornell University Press, 1991).

Benson, Larry, "The 'Queynte' Punnings of Chaucer's Critics," *Studies in the Age of Chaucer, Proceedings*, 1 (1984), 23–47.

Bradbrook, Muriel, *Themes and Conventions of Elizabethan Tragedy* (Cambridge: Cambridge University Press, 1935).

Brenkman, John, *Culture and Domination* (Ithaca, N.Y.: Cornell University Press, 1987).

Camille, Michael, *Image on the Edge: The Margins of Medieval Art* (Cambridge, Mass.: Harvard University Press, 1992).

Carruthers, Mary, "Locational Memory in Chaucer's Knight's Tale," in *Art and Context in Late Medieval English Narrative*, ed. Robert Edwards (London: D.S. Brewer, 1994).

Chrimes, S.B., *English Constitutional Ideas in the Fifteenth Century* (New York: American Scholar Publications, 1966).

Ciardi, John (trans.), *Dante's Inferno* (New York: New American Library, 1954).

Cohen, Walter, "The *Merchant of Venice* and the Possibilities of Historical Criticism," *ELH*, 49 (1982), 765–89.

Coleman, Janet, *Medieval Readers and Writers: 1350–1400* (New York: Columbia University Press, 1981).

Cressy, David, *Education in Tudor England* (London: Edward Arnold, 1975).

Daniell, David, *William Tyndale: A Biography* (New Haven and London: Yale University Press, 1994).

David, Richard, Introduction and notes for Shakespeare's *Love's Labors Lost* (Arden Edition; London: Methuen, 5th edn 1956).

Davlin, Mary Clemente, "*Kynde Knowing* as the Middle English Equivalent for 'Wisdom' in *Piers Plowman B*," *Medium Aevum*, 50 (1981), 5–17.

Delany, Paul, "*King Lear* and the Decline of Feudalism," *PMLA*, 94 (1979), 429–440.

Delany, Sheila, "Anatomy of the Resisting Reader: Some Implications of Resistance to Sexual Wordplay in Medieval Literature," *Exemplaria*, 4 (March 1992), 7–34.

Derrida, Jacques, "Plato's Pharmacy," in *Dissemination*, trans. Barbara Johnson (Chicago: University of Chicago Press, 1981).

Duby, Georges, *Medieval Marriages* (Baltimore: Johns Hopkins University Press, 1978).

Duby, Georges, *The Chivalrous Society*, trans. Cynthia Postan (Berkeley and Los Angeles: University of California Press, 1977).

Duby, Georges, *The Three Orders: Feudal Society Imagined*, trans. Arthur Goldhammer (Chicago: University of Chicago Press, 1980).

Duffy, Eamon, *Stripping the Altars: Traditional Religion in England, 1400–1580* (New Haven and London: Yale University Press, 1992).

Elias, Norbert, *The Civilizing Process: State Formation and Civilization* (Oxford: Blackwell, 1982).

Empson, William, *The Structure of Complex Words* (New York: New Directions, 1951).

Engle, Lars, "'Thrift is a Blessing': Exchange and Exploration in *The Merchant of Venice*," *Shakespeare Quarterly*, 37 (1986), 20–37.

Freud, Sigmund, *Jokes and their Relation to the Unconscious*, trans. and ed. James Strachey (New York: W.W. Norton, 1960).

Gadamer, Hans-Georg, *Philosophical Hermeneutics*, trans. David E. Linge (Berkeley: University of California Press, 1976).

Gibbons, Brian, *Jacobean City Comedy: A Study of Plays by Jonson, Marston, and Middleton* (London: Rupert Hart-Davis, 1968).

Green, Richard Firth, *Poets and Princepleasers: Literature and the English Court in the Late Middle Age* (Toronto: University of Toronto Press, 1980).

Greenblatt, Stephen, *Renaissance Self-Fashioning* (Chicago: University of Chicago Press, 1980).

Greenblatt, Stephen, *Shakespearian Negotiations: The Circulation of Social Energy in Renaissance England* (Berkeley and Los Angeles: University of California Press, 1988).

Gurr, Andrew, *The Shakespearean Stage, 1574–1642*, 3rd edn (Cambridge: Cambridge University Press, 1992).

Habermas, Jürgen, "A Review of Gadamer's *Truth and Method*," in *Understanding Social Inquiry*, ed. Fred Dallmayr and Thomas McCarthy (South Bend, Ind.: Notre Dame University Press, 1977).

Hall, Stuart, "On Postmodernism and Articulation: An Interview with Stuart Hall," ed. Lawence Grossberg, *Journal of Communication Inquiry*, 10 (1986), 53.

Hall, Stuart, "The Problem of Ideology—Marxism without Guarantees," in *Marx 100 Years On*, ed. B. Matthews (London: Lawrence and Wishart, 1983).

Haller, William, *The Elect Nation: The Meaning and Relevance of Foxe's "Book of Martyrs"* (New York: Harper and Row, 1963).

Hanning, Robert, "'I Shal Finde It in a Maner Glose': Versions of Textual Harassment in Medieval Literature," in *Medieval Texts and Contemporary Readers*, ed. Laurie A. Finke and Martin B. Shichtman (Ithaca: Cornell University Press, 1987), 27–50.

Harwood, Britton J., "Langland's *Kynde Knowing*, and the Quest for Christ," *Modern Philology*, 80 (1983), 242–255.

Harwood, Britton J., *Piers Plowman and the Problem of Belief* (Toronto: University of Toronto Press, 1992).

Heineman, Margot, *Puritanism and Theatre: Thomas Middleton and Opposition Drama under the Early Stuarts* (Cambridge and New York: Cambridge University Press, 1980).

Hexter, J.H., *The Vision of Politics on the Eve of the Reformation* (New York: Basic Books, 1973).

Hill, Christopher, *The English Bible and the Seventeenth-Century Revolution* (Harmondsworth: Penguin, 1993).

Hill, Christopher, *The World Turned Upside Down: Radical Ideas during the English Revolution* (New York, 1972).

Hock, Hans Henrich, *Principles of Historical Linguistics* (Berlin: Mouton de Gruyter, 1986).

Hopper, Paul and Elizabeth Closs Traugott, *Grammaticalization* (Cambridge: Cambridge University Press, 1993).

Hopper, Paul, "Some Principles of Grammaticalization," *Approaches to Grammaticalization* (Amsterdam: John Benjamins, 1991).

Jauss, Hans Robert Jauss, *Question and Answer: Forms of Dialogic Understanding*, ed. and trans. Michael Hays (Minneapolis: University of Minnesota Press, 1989).

Jones, Terry, *Chaucer's Knight: Portrait of a Medieval Mercenary* (London: Weidenfeld and Nicolson, 1980).

Kegl, Rosemary, *The Rhetoric of Concealment* (Ithaca, N.Y.: Cornell University Press, 1994).

Knapp, Jeffrey, *An Empire Nowhere: England, America, and Literature from Utopia to the Tempest* (Berkeley, Los Angeles, Oxford: University of California Press, 1992).

Kolve, John, *Chaucer and the Imagery of Narrative* (Stanford, Cal.: Stanford University Press, 1984).

LaCapra, Dominick, "Habermas and the Grounding of Critical Theory," *History and Theory*, 16 (1977), 237–264.

Lee, Maurice, "James VI and the Revival of Episcopy," *Church History*, 43 (1974), 50–62.

Lewis, C.S., *Studies in Words* (Cambridge: Cambridge University Press, 1967).

Lewis, C.S., "What Chaucer Really Did to *Il Filostrato*," *English Institutes Essays*, 17 (1932), 56–75; rpt. in *Chaucer Criticism: Troilus and Criseyde and the Minor Poems*, ed. Richard Schoek and Jerome Taylor (Notre Dame, Ind.: Notre Dame University Press, 1961), pp. 16–33.

Lupton, Donald, *London and the Country Carbonadoes and Quartered into Several Characters* (London, 1632).

MacCabe, Colin, "Language, Linguistics, and the Study of Literature," *Theoretical Essays* (Minneapolis: University of Minnesota Press, 1985).

Marx, Karl, *The Communist Manifesto*, ed. Frederic L. Bender (New York: W.W. Norton, 1988).

Mendle, Michael, *Dangerous Positions: Mixed Government, the Estates of the Realm, and the Making of the Answer to the xix Propositions* (University, Al.: University of Alabama Press, 1985).

Miller, J. Hillis, "The Critic as Host," *Critical Inquiry*, 3 (1977), 439–447.

Montrose, Louis, "The Work of Gender in *The Discourse of Discovery*," *Representations*, 33 (Winter 1991), 1–41.

Mosse, George, *The Holy Pretense: A Study in Christianity and Reason of State from William Perkins to John Winthrop* (Oxford: Blackwell, 1957).

Mueller, Janel, *The Native Tongue and the Word: Developments in English Prose Style, 1380–1500* (Chicago: University of Chicago Press, 1984).

Mulvey, Laura, "Visual Pleasure and Narrative Cinema," in *Visual and Other Pleasures* (Bloomington: Indiana University Press, 1989), pp. 14–26.

Myers, A.R., *The Household of Edward IV: The Black Book and the Ordinance of 1478* (Manchester: Manchester University Press, 1959).

Nerlich, Michael, *Ideology of Adventure: Studies in Modern Consciousness, 1100–1750*, trans. Ruth Crowley (Minneapolis: University of Minnesota Press, 1987).

Owst, G.R., *Literature and the Pulpit in Medieval England* (Cambridge: Cambridge University Press, 1933).

Owst, G.R., *Preaching in Medieval England* (New York: Russell & Russell, 1926).

Pantin, W.A., *The English Church in the Fourteenth Century* (Cambridge: Cambridge University Press, 1955).

Parker, Patricia, "*Othello* and *Hamlet*: Dilation, Spying, and the 'Secret Place' of Woman," *Representations*, 44 (Fall 1993), 60–95.

Pierce, William, *An Historical Introduction to the Marprelate Tracts* (New York: Burt Franklin, 1908).

Plamenatz, John, "In Search of Machiavellian *Virtù*," in *The Political Calculus*, ed. Anthony Parel (Toronto: University of Toronto Press, 1972), 157–78.

Pocock, J.G.A., *The Machiavellian Moment: Florentine Political Thought and the Atlantic Republican Tradition* (Princeton, N.J.: Princeton University Press, 1975).

Powicke, Maurice, *The Reformation in England* (London: Oxford University Press, 1941).

Rappaport, Steven, *Worlds within Worlds: The Structure of Life in Sixteenth-Century London* (New York: Cambridge University Press, 1988).

Rollins, Hyder E. and Herschel Baker, *The Renaissance in England* (Boston, Mass.: D.C. Heath, 1954).

Schwartz, Murray, "Leontes' Jealousy in *The Winter's Tale*," *American Imago*, 30 (1973), 250–273.

Schwartz, Murray, "*The Winter's Tale*: Loss and Transformation," *American Imago*, 32 (1975), 145–199.

Sinfield, Alan, *Literature in Protestant England, 1560–1660* (Totowa, N.J.: Barnes and Noble, 1983).

Slack, Paul, *The Impact of Plague in Tudor and Stuart England* (London: Routledge and Kegan Paul, 1985).

Smith-Rosenberg, Carroll, "Coquettes and Revolutionaries in Young America," *Literature and the Body: Essays on Populations and Persons*, ed. Elaine Scarry, English Institute Essays (1986).

Stallybrass, Peter and Allon Whyte, *The Politics and Poetics of Transgression* (Ithaca: Cornell University Press, 1986).

Stone, Lawrence, *The Crisis of the Aristocracy, 1558-1641* (Oxford: Clarendon Press, 1965).

Stone, Lawrence, *The Family, Sex, and Marriage, in England, 1500-1800* (New York: Harper & Row, 1977).

Strong, Roy, *Portraits of Queen Elizabeth* (Oxford: Clarendon Press, 1963).

Symonds, Arthur, *Shakespeare's Predecessors in English Drama* (London: Smith, Elder, 1884; rpt. New York: AMS Press, 1968).

Szittya, Penn, "The Anti-Fraternal Tradition in Middle English Literature," *Speculum*, 52 (1977), 287–313.

Theweleit, Klaus, *Male Fantasies*, trans. Stephen Conway (Minneapolis: University of Minnesota Press, 1987).

Tillyard, E.M.W., *Shakespeare's History Plays* (New York: Barnes & Noble, 1969).

Tillyard, E.M.W., *The Elizabethan World Picture* (New York: Random House, 1960).

Walzer, Michael, *The Revolution of the Saints: A Study in the Origins of Radical Politics* (Cambridge: Harvard University Press, 1965).

Weston, Corinne Comstock and Janelle Renfrow Greenberg, *Subjects and Sovereigns: The Grand Controversy over Legal Sovereignty in Stuart England* (Cambridge: Cambridge University Press, 1981).

Wiener, Andrew D., "Moving and Teaching: Sidney's *Defence of Poesie* as a Protestant Poetic," in *Essential Articles for the Study of Philip Sidney*, ed. Arthur Kinney (Hamden, Conn.: Archon Books, 1986).

Williams, Raymond, *Keywords: A Vocabulary of Culture and Society* (New York: Oxford University Press, 1976).

Williams, Raymond, *Marxism and Literature* (Oxford: Oxford University Press, 1977).

Williams, Raymond, *Writing and Society* (Thetford, Norfolk: Verso, n.d.).

Womack, Peter, "Imagining Communities: Theatres and the English Nation in the Sixteenth Century," in *Culture and History, 1350–1600*, ed. David Aers (Brighton: Harvester Press; Detroit: Wayne State University Press, 1992).

Ziolkowski, Jan (ed.), *On Philology* (University Park: Pennsylvania State University

Index

Adams, Robert, 179
Aers, David, 53
Agnew, Jean-Christophe, 60, 62, 75, 95, 206 n.5
Anderson, Benedict, 11, 73, 96, 101, 105, 139, 191
articulation, 5, 7, 11
Augustine, Saint, 66, 67

Bakhtin, M.M., 104, 139
Baldwin, Frances Elizabeth, 29
Bale, John, 18, 197 n.4
Barroll, Leeds, 197–98 n.8
Beaumont, Francis, and John Fletcher, 110, 155, 205 n.5
Benson, Larry, 137
Bible, Geneva, 68, 72, 79, 117, 118, 173
Bible, Authorized, 72, 117, 173, 196 n.3
Bible, Wycliffite *see* Wyclif
Book of Common Prayer, 105, 119, 139, 164
Bradbrook, Muriel, 126
Brenkman, John, 3
Brown Carleton, 192, 198 n.1

Calvin, John, 6, 8, 114, 117–20, 157, 164, 203 n.6
Castle of Perseverance, 131–32, 206 n.3, 220 n.4
Chapman, George, 75, 155–56, 167, 187–88
Chaucer, Geoffrey,
  Boece, 15, 50, 70, 114–15, 194 n.2, 198 n.3
  Book of the Duchess, 84, 137, 194 n.2, 198 n.3
  Canterbury Tales, 71, 79, 194 n.2
  Clerk's T., 34-35, 36, 16, 147
  Canon's Yeoman's T., 103, 137, 147, 163
  Franklin's T., 49–50, 83, 116, 163

Friar's T., 103
Gen. Prol., 15–16, 102–03, 178, 205 n.2
Knight's T., 55, 115, 137–38, 198 n.3, 202 n.2
Manciple's T., 198 n.4
Man of Law's T., 103, 116, 146, 163, 178
Merchant's T., 14, 16–17, 55, 103, 148, 163
Miller's T., 103–04, 110, 111, 116, 136–38, 142, 148, 163–64, 170, 192, 202 n.2
Monk's T., 198 n.4
Nun's Priest's T., 147
Parson's T., 34, 35–36, 52, 71, 84, 197 n.1
Physician's T., 147, 178
Prioress's T., 147, 178
Reeve's T., 148
Sec. Nun's T., 84, 103, 147, 153, 178
Shipman's T., 147, 163
Summoner's T., 71, 147
Wife's T., 54, 70–71, 73, 84, 100, 116. 136, 148, 203 n.2, 205 n.2
Legend Good Women, 145
Rom. Rose, 15, 134, 194 n.2
Troilus and Criseyde, 17, 34, 36–38, 50, 54–55, 84–85, 104, 115, 146, 155, 161–63, 194 n.2, 203 n.3
Chrimes, S.B. , 30, 37, 48–49, 176, 195 n.1, 196 n.4
Ciardi, John, 10
Cohen, Walter, 169
Coleman, Janet, 101
Coverdale, Miles, 159, 173
critical theory, 2–4
Cressy, David, 205 n.3

Daniell, David, 39, 72
David, Richard, 78

Dekker, Thomas, 22, 155, 167, 181
Delany, Sheila, 134, 203 n.3
Derrida, Jacques, 9
Duby, Georges, 195 n.1
Duffy, Eamon, 176, 201 n.3, 201–02
n.7

Elizabeth I, queen of England, 26, 28,
108, 117, 119–20, 139, 174, 195
n.11, 197 n.6, 201 n.2, 202 n.4
Elias, Norbert, 108, 142
Elyot, Thomas, 19, 20, 82, 195 n.9,
199 n.6
emergent, 7, 38, 39, 41, 46, 62, 90,
96, 103, 124, 146, 149, 155, 160,
161, 162, 178, 198 n.1
Empson, William, 9
Engle, Lars, 169

Florio, John, 55, 74–75, 138, 154,
181, 195 n.6
Fortesque, John, 161, 176
Foxe, John, 105, 119, 121, 139, 149,
199 n.6
Freud, Sigmund, 133, 141

Gadamer, Hans-Georg, 2–4, 27, 79,
189–90, 192
Gesta Romanorum, 82, 176
Golding, Arthur, 59, 64, 107, 121,
122, 154, 181, 199 n.8, 202–03
n.6
Gosson, Stephen, 49, 75, 107, 166,
181
Gower, John, 14, 83, 113, 115, 116,
131
Greenberg, Janelle, and Corinne
Weston, 30
Greenblatt, Stephen, 119, 126, 151,
154
Greene, Thomas, 43, 189, 195 n.7
Gurr, Andrew, 107, 166

Habermas, Jürgen, 2–4, 13, 27, 190,
192
Hakluyt, Richard, 120–21, 183–84
Hall, Stuart, 4, 5–7, 9, 67, 117, 164
Haller, William, 117, 120
Harvey, Gabriel, 75, 108, 178, 199 n.9

Harwood, Britton, 86, 87, 198 n.2
hermeneutics, 2–4, 6, 13
Hexter, J.H., 179, 186
Hill, Christopher, 59
Hoby, Thomas, 56–57, 90, 153–54,
163, 181, 195 n.6
Hoccleve, Thomas, 68, 102, 134, 160
Hock, Hans Henrich, 130–31, 138
Holinshed, Raphael, 205 n.4, 206 n.5
Hopper, Paul, and Elizabeth Closs
Traugott, 81–82
Hooker, Richard, 89–90, 107, 121–22,
181, 199 n.6, 200 n.9

James I, King of England, 8, 30, 38,
40, 47, 72, 82, 108, 117, 121,
167, 197 n.3, 206 n.5
Jauss, Hans Robert, 194 n.2
Jones, Terry, 137
Jonson, Ben, 60–62, 65, 124, 125,
155–56, 180, 195 n.8, 196 n.11,
198 n.10
Julian of Norwich, 50–51, 83, 87–89,
115

Kegl, Rosemary, 108
Kempe, Margery, 53–54, 101, 139,
197 n.2, 200 n.4
Kinney, Arthur, 107, 154–55, 167,
195 n.7
Knapp, Jeffrey, 21
Knox, John, 39–40, 49, 82, 121, 199
n.6
Kolve, John, 55

LaCapra, Dominick, 4–6, 161, 164,
170
Langland, William, 51, 70, 80, 84–89,
135, 200 n.7, 200 n.8
Lewis, C.S., 36
Liber Niger (*The Black Book*), 32–33,
114
Lindsay, David, 39–40, 160, 200 n.3
Lodge, Thomas, 158, 180
Luther, Martin, 39, 11, 68, 74, 104,
117, 151, 164, 165
Lydgate, John, 14, 82, 83, 114, 133,
134, 160, 174–75, 177, 200 n.6,
204 n.2

MacCabe, Colin, 6
Machiavelli, Nicolo, 120, 178–81, 186
Malory, Thomas, 17–19, 14, 84–85, 194 n.3
Mandeville, John, 131, 175
Marlowe, Christopher, 17, 20–21, 43–44, 76–77, 155, 156, 178, 180, 184, 194–95 n.5, 204–05 n.7, 206 n.7
Marprelate Tracts, 40, 78, 197 n.5, 202 n.8, 202 n.5
Marston, John, 49, 109–10, 155
Marx, Karl, 30, 32
Mendle, Michael, 29, 30, 38, 195 n.1
Middleton, Thomas, 22, 44, 49, 60–61, 65, 155, 184, 195 n.8, 198 n.9, 203 n.8, 205 n.5
Miller, J. Hillis, 2, 9
Montrose, Louis, 183
More, Thomas, 2, 10–11, 21, 43, 58, 60, 56, 65, 72–73, 104, 105–07, 150–51, 165–66, 178, 188, 194 n.4, 197 n.3, 199 n.3, 204 n.5
Mosse, George, 180, 202 n.4
Mueller, Janel, 10–11
Mulvey, Laura, 133

Nerlich, Michael, 9–10, 45, 168

Owst, G.R., 196 n.5, 201 n.1

Pantin, W.A., 201 n.1
paronomasia, 4, 5
Pearl-poet, 28, 84, 113, 135–36, 145–46, 159, 175, 194 n.1
Perkins, William, 39, 206 n.5
philology, 1–4, 194 n.1
Pocock, J.G.A., 173, 175–76, 179, 182, 190
Powicke, Maurice, 104
Protestant Reformation, 8, 10–12, 30, 38–40, 82, 99, 100, 104, 106, 110, 111,117–24, 144, 148–49, 151, 157, 159, 164, 165, 170–71, 180, 197 n.4
Prothero, G.W., 117
Puttenham, George, 90, 109, 120, 181

Ralegh, Walter, 40, 59, 183–84
Rappaport, Steven, 60, 108, 196 n.9
residual, 7, 15, 26, 29–30, 46, 92, 96, 149, 156, 190

Schwartz, Murray, 63
Shakespeare, William,
    Ant. and Cleo., 24–25
    AYLI, 24, 25, 109, 140, 165, 203 n.4
    Cymbeline, 25, 26, 141
    Hamlet, 62–63, 93, 124–25, 141, 169–70, 180, 185
    Henry IV, (I), 112, 168, 190–91
    Henry IV, (II), 112
    Henry V, 77
    Jul. Caesar, 124
    Lear, 93–96, 180
    LLL, 78–79, 174
    Macbeth, 24, 25
    M for M, 126, 170–71, 185–87
    MV, 9, 24, 44–45, 93–95, 142, 168–70, 196–97 n.12
    Merry Wives, 141–42, 171
    MND, 22–23, 30, 140, 142
    Much Ado, 8, 185
    Othello, 62, 63–64, 112, 155, 185, 206 n.9
    Pericles, 78, 185
    Rich. II, 75, 111, 144
    Sonnets, 92
    Taming, 111, 141, 155
    Tempest, 30, 62, 68, 78, 125–26, 140, 142
    Timon, 44, 46–47, 104, 170
    Titus, 78
    Troilus, 25, 77–78, 126, 141, 170
    Twelf. Night, 155, 205 n.7
    Two Gent., 149, 157
    Winter's T., 62–63, 155, 185
Sidney, Philip, 22–24, 41–43, 58–59, 90, 91, 92–93, 110, 140, 152–53, 181–83, 195 n.9, 195 n.10, 200 n.13, 206 n.6
Sinfield, Alan, 149
Slack, Paul, 123–24
Smith-Rosenberg, Carroll, 188
Spenser, Edmund, 22–23, 41, 75–76, 79, 91, 99, 108, 110, 121,

Spenser, Edmund – *continued*
139–40, 151–52, 158, 197 n.6,
199 n.2, 201 n.12, 203 n.7, 204
n.6
Stallybrass, Peter, and Allon Whyte,
149
Stone, Lawrence, 40, 111, 171
structures of feeling, 4, 7, 10, 21, 58,
60, 62, 112, 119, 129, 151, 156,
190, 194 n.2
Szittya, Penn, 147

Theweleit, Klaus, 13, 21, 22, 27, 133,
195 n.9
Thirning, William, 48–49, 37
Tillyard, E.M.W., 119–20
Tourneur, Cyril, 126–29, 203
nn.5, 9
Trevisa, John, 13, 33, 83, 99, 158,
173, 175, 176, 99 n.1, 199 n.2,
201 n.4
Tyndale, William, 10–11, 21, 39–40,

43, 51, 56, 57–58, 65, 68, 72 74,
79, 104–05, 117, 165
Udall, Nicholas, 68

Walzer, Michael, 39, 196 n.8
Webster, John, 141, 155, 167,
184–85, 203 n.5, 206 n.8
Williams, Raymond, 4, 7, 30, 47, 56,
99, 194 n.3
Wimbledon, 173, 196 n.5, 200 n.6,
201 n.3, 206 n.8
Womack, Peter, 119
Wyatt, Thomas, 58, 74, 90-91, 165,
199 n.7, 200-01 n. 11
Wyclif, John, and Wycliffite writing,
10, 14, 31–33, 51–53, 67–70, 73,
77, 79, 83, 99, 100, 105, 113,
115, 117, 121, 132, 135, 145,
173, 196 n.6, 198 n.5, 199 n.1,
200 n.4, 204 n.3

Ziolkowski, Jan, 194 n.1